S0-ADO-235

ILL FEELING IN THE ERA
OF GOOD FEELING

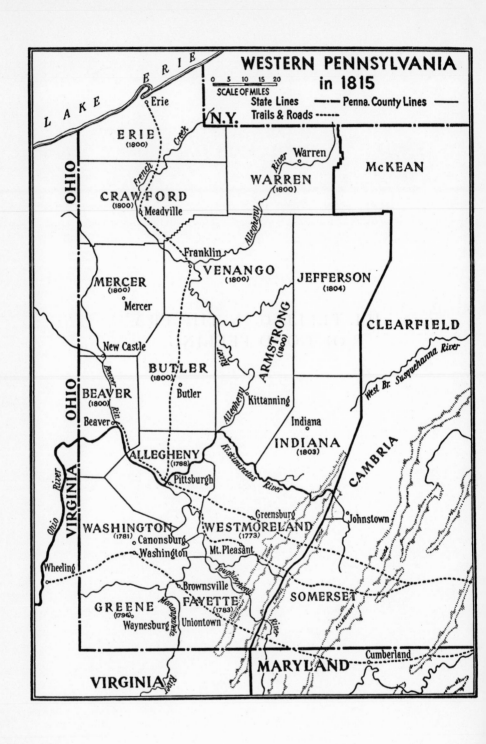

WESTERN PENNSYLVANIA
in 1815

SCALE OF MILES
0 5 10 15 20

State Lines —·—·— Penna. County Lines ——
Trails & Roads ------

LAKE ERIE

N.Y.

OHIO

ERIE
(1800)

Erie

CRAWFORD
(1800)

Meadville

French Creek

WARREN
(1800)

Warren

Allegheny River

McKEAN

MERCER
(1800)

Mercer

Franklin

VENANGO
(1800)

JEFFERSON
(1804)

CLEARFIELD

New Castle

Beaver Riv.

BUTLER
(1800)

Butler

Allegheny River

ARMSTRONG
(1800)

Kittanning

West Br. Susquehanna River

OHIO

BEAVER
(1800)

Beaver

VIRGINIA

Ohio River

ALLEGHENY
(1788)

Pittsburgh

Kiskiminetas River

Indiana

INDIANA
(1803)

CAMBRIA

Greensburg

Johnstown

WASHINGTON
(1781)

Canonsburg

Washington

WESTMORELAND
(1773)

Mt. Pleasant

Youghiogheny

Wheeling

Brownsville

FAYETTE
(1783)

SOMERSET

Allegheny

GREENE
(1796)

Waynesburg

Monongahela

Uniontown

Cumberland

VIRGINIA

River

MARYLAND

ILL FEELING IN THE ERA OF
GOOD FEELING

Western Pennsylvania Political Battles, 1815-1825

by

JAMES A. KEHL

PITT - 1787

UNIVERSITY OF PITTSBURGH PRESS

Library of Congress Catalogue Card Number: 56-6425

LIBRARY
FLORIDA STATE UNIVERSITY
TALLAHASSEE, FLORIDA

© 1956

UNIVERSITY OF PITTSBURGH PRESS

Printed in U.S.A.

FOREWORD

The history of American politics consists of many histories. National party organizations as they are known today are of late growth. They are the product of a long evolution during which a great number of communities and a somewhat smaller number of regions each developed a politics of its own. The process by which these widely scattered local partisanships were welded into the national system is long and intricate. Historians have concentrated too much on the national story and have much oversimplified it. To see the real working of our system of democratic behavior we need a deeper penetration and a closer observation of the experience of many localities and many regions.

Dr. Kehl has made it possible for us to relive the experience of a significant region in a period falsely called an Era of Good Feeling. He has brought back the actors in the drama, placed them on the stage of their activities, and made them speak and act in such a fashion as to give us a vivid and convincing picture of their experience.

Watching this era of contest and sharing its emotions, we get a new sense of the complexity of political behavior and realize more effectively than before the dynamic quality of American local politics.

Most important, we see clearly the basic fact of American politics, that is, its federal system. Our politics is operated on two levels, one national and spectacular, one local and often obscure. But it is on the second level things happen, for there politics most vitally affects the average citizen. Most national political reputations are made in local settings and most national political behavior is conditioned by the folkways of localities. It is the local voice that controls. These pages illustrate graphically the fundamental patterns of the workings of American Democracy.

ROY F. NICHOLS
Vice Provost and Dean
University of Pennsylvania

PREFACE

Transitional periods are always clouded with confusion, false starts, and uncertainty. At times they even defy organization and permit only description. This work treats such an interim, the 1815-1825 decade of Western Pennsylvania politics.

At the outset of this era the organization necessary for healthy party conflict was rapidly passing beyond the horizon; at its end political realignments were only beginning to emerge. The intervening years were doomed to political chaos. Before the relaxed party discipline of this period could be revitalized, both regionalism and localized methods of party control had to be overcome.

The nation had accepted the peace following the War of 1812 with an attitude of optimism, but Richard Rush of Philadelphia warned that in Pennsylvania political good feeling would reign only temporarily. In a letter to Jonathan Roberts he perceived that "something in the seeming uncertainty and profound calm of the present moment . . . fills me with anticipations. It cannot last. Tornadoes that will sweep in opposite courses may be generating." [1] Surprisingly enough, he did not realize the full impact of his observations; Western Pennsylvania was already convulsed with the party chaos and popular bewilderment he predicted.

The region's political life in this decade is analogous to a series of military campaigns in a civil war. Parts One and Two, designated as the Battlefield and the Weapons of Battle, respectively, are intended to present at least seven different profiles of these turbulent years so that the depth and breadth of the political disorder might be understood. Emphasis is focused on these parts, but the logical climax to their operation is not revealed until Part Three, the Major Campaigns. There the interactions of the factors, individually described in the earlier parts, are translated into the actual election results.

In every political battle, like every military encounter, geography, combatants, and the inhabitants of the battle area comprise the study of the battlefield. With every passing year after the mid 18th Century, the geography of the Allegheny Mountains converted the western settlers into a more conscious minority. Those who went westward looked to the West for their future; at the same time they cast an eye to the East

---

[1] Richard Rush to Jonathan Roberts, July 3, 1817. Jonathan Roberts Papers.

for the encouragement which was necessary for success, but generally the East ignored them.

By 1815 the Pennsylvanians west of the mountains had developed a group-consciousness, based on geography and experience, that reflected a more or less common resentful attitude toward the East. On most other topics, however, these western counties were rent with factionalism. There were instruments available to frustrate this disagreement, but these weapons, namely newspapers, local political committees, and other political and social alignments, were not equal to the task, often serving to promote further division. These weapons were used to bombard the public with internal improvement, tariff, bank, and caucus ammunition, the explosive properties of which were not understood.

This indiscriminate use of weapons, along with their ammunition, inevitably led to a series of unsatisfactory political campaigns which found contestants frequently switching allegiance from the time of one skirmish to that of the next. All semblance of party discipline constantly eluded the unhappy region until the very end of the decade.

ACKNOWLEDGMENTS

The extant details of this era in Western Pennsylvania's history are found principally in newspapers which are scattered throughout the Middle Atlantic area. Before this account could be written, materials had to be gathered from many repositories stretching from Pittsburgh and Erie in the west to New York and the nation's capital in the east.

The author is appreciative of the many kindnesses shown him in the course of this research by the staffs of the Library of Congress, the State Library of Pennsylvania, the Carnegie Library of Pittsburgh, the Princeton University Library, the Lehigh University Library, the University of Pennsylvania Library, the Darlington Library of the University of Pittsburgh, the Uniontown Public Library, the Erie Public Library, the Historical Society of Pennsylvania, the New York Historical Society, the Historical Society of Western Pennsylvania, the Crawford County Historical Society, the Washington County Historical Society, the Tribune Review Publishing Company of Greensburg, and the Observer Publishing Company of Washington, Pennsylvania.

Miss Rose Demorest, Miss H. Dorothy English, and Mr. William M. Betcher of Carnegie Library, Mrs. Lois Mulkearn of the Darlington Library, Mr. Earle R. Forrest of the Washington County Historical Society, Mr. James R. Shryock of the Crawford County Historical Society, the late Professor Russell J. Ferguson of the University of Pittsburgh, and Mrs. Agnes L. Starrett, editor of the University of Pittsburgh Press, deserve a word of special thanks for extending much more than professional courtesy and consideration to the many requests made of them.

I am especially grateful to Dean Roy F. Nichols, University of Pennsylvania, and to Professor Philip S. Klein, Pennsylvania State University, for reading the entire manuscript and offering valuable suggestions. The shortcomings that still remain are not to be charged to them, but to my own failure to heed the full meaning of their counsel.

JAMES A. KEHL
Pittsburgh, 1956

TABLE OF CONTENTS

Part One—The Battlefield

Part Two—The Weapons of Battle

LIST OF ILLUSTRATIONS

PART ONE

The Battlefield

I

The Position of Western Pennsylvania

*The State of Pennsylvania—We love her as a parent,
altho' she treats us like a step child.*[1]

AS the year 1814 drew to a close, the fabric of the American nation
was fast becoming frayed at the edges. Both the moral fiber
and the military capacity of the people were grievously challenged during this year of war with Great Britain. The United States
Navy had been swept from the sea, and government officials expected
the next packet from Europe to report the failure of the diplomatic
negotiations which were being conducted at Ghent. Internally, the
anti-war faction in New England had gathered at Hartford to condemn the conflict against Britain; and the nation's capital was humbled
before the invader's torch when defenses were tested and found inadequate.

This burning of Washington alarmed Pennsylvania's nearby metropolis of Philadelphia where the citizens girded themselves to resist what
they believed would be the next British thrust of devastation along the
Atlantic seaboard. The city councils and surrounding communities
appropriated a half million dollars for the defense of the area. In fever-
ish haste new military units were formed, and private citizens volun-
teered unstintingly of their labors to strengthen the fortifications. The
western part of the state, especially the Pittsburgh area, did not experience such pronounced anxiety and gloom. There both the farmer and
the manufacturer enjoyed unprecedented prosperity. The war was now
remote to their area, and following prescribed Federalist principle, the
Pittsburgh Gazette, the most prominent newspaper of the western
counties, saw no harm in the Hartford conclave since peace was prefer-
able to "Mr. Madison's war." [2]

---

[1] Toast proposed at an Independence Day celebration in the borough of Erie.
Erie Gazette, July 14, 1821.

[2] Sanford W. Higginbotham, *The Keystone in the Democratic Arch: Pennsylvania Politics 1800-1816* (Harrisburg: Pennsylvania Historical and Museum
Commission, 1952), p. 295.

Contrary to early predictions, the war had proved anything but disastrous to Pennsylvania farmers. Certainly those of the countryside around Pittsburgh could not complain since a hundredweight of flour was selling for as much in 1814 as a barrel had brought before the war. Other farm products were retailing at correspondingly high prices—leaving the farmer without any deep-seated hatred of the conflict. While this inflation was local and perhaps temporary, it was no doubt conditioned in part by the spectacular progress of Pittsburgh and other Western Pennsylvania communities in the development of domestic manufactures. In Pittsburgh proper the value of manufactured products in 1814 was double that of 1810, inciting no economic objection to the war among these producers.[3]

In spite of these advantages accruing from the conflict with Britain, Western Pennsylvania was perturbed about the ultimate outcome. The mounting war costs and the many obstacles to an honorable peace prompted the greatest concern. At the very end of the year the nation began receiving reports that the British were launching a new offensive in the South—against the city of New Orleans. In Meadville, Pennsylvania, the editor of *The Crawford Weekly Messenger* declared that the fate of this southern city had probably been decided on Christmas. With the enemy in command of the numerous waters surrounding the city and able to disembark a land force superior to the American, he saw no chance for victory, especially since the detachments from Kentucky and Tennessee had probably not arrived in time to help with the city's defense.[4] The public was further prepared for the shock of another American debacle by a James Wilson editorial which found its way, either directly or by reproduction, into many homes throughout Pennsylvania. This editor urged his readers to consider their compatriots in New Orleans:

> Their day of trial has arrived—alas, perhaps it is passed, and the town wrapt in flames!—Wives, husbands, children, massacred! If this is not actually the case, it is their own personal bravery, with a small part of the United States army, and the brave general Jackson that have saved them.[5]

Then with dramatic suddenness the victory at New Orleans and the Treaty of Ghent, reported to the nation in that order, transformed darkness into light. The end of every war, even this indecisive War of

---

[3] Higginbotham, *Keystone in the Democratic Arch,* p. 289.
[4] *The Crawford Weekly Messenger* (Meadville), January 25, 1815.
[5] *Aurora: General Advertiser* (Philadelphia), January 14, 1815.

1812, automatically generates a feeling of hope for brighter days than those experienced immediately before, especially among the people of the conquering nation.

In American minds there was no doubt as to the triumphant nation in this second struggle with Britain. General Jackson's crushing defeat of "Wellington's Invincibles," Commodore Perry's victory on Lake Erie in 1813, and the exaltant ring of such stirring phrases as "we have met the enemy and they are ours" could spell only success for the American forces. The nation dreamed of peace, of national prosperity, and of freedom to trade, to develop industry, and to open new lands. It seemed that an "era of good feeling" had most certainly dawned, but these prospects were abruptly transformed into horrible nightmares. Because of her transmontane position, changing economy, and sparse population, Western Pennsylvania was among the most acute sufferers in the ensuing decade. Throughout this period her people nevertheless continued to talk a superficial language of good feeling, but this was only a thin veil covering many strong and unmanageable undercurrents.

The New Orleans victory contributed substantially to this cloak of good feeling enveloping the American nation as a whole. Not only did the report of this triumph precede the announcement of the Treaty of Ghent and cause many Americans to link peace with Britain's defeat at the hands of Andrew Jackson, but it also reversed the editorial predictions of the outcome. For weeks before the battle it had been anticipated that the British would launch an offensive against New Orleans, and newspapers had circulated widely the possibility of battle and the probability of another American debacle. Conditioned to defeat, the nation heard the "glorious news" which produced an even greater psychological reaction than would have come from the normal announcement of a victory.

When the report from Ghent followed, the nation had achieved a peace that even the Federalists could accept as honorable. Military victory alone had not been enough, but the added knowledge of peace caused the differences concerning the war to be displaced by a burst of national pride. Westmoreland County's soundingboard of Federalism, the *Greensburg Gazette,* reflected this interaction with its comparative treatment of these two national events. In reporting General Jackson's success, the editor was content with a regular-sized headline declaring vaguely "Great News," but the negotiations at Ghent produced the boldface banner "PEACE," and the whole introductory paragraph to the account, covering 15 lines, was set in large type.[6]

As late as February 1, 1815, the Brownsville *American Telegraph* was still waiting to have its "awful apprehensions" concerning the fate of the Louisianans confirmed although it had received rumors of peace. This Fayette County paper refused to give credence to the idea of a truce and injected the prediction that peace on honorable terms would be indefinitely postponed unless the affairs of Europe would influence British council. In denouncing this "gossip of peace" as the probable connivance of "unprincipled merchants" to facilitate their speculations, the editor was suggesting one of the undercurrents that was to dominate the forthcoming decade in which the merchant class was brought under attack by both the farmer and the domestic manufacturer for unpatriotic exploitation.[7]

To the people of the entire Mississippi Valley, especially those of the Pittsburgh area, the New Orleans victory was an economic, as well as a national achievement. They regarded it as a part of their final battle in the struggle to secure the "invaluable right" of free communication with the ocean via the Mississippi River. James Ross, a Pittsburgh civic and business leader, told President James Monroe in a welcoming address on September 5, 1817, that this was "an attainment second in magnitude only to national independence itself, and inseparably connected with it." [8] By the turn of the 19th Century the Monongahela Valley of Western Pennsylvania and Pittsburgh proper had vigorously undertaken the construction of boats to supply the commercial needs of the Ohio River Valley; the area had come to believe that it had a destiny "to supply a western world with blessings, without dependence on another hemisphere." [9]

As early as 1805 the vision of Pittsburgh commercial leaders, such as James O'Hara and John Wilkins, Jr., went far beyond the Ohio River market. Their *General Butler* carried sundry articles, but chiefly

---

[6] *Greensburg Gazette*, February 11, 18, 1815.

[7] *American Telegraph* (Brownsville), January 25, February 1, 1815.

[8] S. Putnam Waldo, *The Tour of James Monroe, President of the United States, in the Year 1817; . . . together with a Sketch of His Life, His Inaugural Speech and First Message; and Historical and Geographical Notices of the Principal Places through which He Passed* (Hartford: F. D. Bolles & Co., 1818). p. 256.

[9] *Pittsburgh Gazette*, May 29, 1818.

window glass and porter, for the Louisville and Natchez markets, and nominal quantities of both were reserved to try the new market at New Orleans which, it was hoped, would prove a "good experiment." At Natchez the *General Butler* took on a full ocean cargo of cotton, and, after an interim stop at New Orleans, struck out with Liverpool, England, as her destination. There the agent for O'Hara and Wilkins was instructed either to arrange a return cargo for any United States port or to sell the vessel. He was advised that the owners did not wish to sell at considerable loss, but since they were in the process of constructing another ship at Pittsburgh and were "desirous to encourage shipbuilding at this place," they were willing to sell without profit.[10]

Western Pennsylvania dreamed of developing an extensive foreign commerce, and within a short time one of her maritime exploits had became legendary. In 1812 Henry Clay recounted the story in explaining Pittsburgh's thriving commerce to Congress. He told of a Pittsburgh vessel that crossed the Atlantic and entered a European port where the master of the vessel, according to the requirements of law, laid his sailing papers, which included his departure point, before the keeper of the customs-house. The keeper boldly denied the existence of such a port as Pittsburgh and moved to seize the vessel for operating with forged papers. The master procured a map of the United States, and, pointing to the city of New Orleans on the Gulf of Mexico, began to retrace his course up the Mississippi River more than a thousand miles to the mouth of the Ohio. The astonished port authority watched with increasing interest as the captain continued to re-map his route up the Ohio River another thousand miles to the juncture of the Allegheny and Monongahela. "There," he exclaimed, "stands Pittsburg, the port from which I sailed." [11]

The practice of selling vessels abroad or in our own Atlantic or Gulf ports, as suggested by O'Hara and Wilkins to their agent, was commonplace among Pittsburgh merchants at this time because of the hazards of upstream navigation from New Orleans to Pittsburgh. Even

---

[10] James O'Hara to William C. O'Hara, March 8, 1805; James O'Hara and John Wilkins, Jr. to William C. O'Hara, June 9, 1805. Box 48, Denny-O'Hara Papers.

[11] *Annals of Congress: The Debates and Proceedings in the Congress of the United States;* . . . 12th Cong., 1st Sess., I (Washington: Government Printing Office, 1853), 918f.

after the *New Orleans,* the first steamboat built on western waters, was constructed at Pittsburgh in 1811, ships that left Western Pennsylvania for the Mississippi Valley did not return because of the navigation dangers involved. The *New Orleans,* for example, spent its lifetime plying between the city of the same name and Natchez. In 1817 the navigation obstacles were overcome, and the steamboat *Enterprise* completed the first upstream journey from the Gulf to Pittsburgh.[12]

As the up-river trade developed, more and more of the needs of the Mississippi and Ohio Valleys were supplied from New Orleans instead of Pittsburgh. Although this shift reduced the area of Pittsburgh's commercial dominance, Western Pennsylvania's economy was not seriously impaired. Increased settlements in the Old Northwest proved more than an adequate substitute. Furthermore, the one-way Pittsburgh-New Orleans trade had never been a satisfactory one since Pittsburgh sold her products in the Gulf city while being forced to procure her needs from Philadelphia on the Atlantic seaboard. Financial arrangements with New Orleans had been marked, not only by delays in payment, but also by confusion in the type and value of money presented.[13]

In spite of this difficulty, money flowed into Western Pennsylvania from the westward, but it seemed to flow out again with greater facility to meet the demands of the area's eastern creditors. This exodus of the circulating medium across the mountains, chiefly to Philadelphia, helped to produce an antagonism between the two areas of Pennsylvania that was to run uncontrolled through the era of good feeling. With each passing year Western Pennsylvania's economic future seemed more firmly linked with the West, but politically she remained leagued with the section of the state east of the Alleghenies. Western Pennsylvania had founded new industries to meet the demands of the West and resented the competition that came from the influx of foreign goods through the eastern ports, but the commercial East refused to consider legislation to protect the "war-born" industries. The pull of these economic and political forces in opposite directions tended only to heighten the undercurrents in the years after the War of 1812.

---

[12] Sara Killikelly, *The History of Pittsburgh: Its Rise and Progress* (Pittsburgh: B. C. and Gordon Montgomery Co., 1906), pp. 140, 144.

[13] James O'Hara to Messrs. McEwen, Hale, and Davidson, June 22, 1805. Box 48, Denny-O'Hara Papers.

Undoubtedly this war engendered a deeper appreciation and a more practical meaning of independence than was prevalent in 1776. Although the political break with England had come with the Declaration of Independence, the nation's ultimate fate nevertheless remained in the balance because of nearly complete economic dependence on the former mother country. In the 40 years that followed, the United States proceeded to lay her own economic foundations and had now fought a second war—a war supported largely by her own production. To symbolize this economic ascendancy, John Binns of Philadelphia proposed in 1816 to publish an edition of the Declaration of Independence that would be American in all respects: paper, ink, type, designs, and engraving, as well as political concept. This edition was to illustrate that, what the United States had achieved politically, she could now also accomplish in the realms of art and manufacturing.[14]

Although the Americans had announced their independence of Britain in 1776, Binns was aware that they had been literally compelled to borrow "pencil and paper" to record it. Now it was a good feeling to end that dependence. Western Pennsylvania, however, was not so optimistic. She shared the East's enthusiasm for this economic advance, but warned that these gains, although won, were not yet secure. The East refused to accept this admonition which was echoed principally by Pittsburgh's manufacturers.

Within a matter of months after the signing of the Treaty of Ghent cheap British goods appeared in Western markets. The clamor for protection resounded loud and strong, and Pennsylvania became locked in a great tariff debate. This issue, like so many others, found the western counties disunited, but all were willing to look across the Alleghenies to find the source of their economic infirmities. Although not all the western "doctors" diagnosed the sickness as lack of tariff immunity, they heartily agreed that the poison affecting the state's economic health was originating in the eastern counties around Philadelphia.

THE LIMITS OF THE REGION

From this brief introductory description of Western Pennsylvania's position in the stream of national development in 1815 comes the inference that geography was paramount in shaping the area's history

---

[14] *The Mercury* (Pittsburgh), May 4, 1816.

during this era of good feeling. Without further delay this inference should be transformed into a positive declaration although the actual geographical position of the region represents a controversial topic. Many authorities from the various branches of social science do not accept the thesis that the western counties of the state constitute a satisfactory region for study. The bulk of this skepticism is supplied by the economists. They even challenge the validity of the term "region" because in modern social organization large cities, with their surrounding and dependent hinterland, represent the focal points of regions without regard for state lines.

Twentieth Century interstate commerce interpretations have paled political boundaries and localisms into unimportance and have catapulted this new cultural unity based on the large city into the forefront. In 1815, however, political boundaries contributed substantially to the demarcation of cultural and regional units since all areas were more dependent upon their state capitals than in this age of social control by the national government.

Even today, when the economics of the city is the focal point of regional organization, there is much more to history than blind economic surge. Men generally act together because they see and believe together; an inspiring idea or a cringing inferiority gives as much direction to history as a concern for the next meal. In the years following the War of 1812 that part of Pennsylvania, which was bounded on three sides by the state lines of Virginia, Ohio, and New York, and in the east by the natural barrier of the Allegheny Mountains, possessed enough distinctive ideas to be classed a cultural unit.

These mountains, a part of the Appalachian range which extends in a southwesterly direction along the Atlantic seaboard from New England to Georgia, helped form the first boundary between Eastern and Western America. Nowhere were the mountains more formidable than in Pennsylvania. By retarding transportation and migration, they influenced the development of society in Western Pennsylvania in a negative way. This restricted communication prevented an easy exchange of ideas between the people on the opposite sides of the mountains and produced psychological differences between the older civilization and the transmontane pioneers.[15] The localized attitudes and behavior pat-

---

[15] Russell J. Ferguson, *Early Western Pennsylvania Politics* (Pittsburgh: University of Pittsburgh Press, 1938), p. 2; Louis Hartz, *Economic Policy & Democratic Thought: Pennsylvania, 1776-1860* (Cambridge: Harvard University Press, 1948), p. 22.

terns engendered by this separation transformed Western Pennsylvania into a state of mind, as well as a geographic expression.

Many of the economists, who object to this acceptance of Western Pennsylvania of 1815 as a region because it does not conform to the pattern of present-day organization, join with sociologists and an array of historians in their insistence that in the decade of this study the characteristics of the region were not essentially different from those of the Ohio Valley generally. These critics correctly maintain that this area, drained by the western watershed of the Alleghenies, constituted the first area to look westward for a destiny instead of across the Atlantic. Their contention is further corroborated by the greatest geographical determinist, Frederick Jackson Turner, who observed that from the time the mountains rose between the pioneers and the seaboard a new order of Americanism was born.[16] In spite of all this testimony of a community of interest within the Ohio Valley, all the eyes of Western Pennsylvania did not turn westward.[17]

Although Western Pennsylvania's industry was rewarded with good markets in the Ohio Valley, the region was nevertheless dependent upon the Atlantic seaboard for its needs not supplied by the immediate area. Philadelphia merchants and wagoners, meanwhile, continuously pressed this advantage which tied them to the counties across the mountains. Since the state's economy was predominantly agricultural, an added bond of kinship sprang up among the farmers, whether they lived on the Schuylkill, Susquehanna, or Allegheny.[18] Political cooperation, however, was not uniform; political and economic rivalries among these counties produced varied reactions to the many bills considered by the legislature. In a negative sense these changing alignments operated as a cohesive factor and restrained the counties west of the mountains from carrying through a complete political separation.

Antagonisms, however, were dangerously divisive; "no other area

[16] Frederick J. Turner, *The Frontier in American History* (New York: Henry Holt and Co., 1921), p. 18.

[17] Catherine Reiser, *Pittsburgh's Commercial Development 1800-1850* (Harrisburg: Pennsylvania Historical and Museum Commission, 1951), p. 2, denies this contention and emphasizes western economic factors in explaining Western Pennsylvania's development.

[18] Harry M. Tinkcom, *The Republicans and Federalists in Pennsylvania 1790-1800: A Study in National Stimulus and Local Response* (Harrisburg: Pennsylvania Historical and Museum Commission, 1950), p. 19.

in America ever came so near being a separate state without becoming one," as Western Pennsylvania.[19] Because of the divisive character of the Appalachian chain, Pennsylvania is the only state which today em- braces important areas on both sides of the main ridges. Other states had originally been organized with transmontane areas, but all of them broke away in the course of development. Virginia successively lost Kentucky and West Virginia while North Carolina's suppression of the state of Franklin was eventually overthrown in the rise of Tennessee. On numerous occasions the people of Western Pennsylvania threatened similar action, but the cohesive factors always remained predominant.[20]

Although not so formidable as the Allegheny Mountains, state boundary lines in 1815 did represent cultural barriers, and nowhere is this tendency more sharply demonstrated than with the Pennsylvania-Ohio line. In this decade of good feeling Ohio was wholly western and looked to a legislature that was completely western in composition and attitude. Western Pennsylvania, on the other hand, set off from the East by the mountains, was western in attitude, but had to depend upon a legislature at Harrisburg that was largely eastern in sympathy.

Almost inevitably these circumstances produced behavior patterns in Ohio different from those of Western Pennsylvania. Ohio laws regard- ing business transactions and failures favored the debtor while the Pennsylvania laws gave the advantage to the creditor. Ohioans could refuse to pay their debts with eastern paper, or altogether for that matter, and assume the attitude that "Philadelphia may go to the devil." They could sneer at the East with such comments as "You may talk of suing us, but your merchandise is converted into brick houses which, thanks to our appraisement law, you cannot sell."[21]

Western Pennsylvania was no such economic sanctuary for the debtor; she experienced the same hardships as Ohio, but did not enjoy the same facility for dodging or postponing her obligations. Bankruptcy laws were generally localized for the special benefit of creditors resident in the state, and with the increasing volume of supplies sent by seaboard merchants to western areas outside their own state, the problem of debt

---

[19] George Swetnam, *Pittsylvania Country* (New York: Duell, Sloan & Pearce, 1951), p. 36.

[20] *Ibid.*, pp. 36-39.

[21] Anonymous letter dated Pittsburgh, September 21, 1819, quoted in *Aurora*, October 29, 1819.

collection became acute. Since the entire area west of the mountains was a debtor section in transactions with the East, the advantage of the Ohio debtor over his Western Pennsylvania neighbor was considerable in the years following the War of 1812.

This situation proved that the laws of individual states were not competent to render justice between debtor and creditor, but no national regulation existed. Laws of eastern states were frequently disgraced by a mean self-interest in behalf of the creditors while the laws of western states were slanted for the debtor and permitted fraudulent men to escape their just obligations. Obviously there was a need for a system whereby an eastern creditor could readily force a debtor in another state to give his property in payment of his debt and at the same time assure the debtor of Western Pennsylvania a fair price for his real estate or personal property when confiscated to satisfy his creditors.[22]

In the 1819-1820 session of the Pennsylvania House of Representatives six petitions from the western counties were presented urging the passage of a law to prevent the sacrifice of property by process of law at a price far below its actual worth. Each petition had its own peculiar appraisement or stay provisions, but the law, which eventually emerged and went into effect after March 28, 1821, provided that 12 men under oath were required to place a valuation on any real property in question while three men would suffice in cases of personal property. If the property could not be sold for at least two-thirds of this valuation, all further proceedings were to be stayed for one year.[23]

This legislation was designed, not only to give the creditor reasonable assurances of payment, but also to relieve the unfortunate debtor on an equitable basis and enable him to resume his usefulness to society. Until the passage of this law, Western Pennsylvanians who fell into debt were at the unchecked mercy of the eastern creditor while in Ohio the debtor frolicked at the expense of the same agent. In Western Pennsylvania enterprises had to be undertaken with caution; in Ohio they could be assumed with abandon.

This distinction alone was enough to mark the political boundary

---

[22] *Niles' Weekly Register* (Baltimore) quoted in the *Statesman* (Pittsburgh), January 2, 1819.

[23] Pennsylvania, *Journal of the House of Representatives,* 1819-1820, pp. 246, 268, 585, 660, 749; *Crawford Messenger,* April 14, 1820.

between the two as an imposing barrier, but Pennsylvania's rigid legislation regarding imprisonment for debt further handicapped the western counties. This region, which enjoyed no surplus population, suffered a significant loss in productive energies with every conviction, and her constituents petitioned the legislature to abolish debtor imprisonment. No success in this direction was recorded, however, until 1832 when a law declared that imprisonment for sums less than $5.33 be abolished.[24]

The Pennsylvania-Virginia line produced a similar economic inequity for the former's western counties. Western Pennsylvania businessmen charged that western merchants preferred to trade through Wheeling, Virginia, rather than Pittsburgh because under Pennsylvania laws it was easier for the creditor to enforce payment by attaching the goods of the western merchant at the latter city. The actual influence of these business regulations on the growth and commerce of the two towns cannot be accurately weighed, but in the course of their rivalry, particularly in times of depression, Western Pennsylvanians used the differences to place the blame for their failures on the business legislation of their eastern-dominated state government.[25]

The only other state that Western Pennsylvania bordered was New York. The cultural distinctions between the areas adjoining this political boundary were not so clearly-drawn, but nevertheless one area did depend upon Albany and the other upon Harrisburg for the legislation that formulated the rules governing their development. That difference in itself could incite jealous comparisons of state governments and produce dissatisfaction, especially since communities have always shown a tendency to dwell on their disadvantages and ignore the benefits they enjoy because of their position.

Only to a moderate degree did the people of Northwestern Pennsylvania reflect this attitude. They were irritated by the fact that the legislature at Harrisburg was satisfied to give less attention to improvements in the state's western counties than that supplied by the Albany legislature, but these conditions prompted no antagonisms or rivalry with Southwestern New York. The two were tied together by such common avenues of trade as Lake Erie and the Allegheny River and

---

[24] Hartz, *Economic Policy & Democratic Thought,* p. 223f.

[25] *Pittsburgh Gazette,* September 17, October 8, 12, 1819.

by such Western Pennsylvania needs as lumber, salt, potash, and pearl ash which New York could supply.

Shortly before the turn of the 19th Century James O'Hara had begun this community of interest by successfully importing salt from the Onondaga works in New York to Pittsburgh. This necessity of life was transported by way of Lake Ontario and Lake Erie to the borough of Erie from which it was transshipped to the Pittsburgh area by way of French Creek and the Allegheny River. Through this new enterprise a fair quality of salt was delivered into Western Pennsylvania at half the price assessed for carrying it by pack horse across the mountains from Philadelphia.[26]

The Customs House Records at Erie reveal the quick response that was made to this new source of cheap salt: 714 barrels were transshipped in 1800 and 12,000 barrels in 1809. Shipments remained high until abruptly cut off by the War of 1812, but Western Pennsylvania was neither forced to return to dependence upon Philadelphia nor to experience a lack of salt. The New York supply was replaced by a more recent discovery of salt deposits in the Kiskiminetas Valley.[27]

When the war ended, this avenue of trade was re-opened. The Pittsburgh *Mercury* reported that large quantities of lumber were being brought down the Allegheny River from Hamilton, New York, to a Pennsylvania market. It also predicted that potash and pearl ash would soon follow the same route to the Pittsburgh glassworks. The writer, who signed his name "Sylvanus," exhibited a feeling of friendliness toward New York and insisted that Western Pennsylvania was indebted for these products to the liberal aid of her northern neighbor's legislature. The shipments of lumber were only possible, he argued, because of the improvements to the road from Hamilton to Olean on the Allegheny River. In fact, he envisioned products from the East for Ohio and Kentucky taking the same course—being diverted from the old channels because of Philadelphia's failure to improve her trade lane through Pittsburgh.[28]

This prophesy was not beyond the realm of probability as a Western

[26] Eulalia C. Schramm, "General James O'Hara: Pittsburgh's First Captain of Industry" (Unpublished Master's thesis, History Dept., University of Pittsburgh, 1931), p. 66.

[27] *Ibid.*, p. 67.

[28] *Mercury*, September 28, 1815, quoted in *Poulson's American Daily Advertiser* (Philadelphia), October 10, 1815.

Pennsylvania petition to the legislature in the winter 1818-1819 attested. It declared that merchandise was being shipped from the city of New York to Pittsburgh at the cost of five dollars per hundredweight while the existing Philadelphia to Pittsburgh rates were from six to eight dollars for the same quantity.[29] Thus here in 1815 "Sylvanus," consciously or unconsciously, struck a chord on internal improvement that was to reverberate throughout Western Pennsylvania in the ensuing decade: "New York is wide awake. If we dose, we shall have time to repent when repentance will not avail." [30]

This last comment suggests that "Sylvanus's" article was designed more to goad Philadelphia into action on the subject of internal improvements than to praise New York, but there was also a deep sincerity in the commendation. The cooperation of the two areas was well demonstrated by the case of *The Phoenix and Erie Reflector,* a newspaper established by John Morris at Erie in 1819, but printed and edited by Robert I. Curtis at the office of his *Chautauqua Eagle* in Mayville, New York.[31] This relationship presupposed common news coverage and interpretation which helped to draw the two areas closer together.

A few years later their economies were further intertwined through the construction of New York's Erie Canal. When a citizen from Crawford County penned his exaltations concerning the canal to a friend in Harrisburg, he declared that wheat was selling for 75 cents per bushel at his door, and, if he preferred, he could take it to Erie where Buffalo merchants were purchasing all they could get for a dollar a bushel. The net result was an increase in Crawford County land values and an influx of settlers to populate the county's many vacant lands.[32]

Even before the Erie Canal influenced trade and transportation, the Pittsburgh *Statesman* offered practical evidence of the facility by which regular water communication with New York could be opened. The editor gave a detailed description of the voyage of a 35-foot keelboat that had just arrived in Pittsburgh with several families aboard. They

---

[29] Erasmus Wilson (ed.), *Standard History of Pittsburg Pennsylvania* (Chicago: H. R. Cornell & Co., 1898), p. 87.
[30] *Mercury,* September 28, 1815, quoted in *Poulson's Advertiser,* October 10, 1815.
[31] Clarence S. Brigham (ed.), *History and Bibliography of American Newspapers 1690-1820* (Worcester, Massachusetts: American Antiquarian Society, 1947), II, 848f.
[32] *Poulson's Advertiser,* February 26, 1824.

had embarked in *this* vessel at the mouth of Wood Creek at the head of Oneida Lake in New York. The first leg of their journey carried them down the lake, through the Oswego River, and into Lake Ontario. From there they entered the Niagara River and passed to within five miles of the falls. The boat was carried around the falls on wheels and placed in the river again two miles above. After reaching the shores of Lake Erie, the travelers were forced to place their craft on wheels again and moved seven miles over good road to Lake Chautauqua. Launching the boat there, they passed through the lake into Chautauqua Creek and then Conewango Creek; on the last leg of the historic journey they entered the Allegheny River at Warren and descended to Pittsburgh.[33]

A few years later after the Erie Canal was completed, the advantages of this trade lane were being sung at the eastern terminus as well. A citizen from the city of New York joined Western Pennsylvania in painting a similar picture of the communications' potential between his state and the forks of the Ohio. His article, printed by the *Aurora,* reported that a steamboat was being built at Erie to ply between that borough and Buffalo on a schedule that was to be synchronized with that of a line of stages running between Pittsburgh and Erie. These two links, plus the Erie Canal, were expected to divert western travel to New York from the expensive and tiresome route over the mountains to Philadelphia to this more comfortable and economical channel.[34]

The actual purpose for reporting both travel from Oneida Lake to Pittsburgh and this newly-projected transportation system was not intended to encourage either. The attention given by the *Statesman* and the *Aurora,* as well as by other instruments aimed at the direction of public opinion, was designed more to stimulate a fresh motivation in Philadelphia's latent exertions to improve the communication lanes of the state than to promote a community of interest with New York.

Although a Pittsburgh-Erie-Buffalo-Albany-New York trade route had possibilities, they were remote. Generally speaking, the writers were aware of these limitations and desired only to prod the eastern part of the state into the promotion of road and canal improvements within Pennsylvania. Not sincere in their projections, they were nevertheless

---

[33] *Statesman,* November 12, 1822, quoted in *Democratic Press* (Philadelphia), November 19, 1822.

[34] Annonymous letter dated New York, May 4, 1825, quoted in *Aurora,* May 6, 1825.

able to induce many naive citizens in Western Pennsylvania to have faith in a potentially-valuable community of interest with New York. This idea was most easily established in the northern counties where the pioneer spirit predominated. Typical of American pioneers, these people were richly imbued with hope and idealism which made acceptance of this scheme for a new outlet relatively simple in spite of the fact that its promoters were using it chiefly as a lever against the East.

Although this community of interest with Western New York was partly real and partly fictitious, it cannot be overlooked. It showed a tendency to make the limits of our culture area somewhat nebulous because Northwestern Pennsylvania was encouraged to establish bonds of mutual assistance with New York and to anticipate a marked rise in commercial activity and prosperity. This cooperation with a northern neighbor and hope for increased economic development came at a time when neither the southwestern counties nor the more densely-settled East had either the means or the desire to lend a helping hand. From these circumstances the northern counties received inspiration to continue within the political framework of Pennsylvania in spite of their distant and transmontane position.

Aside from the three states of Virginia, Ohio, and New York the culture area, herein called Western Pennsylvania, was bounded by the Allegheny Mountains which traverse the state in a northeasterly-southwesterly direction to hinder and delay communications with the East. The nature of this boundary is different from the political frontiers already described and in a sense is more arbitrarily drawn, but certainly no less formidable. Transportation was a fundamental question in the early history of the area west of the mountains, and in spite of precautions wagons and stages engaged in this travel were overturned daily.[35] Many others were disabled with broken axles and wheels or during the spring thaws were found hopelessly mired in the deep ruts caused by the winter's traffic.

In crossing the mountains from either Baltimore or Philadelphia, an immigrant to Western Pennsylvania customarily saw several loaded wagons upset and heard stories of many more. Wagoners, stage drivers, tavern keepers, and newspaper reports related to the traveler a collection of gruesome pictures of accidents along the mountain roads. En

---

[35] Jeremiah S. Young, *A Political and Constitutional Study of the Cumberland Road* (Chicago: University of Chicago Press, 1902), p. 16.

route stage drivers pointed out scenes of tragedy in tour-guide fashion. Spots where teams had plunged over precipices to their death or where wagons had overturned to kill their occupants, or at least destroy their cargoes, were always landmarks worthy of comment. Such accounts were enough to win the full cooperation of the passengers. When the driver's laconic command of "to the right, gentlemen" or "gentlemen, to the left!" was given to trim the coach, response was immediate. When wash-outs or poor grading had left roadbeds lopsided, the passengers were required to get out and hold up the lower side of the stage until safer ground had been reached.[36]

Either through such arduous experiences or the knowledge of them, the people of the western counties came to recognize the imposing obstacle that the mountains presented to communication with the East. Together with the state lines, the Alleghenies completed the process of marking off Western Pennsylvania as a rather unique culture within the larger cultural pattern of Pennsylvania. Culturally, Eastern Pennsylvania reckoned time in terms of the first settlement, the first inland town, the first college, the first newspaper, and other evidences of a flowering civilization within the state.

To the people of Western Pennsylvania these innovations had no utility and very little meaning. They, meanwhile, thought in terms of the first settlement west of the mountains, the first presbytery west of the mountains, "the original seat of literature in the west," [37] the first newspaper published west of the mountains, the first book written and printed west of the mountains, the appearance of a President of the United States "for the first time upon the western waters," [38] the first foundry and manufactory to turn out the needs of western civilization, and many other proofs of Western Pennsylvania's growing importance and independence. They took pride in and reckoned progress from these

---

[36] Timothy Flint, *Recollections of the Last Ten Years, Passed in Occasional Residences and Journeyings in the Valley of the Mississippi, from Pittsburg and the Missouri to the Gulf of Mexico,* . . . (Boston: Cummings, Hilliard, and Co., 1826), p. 8; John Palmer, *Journal of Travels in the United States of North America, and in Lower Canada, Performed in the Year 1817;* . . . (London: Sherwood, Neely and Jones, 1818), p. 41; *Greensburg Gazette,* January 2, June 11, 1824.

[37] Waldo, *Tour of James Monroe,* p. 248.

[38] *Ibid.,* p. 256.

social and cultural milestones while easterners spoke an entirely different language of advancement.

In experiencing these successes west of the mountains, settlers developed the attitude that their exploits were unique—that they were doing things that had not been achieved before. They were in a new land and automatically, it seems, showed a tendency to look forward, not backward. They were interested in the new, not the old. Of course, as one approached closer and closer to the frontier at any time in American history, this concept grew stronger, but in reality none of the settler's activities was as unusual as he thought. Being unaware of general recurring patterns, the Western Pennsylvanian attached the greatest possible significance to the developments made in his settlements beyond the mountains.

THE LAND ITSELF

In 1815 there were 15 counties within the limits of these boundaries.[39] Covering 29 per cent of the area of Pennsylvania, they were inhabited by only 22 per cent of the state's population. In size these counties ranged from Greene with 597 square miles to Jefferson with 1203. The latter, with less than one person for every two square miles of land, was the most sparsely settled according to 1820 statistics. The concentration of population was in the five southern counties of Greene, Washington, Fayette, Westmoreland, and Allegheny which represented the only counties of Western Pennsylvania above the all-state average of 24 persons per square mile. They covered approximately one-third the area of the region, but embraced roughly two-thirds of the population. According to census figures in 1800, 1810, and 1820, the largest single county west of the mountains in population was Washington, but Allegheny, influenced particularly by the rapid development of Pittsburgh, registered a slightly higher density of settlement by 1820.[40]

The sparse population in the northern counties was the subject of much anxiety among the inhabitants because in six out of ten of these counties the population density was less than half that of the all-state norm. The Philadelphia *Aurora* insisted that Pennsylvania was not being considered for settlement by the average immigrant with the result that the state's overall population was not increasing proportionally

---

[39] For a complete geographic picture of the western counties see *Frontispiece*.
[40] For population details see Appendix A.

with other states. The editor asserted that this trend was the bitter fruit of the insecurity exhibited toward land titles, particularly in Northwestern Pennsylvania. Here, he charged, lands were generally occupied by a class of people called squatters, who had no legal claim to the soil that they cleared, improved and cultivated. If an actual purchaser attempted to settle on the land he had legally procured, his life was immediately endangered by these interlopers. Western Pennsylvania politicians frequently befriended the squatter and sponsored legislation which favored his retention of the land in order to win his political support. Thus "the bargain and sale of the title to property" was often practiced as a means of political advancement without any concern for the sanctity of the established rights of ownership.[41]

A descendant of Benjamin Franklin, who had possessed several large tracts on the Allegheny River, personally realized the threat to the land titles when he went to inspect the patriarch's holdings in 1817 and discovered that several pieces were occupied by "lawless interlopers." One insolently asserted:

> I know the land is yours, and that I have no title—but I have possession, and that is nine points of the law—possession you shall never get *without a good long lawsuit*, and you shall then spend more money than the land is worth.[42]

Such accounts made lasting impressions on the potential western settler in spite of assurances by the inhabitants of the northern counties that the days of insecure land titles had passed. Their efforts were not convincing. Since the people of other areas were not "undeceived" concerning the insecurity of land titles, the population in Pennsylvania's northwestern counties continued to lag.[43]

The conflict over land titles was particularly vexatious in these counties because of the great distances that many of the inhabitants were required to travel before reaching seats of justice where they attempted to have their land claims upheld. Although Warren County had been established in 1800, it had no separate and independent county organization until 1819. Its residents, for example, were forced to trudge from their cabins in the wilderness to Meadville, in Crawford County, to transact their public and legal business. This arrangement lasted for five years. Then a reorganization of the county administration

---

[41] *Aurora*, February 4, 1818. The basis of these conflicting land titles is explained in Chapter II.

[42] *Aurora*, February 4, 1818.

[43] "Agricola," *Crawford Messenger*, April 4, 1818.

sent them on toilsome journeys to Franklin, in Venango County, which was about 65 miles from the center of Warren County.[44]

Since so many residents were involved in litigations concerning land titles, many complaints protesting the inadequacy of this judicial system were registered with the state legislature in these first two decades of the 19th Century. They were, in turn, reported throughout the East with the result that emigrants planned to settle elsewhere.

The people in these northern counties attempted to minimize the importance of the insecurity of land titles in accounting for the sparse population and endeavored to place the responsibility on inadequate turnpike facilities. The *Kittanning Columbian* declared that the citizens of Pennsylvania's eastern counties knew more about Indiana and Illinois than they did the northwestern part of their own state because western immigrants had passed along routes either to the north or south of it. "Agricola" went a step further and insisted that American people generally had a more limited knowledge of Northwestern Pennsylvania than of any other area in the nation. Both insisted that the lack of good roads was responsible for the situation.

The *Columbian* urged the construction of a road from Kittanning, in Armstrong County, to Hamilton, New York, while "Agricola" had more grandiose dreams. He wanted a turnpike from Easton on the Delaware by way of Sunbury, Bellefont, Franklin, Meadville, and Waterford to Erie. He justified this demand with the assertion that Detroit merchants were carrying goods to New York more cheaply than Philadelphia merchants could ship to Pittsburgh. This comparison produced the generalization that Pennsylvania was 20 years behind New York in improvements and, therefore, 20 years behind in population development. "Agricola" was particularly disturbed that many settlers traveled from New York to Ohio and then took up residence on the same latitude as Northwestern Pennsylvania. If, by chance, any of them stopped at Erie, they were likely to settle in the immediate vicinity because of the lack of roads to the interior. The few who were highly charged with the investigating spirit, he pointed out, sought the interior via the Allegheny River. This route afforded a "bad specimen of the country" because of the foreboding hillsides along the river banks and prompted the poten-

---

[44] J. S. Schenck (ed.), *History of Warren County Pennsylvania* (Syracuse: D. Mason & Co., 1887), pp. 125, 141.

tial settler to continue his quest for a home without a true picture of Northwestern Pennsylvania's possibilities for settlement.[45]

Harm Jan Huidekoper, who resided for 50 years in Northwestern Pennsylvania, attributed the lack of progress in his section to a social and cultural lag in relation to other portions of the United States. To him the people, addicted to intemperance and dissipation, demonstrated only a limited capacity for religious and educational improvement. For many years after Huidekoper's arrival in 1804 there was not a single church in the four counties of the extreme northwest. The Reverend Joseph Stockton of the Presbyterian Church settled at Meadville for a time, and the Methodists held occasional camp meetings there, but such was the extent of religious development. Education, too, was limited almost exclusively to the county towns and even that was generally of the poorest kind.[46]

Thomas Atkinson of the *Crawford Messenger* sought to overcome these disadvantages of the northern counties with a bit of well-directed advertising in the winter of 1822-1823. He described the climate of the area as mild for the season, giving both the farmer and the merchant a worthwhile advantage. Slyly he mentioned that crops had been abundant and were now stored away with the firm assurance that the winter market would "afford the farmer a reasonable compensation for his produce." Continuing to reflect on the subject, Atkinson pointed out that:

if we contrast this section of the country with many other parts of the state, Ohio, Indianna, &c. to which the emigrant frequently appears bending his course, and but too late finds his error—we must be incapable of appreciating our own happiness and prosperity. . . . More southern climes, with all their tempting luxuries, when mingled with prevailing disease, are far inferior to our own, always accompanied with health and *plenty*, the real source of contentment.[47]

This limited population in the northern counties of Western Pennsylvania during the decade of 1815 to 1825 represented nothing unique in the westward development of the nation. Never has a population spread itself evenly over a region; a combination of geography, climate,

---

[45] "Agricola," *Crawford Messenger*, March 28, 1818; *Kittanning Columbian* quoted in *Crawford Messenger*, December 10, 1819.

[46] From a manuscript addressed to his children by Harm Jan Huidekoper and extracted in the *Obituary of Harm Jan Huidekoper*, Harm Jan Huidekoper Papers.

[47] *Crawford Messenger*, December 3, 1822.

minerals, means of communication, and disposition of the settlers had invariably produced clusters of residences. Even within these counties settlement was not uniform. The greatest single factor contributing to the rise of these clusters in Western Pennsylvania at this time was a large-scale dependence upon water transportation. Settlements sprang up along the shores of the Allegheny, Monongahela, and Ohio Rivers to supply the needs of travelers and to handle the commerce of the hinterland. The Allegheny was the principal connecting link between the northern and southern counties of the region, and along its banks were the seats of government for three counties. From these towns of Warren, Franklin, and Kittanning the counties of Warren, Venango, and Armstrong, respectively, were administered. At Franklin the river gained one of its two most significant tributaries, French Creek,[48] which flowed southward from New York through Crawford County and its progressive little community of Meadville.

The Monongahela River, on the other hand, flowed northward from the present state of West Virginia to Pittsburgh and tapped the trade of the extreme southern counties of the region as the Allegheny did in the north. It passed through such settlements as New Geneva, Brownsville, Williamsport (Monongahela), Elizabeth, and McKeesport, all of which conducted thriving boat-building industries. The variety of shapes and structures of water-craft that they turned out was most striking to the stranger recently arrived from the Atlantic. He viewed specimens ranging from the stately barge with its raised deck to the Kentucky flats, "a species of ark, very nearly resembling a New England pig-stye." If the traveler or potential settler desired to have his own transportation for further western travel, he generally priced these models and then consulted his pocketbook before making a purchase.[49]

More people embarked on western waters in the southern counties than in the north because of the direct flow of migration across the mountains from Philadelphia and Baltimore. Those that passed through New York generally used the Great Lakes as their avenue to the expanses of the West. The few, however, who did descend the Allegheny were either treated to their first sample of western travel at

---

[48] The other is the Kiskiminetas River.
[49] Zadok Cramer, *The Navigator* (Pittsburgh: Zadok Cramer, 1808), p. 19; Timothy Flint, *Recollections*, p. 13.

Oleanne Point, New York, or crossed by land from Pennsylvania's lake port of Erie to French Creek.

On the Monongahela the borough of Brownsville was the leading port of embarkation. Since the borough was also situated on the National Road, it possessed advantages for both industrial and transportation development, not enjoyed by many other areas, and at an early date attracted an enterprising class of citizens, including many Quakers. By 1820 the borough's population had reached 976, all of whom firmly believed that their community was destined to become the most important center in Western Pennsylvania except for Pittsburgh. Actually Brownsville was already the fourth largest urban area in the region, being surpassed by only Washington and Uniontown, aside from the city of Pittsburgh. Furthermore, it was the largest borough in Western Pennsylvania not aided by the presence of a county government.[50]

This remarkable growth may be attributed to the fact that at Brownsville the westward traveler had three choices: he could continue to Pittsburgh at the confluence of the Allegheny and Monongahela Rivers by either land or water or he could by-pass the city altogether and follow the National Road some 57 miles to Wheeling, Virginia. This last alternative permitted the traveler to reach the Ohio River 96 water miles below Pittsburgh. Nevertheless, the forks of the Ohio was preferred to Wheeling as an embarkation point because it was nearer Philadelphia and Baltimore. The chief geographic factor recommending Wheeling was the consistently high water of the Ohio in that area which favored navigation in all seasons while neither Pittsburgh nor Brownsville could make a similar claim. Brownsville, particularly, was embarrassed at times by the low waters of Monongahela. The threat of losing time and accumulating a great expense during the delay caused travelers to limit their embarkations from this point almost exclusively to the spring and early summer.[51]

Incorporated in 1816, Pittsburgh, the only area of Western Pennsylvania to be classified a city, enjoyed much better water transportation to the West than Brownsville. Strategically located at the juncture of two rivers, this "natural metropolis" temporarily served the Ohio Valley as

---

[50] Anonymous letter of a traveling friend to the editor, *Monongalia Spectator* (Morgantown), July 20, 1816. For further information on urban development see Appendix A.

[51] Cramer, *Navigator* (1808), p. 19f.

a depot for virtually everything, ranging from the material necessities to carve a home out of the wilderness to the Bibles sent by eastern missionary societies to advance the moral and spiritual life of the frontier.[52]

The city was able to perform in this capacity not only because of its rivers, but also because it was the terminus of several roads from the East which approached through such towns as Greensburg, Uniontown, and Washington. Like the people of Brownsville, Pittsburghers believed that nature had charted a destiny for their city far beyond that of a "mere depot of western merchandize."

> The immense beds of coal, the inexhaustible forests that fringe the borders of our rivers, the majestic stream that flows from our doors, all combine to prove that Pittsburgh was formed for the metropolis of a great tract, as the soul of a flourishing country.[53]

Motivated by this inspiration, the inhabitants proceeded to build a thriving city. By 1817 Pittsburgh could boast of eight churches, a courthouse, three banks, and above all, factories more numerous and more varied than those in places which had been developing three times as long.[54] Approximately 1500 men,[55] engaged in 41 different trades, annually produced manufactures valued at $2,000,000. Indeed it was surprising to visitors from the East to witness this diversity of business which afforded the surrounding countryside a great measure of independence.

Such enterprise was quick to affect the city's population. The census of 1810 reported only 4,740 residents and a decade later 7,248 were

---

[52] Samuel J. Mills to the Committee appointed by the Trustees of the Massachusetts Missionary Society quoted in Samuel J. Mills and Daniel Smith, *Report of a Missionary Tour through That Part of the United States Which Lies West of the Allegany Mountains;* . . . (Andover: Flagg and Gould, 1818), p. 6.

[53] *Pittsburgh Gazette,* July 3, 1818.

[54] Waldo, *Tour of James Monroe,* p. 260.

[55] Conflicting reports on the number of employees exist, partly because of the different meanings given to the term "manufactory" and partly because estimates were made at different times. A committee appointed in 1819 to study the decline in employment reported in the *Mercury,* January 14, 1820, 1,960 employees for the year 1815. Isaac Sharpless, *Two Centuries of Pennsylvania History* (Philadelphia: J. B. Lippincott Co., 1900), p. 280, reported 1,280 hands employed in 1817. John T. Holdsworth, *Financing an Empire: History of Banking in Pennsylvania* (Chicago: S. J. Clarke Publishing Co., 1928), I, 255, held that there were 1,637 employees in 1816 and the *Pittsburgh Gazette,* March 5, 1819, quoted the same figures for 1818.

listed, but the interim witnessed an erratic population fluctuation. The rapid development of manufactures had caused Pittsburgh's population to increase 110 per cent in seven years and give the city 10,000 residents in 1817, but a subsequent slump of 75 per cent in business activity forced 30 per cent of the people out of the city and back to the farm by 1820.[56]

The depression brought similar repercussions in the borough of Washington which had an estimated 2,500 residents in 1817, but three years later the census reported only 1,687, indicating a similar 30 per cent urban decrease.[57] This trend caused the farmers, who had always been skeptical of the security offered by any endeavor other than agriculture, to denounce the "false economy" of the town with renewed vigor. During the depression years, however, a larger bloc of farmers recognized the growing importance of developing a greater interdependence between town and country, between industry and the farm, in order to promote the prosperity of the region. Such a realization not only encouraged urban expansion for the future, but also strengthened the regional solidarity of Western Pennsylvania on many topics.

Pittsburgh was the hub of this urban and industrial activity west of the Alleghenies and the counterpart to Philadelphia in the East. So significant were these cities that they were frequently regarded as symbols of the sections they represented.[58] To many people along the Atlantic coast Pittsburgh was Western Pennsylvania while Philadelphia, the eastern metropolis, was the target of all Western Pennsylvania attacks. When the state legislature's action on internal improvements did not coincide with the demands of the western counties, they blamed Philadelphia for sabotaging their future. When eastern banks all along

---

[56] Killikelly, *History of Pittsburgh,* pp. 140, 153, 173; *Poulson's Advertiser,* October 18, 1821.

[57] See Appendix A and Morris Birkbeck, *Notes on a Journey in America from the Coast of Virginia to the Territory of Illinois* (2d ed.; Philadelphia: M. Carey & Son, 1819), p. 54.

[58] This statement, suggesting that Pennsylvania was divided into only two regions, can be misleading. To the people of Western Pennsylvania in this period the mountains afforded the only division of importance, and since the primary concern of this work is the western counties, we will arbitrarily accept that interpretation. If a systematic study of the whole state were undertaken, the area east of that discussed in this work could appropriately be subdivided into two or even three sections.

the coast discounted western paper, it was still Philadelphia that was forced to bear the brunt of western denunciation because a high percentage of the business done by men from the western end of the state was through this city. The establishment of the Bank of the United States in Philadelphia further helped to intensify the situation. It was quite natural for the minority west of the mountains to assume that their interests would be respected and promoted by their eastern brethren, but when calamities befell the westerners, they were always quick to recognize the exploitive hand of the majority.

Low tariffs, panics, and high discount rates could not, directly or indirectly, be the result of their own negligence and mistakes. They opposed all of them, but knew that in Philadelphia, where they transacted most of their business, merchants favored low tariffs and gave them perhaps 90 cents for their western dollars. This was the only logic necessary to explain their distress. The majority, centering in Philadelphia, which attracted more than 15 times the population of Pittsburgh, had wantonly disregarded the few struggling under adverse conditions in Western Pennsylvania.

In every way this region was the minority section of the state. In size, population, means of communication, educational facilities, and other social and cultural opportunities it could not compete. Inevitably Western Pennsylvania became conscious of this position, and the counties felt impelled to react vigorously—to let the eastern part of the state know that they were "no longer to be treated as colonies." [59]

The region was particularly anxious to demonstrate that it had risen above this "colonial" status when officers representing the state as a whole were to be chosen or elected. The only test that it regarded as valid, however, was to "share and share alike" in the state offices. In 1822 this attitude dramatically revealed itself when three western newspapers, the *Mercury, Statesman,* and *Western Argus,* quoted by the *Aurora,* demanded that the next governor be a westerner since the current one was from Berks County. The *Mercury* went so far as to suggest that a western convention be held to assure such a choice. Almost at once the proposal was attacked in the East as a new type of caucus and denounced for the proposition that, if a man of superior ability lived in the East, he should be rejected because he came from the wrong end of the state.[60]

[59] *Pittsburgh Gazette,* July 3, 1818.
[60] *Aurora,* November 2, 9, 1822.

Two years later similar excitement was stirred up over the choice of a United States Senator to replace Walter Lowrie. To the consternation of Western Pennsylvania, Samuel D. Ingham had more than noticeable support for the position among the members of the state legislature. His appointment would have given Pennsylvania one senator from the middle counties, William Findlay of Franklin, and one from the eastern counties, Ingham of Bucks. John McFarland of the *Allegheny Democrat* pointed out that his county had no candidate of its own to contend with Ingham, but that other counties in the western sector of the state did have. He warned the eastern counties:

> We do not speak from any local feeling [61] when we say, that the western country is certainly entitled to the representative. We have men as capable and better qualified for the office than Mr. Ingham, and any attempt to wrest from us the right of a member of Senate, will be resented at a future day, with some effect. [62]

Since no rival to Ingham was suggested in the editorial, McFarland's opposition could not possibly have been on the basis of personal preference or political alignment. Regional loyalty undoubtedly dictated to his pen.

The tendency toward regional inferiority was not simply the result of the mountains which cast Western Pennsylvania in the role of the minority section of the state. Since the people of these counties also regarded themselves as a part of the West, the minority section of the nation, the feeling was intensified. Certainly they did not believe that their interests were coincident with those of either southern planters or eastern merchants, but assumed the typically western attitude that they were attending to something peculiarly their own. [63]

Easterners, on the other hand, did not identify Western Pennsylvania with the new "Western Country" with which they had become concerned. To them the term was more political than physical in the limits it defined. At first it was used to indicate areas that were not a part of the original 13 colonies and gradually it evolved to imply western areas that were not yet states, but at no time in eastern usage was the term applicable to Western Pennsylvania. The East just never realized that

---

[61] By "local feeling" the editor obviously meant the sentiment of either Pittsburgh or Allegheny County. He thus drew a sharp distinction between local and regional areas and feelings.

[62] *Allegheny Democrat* (Pittsburgh), November 30, 1824.

[63] *Pittsburgh Gazette,* July 3, 1818.

any part of the original states was in need of special legislation by the central government while Pennsylvania's western counties believed that they qualified as Western Country.

This confusion in definition led to continuous misunderstandings. In the name of promoting the Western Country, for example, the national government formulated plans at the turn of the 19th Century to advance Ohio. Part of the proceeds from the sale of federal lands in that territory was to be set aside for the construction of roads within while another percentage was allocated to the establishment of a turnpike between Ohio and the Atlantic coast.[64] All this was undertaken without any consideration for Western Pennsylvania, a region that had been an integral part of the nation since 1776. Nothing was more galling to the state's western counties than to see this new territory preempt the attention of the national government, especially since they had the same needs and interests as Ohio.

The *Pittsburgh Gazette* did not remain quiet about the region's pressing needs and interests. It pointed out that geography placed Western Pennsylvania at a disadvantage. The southern planter, whose tobacco and cotton could very quickly be transported to tidewater and shipped to Europe at an enormous price, could afford to "loll in his coach, preach up agriculture and damn manufactures and monopolists." The climate, as well as this remoteness from ocean ports, deprived Western Pennsylvania of a chance to raise the products of the South which brought high prices in Europe. Accordingly the Southerner owed his wealth to foreign manufactures as did the eastern importing merchant who advised western dealers to tend their farms and let manufacturing alone.

Together these factors rendered it impossible for Western Pennsylvania to compete advantageously with areas either to the east or to the west in the products she did have available for export. Although Western Pennsylvania was well adapted to the growing of grain, so were Kentucky, Tennessee, and Ohio. Their proximity to the Gulf of Mexico and their laws, which enabled them to command labor at half the cost in Western Pennsylvania, gave them control of the United States markets in New Orleans and the West Indies.[65]

This picture suggests that Western Pennsylvania was not only a part

---

[64] Young, *Study of the Cumberland Road,* p. 14f.
[65] *Pittsburgh Gazette,* May 29, 1818.

of the minority section, but also a hapless area within it. As stated above, all the other western areas were controlled by legislatures that were predominantly western in attitude. Western Pennsylvania was frustrated at her inability to act, especially since she witnessed western states, like Kentucky, maneuvering to safeguard and promote their interests. There the house of representatives had passed a bill placing a six-cent tax on every hundred dollars' worth of goods brought into the state for sale by any channel other than the Mississippi River. The purpose of this bill, as tragically recognized by Pittsburgh merchants, was to stop Kentucky purchases in the Atlantic cities and make New Orleans the capital of the West.[66] Western Pennsylvania realized that she was caught in the middle and feared that she would find herself nothing more than a terminus for trade from both Philadelphia and New Orleans. Although the subsequent course of history did not justify these fears, they were very real to those experiencing them in the second decade of the 19th Century.

---

[66] *Aurora*, February 22, 1817.

II

The People and Their Background

May party faction dissolve and we become again a united people.[1]

NOTWITHSTANDING the commercial and industrial progress between 1815 and 1825, Western Pennsylvania remained predominantly agrarian throughout this decade. With each succeeding year the energies of agriculture diffused themselves more widely over the backcountry. While these farm lands were being developed away from the principal roads and streams, the energies of the business community were being concentrated in certain confined localities. As characteristic of westward expansion generally, this trend gave rise to two cultures in the region: the agrarianism of the countryside and the business pursuits of the town or village.

Development in Western Pennsylvania followed a pattern of gradual infringement or domination of the agrarian community by the urban cultures that sprang up at strategic points. Newspaper editors, merchants, lawyers, apothecaries, bankers, and other urban workers carried their concepts of an urban culture from an old town to a frontier town. As western population grew and society became more complex, this group extended its control over broader and broader areas until much of the countryside was influenced by or was dependent upon life in the urban centers. Other immigrants to the western counties had forsaken eastern farms for western or immediately upon arrival in America had journeyed across the mountains to establish their new homes. In either event they brought at least a desire to exploit the opportunities offered by the rich soil and favorable climate.

All of these people who came into Western Pennsylvania seemed to be motivated primarily by one of two ambitions: to pursue their own lives in their own way or to establish themselves as business or political

---

[1] Toast proposed at an Independence Day celebration of the Greensburg mechanics. *Greensburg Gazette,* July 8, 1815.

leaders. Those in the urban centers were, generally speaking, inspired by the latter objective while the farm element was undecided between the two alternatives. If a farmer were aggressive and energetic upon arrival, his enthusiasm was frequently dulled by the new and challenging conditions he found in the region.

Of the people who came into the region those of Scotch-Irish origin predominated. Either the actual settlers or their forebears had been temporarily domiciled in Northern Ireland under the heel of British mercantile policy where their love of liberty grew in intensity. Even before they struck out for America, they were "more Scotch than the Scotch." Although they constituted the largest national group to populate the western counties, the Scotch-Irish were reenforced with a strong leaven of German. This group had likewise been persecuted in Europe before it found refuge in William Penn's colony, and the further desire for freedom from the Quakers impelled many of them to move to the western end of the state.[2]

The enterprising Scotch-Irish were joined by their English brethren and "the low Irish, as they are called even here," in supplying the major portion of Pittsburgh's industrial manpower. The love of whiskey, to which so many of the Irish emigrants were addicted, relegated them generally to the most menial of factory tasks.[3] In numbers they joined the English and the Germans of Western Pennsylvania as the most serious competitors of the Scotch-Irish for population dominance, but throughout this decade the western counties continued to be populated chiefly by Scotch-Irish with Virginia, New Jersey, and Eastern Pennsylvania backgrounds.[4]

In spite of the fact that the primary economic pursuit of Western Pennsylvania was agriculture, travelers, local newspaper editors, and life-long residents such as Harm Jan Huidekoper and William Reynolds were agreed that farm conditions were generally deplorable. The region's distance from markets, the character of the farmers, and the inconveniences of backcountry life conspired to produce this careless

[2] William J. Holland, "The Educational Needs of Appalachia," *The Transallegheny Historical Magazine*, I (1902), 216.

[3] Birkbeck, *Journey in America*, p. 47; *Pittsburgh Gazette*, March 2, 1799; April 12, 1800.

[4] James M. Miller, *The Genesis of Western Culture: The Upper Ohio Valley, 1800-1825* (Columbus: The Ohio State Archaeological and Historical Society, 1938), p. 23.

inefficiency. Many farmers had no desire to advance their occupation beyond the subsistence level; as long as the harvest was sufficient to meet the family's needs through the winter months, they were satisfied. A surplus only complicated the farmer's life because of the difficulty he often encountered in finding a market. Support was all he asked of the soil; he was stimulated with no impulse for improvement or experimentation.[5]

Morgan Neville of the *Pittsburgh Gazette* was one of the farmer's most outspoken critics. He charged that the farmer's greed for land caused him to undertake farming on a large scale when his manpower and methods of cultivation dictated a small-scale operation. The farmer would not accept the idea that 20 acres properly cultivated would produce a larger crop and require less labor than 40 acres worked in the manner to which the farmers of the Pittsburgh area were accustomed. The editor admitted that the improvement of agriculture was inevitably one of slow progress, but insisted that from 1811 to 1819 there was no change for the better in Western Pennsylvania. Actually conditions grew worse. Since the climate and soil were above average, the fault was traced to the farmer who was charged with a lack of enterprise and no vision for improvement. According to Neville the first farmers of the region instituted a system of agriculture which was "persevered in with Chinese devotion" by succeeding generations. The father sowed so many fields in rye and wheat, kept so many cows, and churned so many pounds of butter; his son fell into the same pattern to leave the farm "the same yesterday, today, and to-morrow." [6]

In order to keep fields continuously in good condition, a farmer was required to practice crop rotation and to restore fertility to the soil systematically by planting red clover or by scattering the manure from his barnyard through the fields. This took equipment, effort, and care which the Western Pennsylvania farmer tried to avoid.[7] System, forethought, and pride in a job well done were seldom apparent. To clear and cultivate a farm in this region was an arduous undertaking, and the farmer attempted to accomplish the task as quickly and easily as possible. Because he wished to cultivate a large area, much of the

---

[5] *Pittsburgh Gazette,* May 29, 1818.
[6] *Ibid.,* July 31, 1818; March 23, 1819.
[7] Anonymously translated letter to Harm Jan Huidekoper from his brother in Amsterdam dated October 20, 1820. Huidekoper Papers.

farmer's work was performed in a haphazard manner. Trees that would die by girdling were permitted to stand until a more convenient time for removal, and frequently that time never came. Growing crops were occasionally injured by the fall of a tree or its decaying branches during the windstorms of the summer. When rotten or superfluous branches were pruned from trees, they were often used as fences which remained intact until strewn about the fields by the first heavy wind.[8]

If the farmer's wheat was not threatened by fallen trees, it was likely to be so overgrown with weeds that at a distance the verdure could be easily mistaken for a pasture. A little foresight would have recognized that it was more efficient to sow clover or some other useful grass among the crops, not only to restore fertility to the soil, but also to check the spread of the weeds to adjoining fields.[9] William Reynolds corroborated this careless treatment of the soil in his Reminiscences of the Olden Times:

> Exhaustion of the fertilizing elements in the soil was the effect of ceaseless culture without manure, which was permitted to accumulate in the barnyard, until it became a question of economy whether to remove the barn or the manure. I remember a notable instance of a farmer who had so great an accumulation, that he became weary of making paths through the piles to reach his stable door, and at a safe distance built a new barn, removed the old one . . . and taking advantage of a spell of dry weather, put fire to and consumed the manure heap.[10]

The Western Pennsylvania farmer exhibited the same indifference toward the care of his livestock that marked the cultivation of his field crops. Neville urged him to pay particular attention to the raising of horses and hogs. The region imported almost all its horses while the general appearance of the hogs produced in these western counties was tangible evidence that they, too, should have been imported. The editor called upon the farmers to improve the breed of this "miserable, gaunt, long-legged race that disgraces our woods" as soon as possible. Mean-

[8] William Reynolds, "Reminiscences of the Olden Times" [an unpublished account], quoted in John E. Reynolds, *In French Creek Valley* (Meadville: The Crawford County Historical Society, 1938), p. 76.

[9] James Flint, *Letters from America, Containing Observations on the Climate and Agriculture of the Western States, the Manners of the People, the Prospects of Emigrants, &c, &c.,* Vol. IX of *Early Western Travels 1748-1846,* ed. Reubon G. Thwaites (32 vols.; Cleveland: The Arthur H. Clark Co., 1904-1907), p. 80f.

[10] John E. Reynolds, *French Creek Valley,* p. 76.

while the itinerant missionary, Timothy Flint, thought that such improvement should be extended to include other species of livestock in Western Pennsylvania as well. During his travels through the region he passed droves of large cattle on their way from Ohio to a Philadelphia market. In spite of the rigors of such a journey, they appeared to be in good condition. "In size and even fat, they are much superior to the Pennsylvania stock by the side of the road. Indeed, it is somewhat surprising to see such bad cattle on the rich lands of this State." [11]

Animal husbandry dipped to this regrettable level because of the farmer's apathy and lack of patience. Selective breeding seemed foreign to his understanding, and the little planning necessary to have calves in the early spring, when the climate was more favorable, required too much forethought. The farmer knew that well-ventilated stables were essential during the winter months for the good health of his cattle, but was content, however, to have that ventilation come from wherever cracks or holes in the structure would develop, even though wind, rain, or snow would blow across the backs of his cattle. [12]

Harm Jan Huidekoper of Meadville contrasted the prosperity of farmers in Eastern Pennsylvania with the subsistence farming of the western counties and concluded that the western lag was attributed to the failure to experiment or to adopt scientific methods of agriculture. [13] Meanwhile Editor Neville went further in his comparison. He asserted that "in no part of the Union, perhaps, are the farms worse cultivated, or the improvement of stock less attended to" than in the vicinity of Pittsburgh. His concern for the farmers' output stemmed from the temporary failure of local products to supply the needs of his city. "By the magic influence of manufactures and internal commerce," Pittsburgh had more than doubled its population in a few short years while farm development languished. The ratio that had existed between town and country was destroyed with the inevitable result that agricultural prices increased. According to the editor, when the butter supply was insufficient to meet the demands of the Pittsburgh market and when veal, beef, and potato prices soared, the cost of living in the city was higher

---

[11] *Pittsburgh Gazette,* July 31, 1818; Flint, *Letters from America,* p. 80.

[12] Anonymously translated letter to Harm Jan Huidekoper from his brother in Amsterdam dated October 20, 1820. Huidekoper Papers.

[13] *Ibid.*

than that of any Atlantic seaboard community, except the nation's capital.[14]

This circumstance itself went a long way toward arousing the farmer from his lethargy, but by no means did it stand alone. Although the foregoing picture represents the general conditions of farming in Western Pennsylvania, there were notable exceptions which spearheaded the trend toward experimentation and scientific development. Heading this list were the sheep-raisers of Washington and Greene Counties. The expense of shipping grain across the mountains had originally prompted the rise of this occupation, and the War of 1812 increased its importance when the nation was forced to depend almost wholly on the domestic manufacture of textiles. After the war the cloth-manufacturing industry was firmly enough established to provide a permanent market for domestic wool, and the sheep-raisers in the extreme southwestern corner of the state supplied the market abundantly. In 1820 Washington was the leading agricultural county of the state, and in the decade that followed, the county's sheep occupied one-fourth of the entire cleared area and accounted for an annual income of almost a half million dollars, much of which came from breeding fine merino sheep for sale in Ohio.[15]

In the vicinity of Franklin, Venango County, Horatio Gates Spafford was responsible for a different type of agricultural progress. He had received samples of four species of wheat and some invaluable Lupenella grass seed from Italy through the courtesy of Secretary of the Treasury William H. Crawford and experimented with their adaptability to the soil and climate of Western Pennsylvania. Interest in the Lupenella grass ran especially high because it was sufficiently nutritive to be given to fatting or working cattle without grain. Spafford encouraged others to join him in this experimental planting and as an inducement offered them a part of his samples.[16]

The spirit of men like Spafford, combined with the growing demands of urban economies, particularly that of Pittsburgh, gradually stirred the farmer's interest in greater efficiency. He began seeking new agri-

---

[14] *Pittsburgh Gazette,* August 7, 1818; March 23, 1819.

[15] Philip S. Klein, *Pennsylvania Politics 1817-1832: A Game without Rules* (Philadelphia: The Historical Society of Pennsylvania, 1940), p. 18f.

[16] Anonymous article dated Meadville, January 23, 1818, quoted in *Poulson's Advertiser,* February 3, 1818.

cultural knowledge directly through experimentation and indirectly through the formation of agricultural societies. The newspapers of Westmoreland, Washington, and Allegheny Counties popularized the cause of such societies well. The *Greensburg Gazette* argued that the best way to correct the balance of trade against Western Pennsylvania was through improved methods of farming and that that, in turn, could be most readily achieved through agricultural societies.[17]

The *Gazette* at Pittsburgh sparked the drive by pointing out that Bible societies were springing up in every village and canal and bridge companies were exerting every nerve for the welfare of the region while the farmer failed to be aroused with the same spirit. He made no effort to organize societies or associations in his own behalf. The editor suggested the promotion of such societies to conduct agricultural exhibits and cattle shows. They would serve, not only to stimulate competition, but also to diffuse agricultural knowledge for which Zadok Cramer had demonstrated a pressing need. In his *Navigator* he declared that the manufacture of brushes had been successfully established at Pittsburgh, but predicted that more progress was possible if the farmers would be more careful of their hogs' bristles.[18] Knowledge of the use and care of this and other by-products had not systematically reached the farmer, but this could have been easily carried out by farm associations. Such an assist to the brush industry would have prompted its expansion and brought both lower prices to farm purchasers of brushes and increased demands for agricultural products from the added personnel of the industry.

The organization of farm societies, however, proceeded slowly. Many farmers exhibited no willingness to join, preferring instead to wait and see the kind of success a society would enjoy before they took out membership.[19] This hesitancy is not only indicative of the farmer's conservatism, but also of his desire to remain independent of the life developing around him.

Generally a threat to his way of life was required to incite the farmer to action. Elections always posed such a threat. Either the possibility of having county tickets dominated by the townspeople or the fear that state offices and legislation were falling under the direction of Eastern

[17] *Greensburg Gazette,* February 8, 1817.
[18] *Pittsburgh Gazette,* July 31, 1818; Cramer, *Navigator* (1817), p. 59.
[19] *The Reporter* (Washington, Pennsylvania), April 22, 1822.

Pennsylvania was sufficient to arouse the farmer for several months preceding every election. For that short time the newspapers appealing primarily to the farm element bristled with political arguments, only to be shunted into oblivion during the nine or ten months following the campaign. A few kept a constant vigil over the affairs of the state and nation, but the average farmer was only sporadically concerned. The diffusion of the farm population over ever broader areas with hazardous means of communication between them and the general attitude of freedom from government regulation and control that so many immigrants brought to the farmlands of Western Pennsylvania combined to label the farmers the most important guardians of the status quo.

COUNTRY VS. TOWN

In contrast to this monotonous life of the farm the business tempo of the town brought new excitements daily. This feeling was most firmly planted in the minds of those who observed town life only occasionally or vicariously from their homes in the countryside. The bustling of travelers as they went about procuring the supplies necessary to continue their journeys, the loading and unloading of merchants' wagons, the sound of the mechanic's hammer, were all symbols of the enveloping life of the region.

The conservative among the farmers resented the growing influence of this town culture. When they saw one merchant buy the corn or wheat of many farmers or a wool manufacturer take the raw product of numerous producers, they became alarmed. A wool growers' committee in Washington County charged that since there were so many wool growers in comparison with wool manufacturers, the latter could more easily act in concert and fix the price of wool so as to engross all profits. Arguing that they had to accept whatever price was offered, the multitude of unorganized and scattered growers feared that they were at the mercy of the manufacturers.[20] Their most favorable attitude toward this concentration of business control in the town was a constant suspicion of being exploited, but more frequently they denounced commerce and manufacturing as unnatural and immoral occupations.

The comparative density of population in the towns also aroused the political distrust of the countryside, but the towns, particularly Pitts-

---

[20] *Reporter,* September 25, 1815.

burgh, made equally scathing countercharges. In the urban areas where the people had many contacts with each other and where inter-dependence was practiced widely, there was a healthy climate for the growth of political organization and leadership. In Fayette County the resentment of Uniontown's control of county politics so distressed George Dearth, a farmer and assemblyman, that he proposed a bill for the formation of a new county. His projected county of Jackson, to be assembled out of parts of Fayette, Westmoreland, and Allegheny Counties, was intended to give greater farm control to politics, but the measure failed. Fayette's other two assemblymen, Daniel Sturgeon of Uniontown and John B. Trevor of the borough of Connellsville, led the fight against it.[21]

Differences of a similar nature existed in all the counties. The siege guns were leveled more frequently on Pittsburgh than any other urban area because of its size and role in western development. The barrage attack came from all sides: from the farmers of the surrounding county, from travelers, from the jealous boroughs of Western Pennsylvania, and from the West generally. By their personal observations Pitts-burghers believed that it was fashionable "in almost every little town in the western country to decry Pittsburgh, to envy its rising greatness and devise every possible means of doing it an injury." [22]

Such a comment served only to emphasize Pittsburgh's insecurity. In the decade following the War of 1812 the inhabitants watched intently to see if the foundation of the city's "rising greatness" could endure the challenges hurled against it. Until this time progress had been rapid because of the city's industrial development and its role as the "Em-porium of the West," but in 1815 both of these pillars were threatened.

Encouraged and necessitated by the enactment of the embargo and the War of 1812, manufacturing had been undertaken in Western Pennsylvania, particularly at Pittsburgh, but the end of the war brought a fear of competition from renewed English importations. Since these war-born industries were at least a half century behind those of England in experience, their owners were painfully aware of their inferior posi-tion and the inevitability of a struggle for survival. Such thoughts were constantly haunting them, and English utterances and trickery served only as added reminders.

---

[21] George H. Roadman, "Daniel Sturgeon, A Political View" (Unpublished Master's thesis, History Dept., University of Pittsburgh, 1950), p. 14.

[22] *Pittsburgh Gazette,* August 7, 1818.

In 1816 Lord Brougham contributed to this anxiety with his famous forthright comment to Parliament that England's economic objective must be aimed "to stifle in the cradle those rising manufactures in the United States, which the war has forced into existence contrary to the natural course of things." [23] In America this frank warning was quoted in nearly every newspaper and indelibly inscribed on every manufacturer's mind while in England Lord Brougham's address provoked an appropriate plan of action to implement this policy at once. English goods were dumped on the American market far under manufacturing costs in an effort to drive local producers out of business. The value of United States imports in 1816 was not surpassed in any subsequent year until 1850. Henry Fearon was moved to comment during his visit to Pittsburgh in 1817 that retail stores there were "literally stuffed with goods of English manufacture." [24]

The British also demonstrated that they were even willing to sacrifice national honor to regain their American markets. They stamped their calicoes and chinaware for sale in the United States with symbols of American victories in the War of 1812 to encourage purchases of their products in this country.[25] Although this psychological appeal to American patriotism could conceivably be regarded as ethical advertising, later British actions lacked all integrity.

When these early methods failed to destroy manufacturing in the United States, new and more ingenious plans were adopted. British agents in the United States bought and sent to England patterns of various "homespuns," particularly cotton goods, either white or colored. When the goods arrived, manufacturers used them as models to produce articles of similar appearance, but of inferior quality, especially durability. This "hybrid cloth" was then sent to the United States where large quantities were sold at public auction and to retail stores, eventually reaching the consumer under the guise of American manufactured goods.

---

[23] T. C. Hansard, *The Parliamentary Debates from the Year 1803 to the Present Time,* XXXII (1816), 1099.

[24] William MacDonald, *From Jefferson to Lincoln* (New York: Henry Holt and Co., 1913), p. 26; Henry Bradshaw Fearon, *Sketches of America: A Narrative of a Journey of Five Thousand Miles through the Eastern and Western States of America;* . . . (2d ed.; London: Longman, Hurst, Rees, Orme, and Brown, 1818), p. 205f.

[25] *Democratic Press,* June 5, 1816.

According to the plan it would wear badly and incite a prejudice against the purchase and consumption of domestic manufactures.[26]

In exposing this practice, the editor of the *Pittsburgh Gazette* extended an invitation to all who doubted the truthfulness of his account to visit his newspaper office. There he displayed some of this "ersatz homespun" which could be compared with genuine domestic cloth. While carrying the fight, especially for the manufacturers in Western Pennsylvania who believed they were being engulfed by the tremendous output of England's mills, Editor Neville was only a "voice in the wilderness" for several years. The importers seemed to captivate the American consumers until the depression of 1818-1822 shook the whole economy. Both American industry and the importing business suffered; but as prosperity returned, there was a gradual swing to the consumption of domestic production. The British recognized their ultimate failure to recapture the market, and in a last desperate effort "to stifle . . . those rising manufactures," they forged American markings, numbers, and even manufacturers' names to foist their imitations on us.[27]

The economy of Pittsburgh was required, not only to hurl back this threat to its continued prosperity, but was also forced to grapple with the problem of possible liquidation of its markets in the West. In the first stages of their development western communities of necessity were economically dependent on Western Pennsylvania. Manufacturers, shipbuilders, and merchants, especially those of Pittsburgh, profited handsomely from the settlement of the Northwest Territory, Tennessee, and Kentucky. By 1815 these businessmen were beset with the fear that their wealth, business, and glory were fast passing away, being transferred to Cincinnati, Louisville, and other points along the Ohio. As these new areas grew, they supplied more and more of their own needs and became the hubs for the next waves of settlement.[28]

The drain on Pittsburgh's economy was rendered all the more acute by the increased use of steamboats, which connected the Ohio Valley towns with the Atlantic ports by way of the Mississippi River. Also with the construction of the National Road it seemed certain that

---

[26] *Pittsburgh Gazette,* November 6, 1818.

[27] *Democratic Press,* September 13, 1822.

[28] Timothy Flint, *Recollections,* p. 17; Juliet G. Gray, "Early Industries and Transportation in Western Pennsylvania 1800-1846" (Unpublished Master's thesis, History Dept., University of Pittsburgh, 1925), p. 35.

Wheeling and Steubenville would pre-empt much of Pittsburgh's western trade. The *Cincinnati Gazette* added to the city's discomfort with a "Farewell! poor Pittsburgh" editorial. The writer reported the establishment of Cincinnati's first foundry, the most modern west of the mountains, which, he predicted, would replace Pittsburgh foundries in meeting the demands of the West.[29]

Since there was a general resentment against Pittsburgh in the West, this view did not seem at all unlikely. Many believed that the city had taken unfair advantage of them when they passed through on the way to their new homes. They charged that Pittsburghers fattened themselves on the spoils of the poor immigrants who had surged across the mountains and stopped there to buy the necessary equipment for a new life in the West. Many, like the people of Cincinnati, wanted to free themselves of this suspected exploitation.

These western settlers frequently recalled that they had been exposed to transportation and financial difficulties at Pittsburgh before they continued toward their destinations. A large percentage of the migrants sold their horses and wagons when they reached this "Emporium of the West" and elected to complete the journey by water. They purchased boats, laid in the provisions necessary for their passage down the Ohio and for their new homes, and waited for the river to rise. Before all was in readiness to depart, the delay at Pittsburgh was long and the expenses high.

At this busy depot the traveler had to pay dearly for every service performed for him; and, most assuredly, he was obliged to purchase more than he sold of his labor and services. He was shocked to find that he was financially worse off in Pittsburgh than he had been either in the East or in England. Lodging at a Pittsburgh hotel, for example, was a hundred per cent higher than the same accommodations in Boston. Many an immigrant went west with a little money thinking that it was sufficient, but too often the little was spent before he began living as a settler. His plight was generally attributed to Pittsburgh where the people were presumed to spend all their energies in making money. According to the westerner many had taken up residence at the forks of the Ohio solely to exploit the unsuspecting immigrant.[30]

---

[29] Timothy Flint, *Recollections*, p. 17; *Cincinnati Gazette*, May 27, 1818, quoted in the *Statesman*, June 13, 1818.

[30] Timothy Flint, *Recollections*, p. 18; Birkbeck, *Journey in America*, p. 48.

Since many of these immigrants discarded their horses and wagons at this junction, the selling price was low. It was further depreciated by the fact that travelers from the West also frequently sold their horses in Pittsburgh and continued eastward by stage. Conversely, since many were buying boats, the price was high, leaving the immigrant the victim of falling prices on what he had to sell and rising costs on what he bought. The situation proved all the more galling when he reached his destination and was forced to sell his boat for a sum far below its cost or perhaps to abandon it on the river bank to rot.[31]

Timothy Flint, one of Pittsburgh's most outspoken critics, believed that the city's anticipated decline was not to be regretted. He insisted that there was little hospitality to be found in the city because "unprincipled men" had gained control of the key positions from which the immigrant could be exploited. He cited a personal experience with one of these hoaxes to demonstrate his point. After purchasing a skiff at Pittsburgh to continue his missionary journey into the West, Flint discovered that it was too weak to carry any considerable weight.

> It is so much strained, that many of the nails have their heads drawn half an inch out of the timber, and others much more. . . . The system of boat building at Pittsburg cannot be too strongly reprobated. Defects in caulking, in the number, and in the strength of nails, were in the case of my boat, disgraceful.[32]

Except for Pittsburgh and the roadside taverns, however, town and country alike in Western Pennsylvania were noted for their hospitality. Flint himself remarked about the kindness tendered him at Washington, Pennsylvania, on his return from a tour of the West and declared that the whole region had received him just as graciously.[33] This report reflected the general attitude of the traveler west of the mountains; when night overtook him in the country, he could reasonably assume that the first cabin door he reached would be open to him. The limited outside contacts of people living in isolated communities or on lonely farms prompted this friendliness, but the desire for companionship and a curiosity about the affairs of the state and nation were not so acute among the people of Pittsburgh and the tavernkeepers along the turnpikes. Many of them had established their enterprises at these points in

[31] Birkbeck, *Journey in America*, p. 50f.; James Flint, *Letters from America*, p. 98.
[32] James Flint, *Letters from America*, p. 94.
[33] Timothy Flint, *Recollections*, p. 380.

order to gain a livelihood by performing services for the immigrants and travelers that passed their way. Their hospitality, naturally, seemed tinged with "mercantile feelings," which aroused the resentment of the migrants.[34]

The travelers, looking expressly for impressions to record in their notebooks, were the most caustic adversaries of business practices in Pittsburgh and at the taverns. Almost to a man they failed to comprehend that the transient residents of both, as well as the comparative density of the population in the case of the city, had prompted the "unsociability" and impersonal character of these business people.[35]

They failed also to evaluate Pittsburgh's "mercenary tactics" in the light of the labor supply. Being located in the midst of cheap land and agricultural opportunities, the city was forced to pay high wages which resulted in high prices, or run the risk of losing its workers skilled in the trades. In 1815 when the journeyman shoemakers "turned out" for higher wages, the Pittsburgh newspapers took cognizance of the effect of high prices on their society. They called upon the general citizenry to suppress this "unlawful combination" of shoemakers which was hindering the trade and commerce of the city and urged, as judiciously as possible, that the favor of areas west of Pittsburgh be courted.[36]

The challenge to Pittsburgh's industrial and commercial development came not only from western areas, but also from the countryside around the city. The local problems were basically political and were generated largely by the uneven spread of population. By 1815 it was apparent that the political machinery of the region had not been modified to keep pace with this population trend. Candidates for political office were still selected and recommended by an equal number of Democratic-Republican delegates from the several townships of Allegheny County. In these years of an impotent Federalist Party, Democratic-Republicans were encouraged to exploit the differences within their own ranks.

A significant bloc of Republicans in Pittsburgh voiced their dissatisfaction with the proceedings of the county meeting in 1816. They registered their disapproval of the ticket formed by the township delegates because the townships had not been represented at the county meeting on any of the three acceptable bases: namely, population, tax-

---

[34] John E. Reynolds, *French Creek Valley,* p. 80.
[35] Miller, *Genesis of Western Culture,* p. 24f.
[36] *Mercury,* October 14, 1815; *Pittsburgh Gazette,* October 14, 21, 1815.

able inhabitants, or the amount of taxes actually paid. According to their charge, the persons nominated were chosen from parts of the county containing a small percentage of the inhabitants—violating the fundamental principle of the American forefathers that taxation and representation should go together. In both population and tax payments Pittsburgh almost equaled the combined total of 11 townships, but the city had no representation at all on the ticket. The situation proved all the more disturbing when the city's 1483 taxable inhabitants compared favorably with the number of taxables in seven townships.[37]

This obvious discrimination, plus Pittsburgh's economic development which was unique throughout the whole of the West at this time, caused the city to counter with a rival ticket, headed by Henry Baldwin as candidate for Congress from the district composed of Allegheny and Butler Counties. The delegate meeting of Allegheny County had earlier nominated Walter Lowrie of Butler County for the Congressional post, but one writer argued that it would be impossible for a man from such a "remote" county to be familiar with the true interests and factories of Pittsburgh and vicinity. He insisted that the rules of fair play entitled Allegheny County to the seat in the House since it was unrepresented at the time in the Pennsylvania Senate and contained more taxable inhabitants than the combined total of Armstrong, Beaver, and Butler Counties, the other three counties of the senatorial district.[38]

The Baldwin or Coalition ticket, needless to say, was denounced by the regular committee of correspondence for the Democratic-Republican Party which had sponsored the delegate meeting and nominations. It charged that this faction, while actually claiming to be Republican, desired

to establish a species of aristocracy in which certain rich individuals in the *city* shall have a predominating influence; an *aristocracy* by whose property and influence it is expected to rule Butler and Allegheny Counties, and to give to the city of Pittsburgh the whole *management of elections and appointments* to office.[39]

The Baldwin ticket was further pictured by the committee as the connivance of bankers and speculators. Farmers of the countryside were assured that this "city wisdom" and intrigue did not hold their welfare uppermost.[40] Not only the ones surrounding Pittsburgh, but also the

---

[37] *The Commonwealth* (Pittsburgh), September 3, 1816.
[38] "A Republican Voter," *Mercury,* August 17, 1816.
[39] "A Democrat," *Commonwealth,* September 3, 1816.
[40] "Nemo Non," *Commonwealth,* September 17, 1816.

farmers throughout Western Pennsylvania were suspicious of the county towns, and this type of rivalry simply strengthened their apprehensions. To these points they were forced to come to transact business and to receive justice before the county courts, but frequently they left with a feeling of mistreatment.

Washington, Greensburg, Uniontown, and Meadville, as well as Pittsburgh, stood out among the county towns that clashed sharply with the countryside. If election results were used as the barometer, it would appear that in a majority of cases the vote in the county towns did not agree with the general results throughout the rest of the counties in this decade. In the gubernatorial election of 1823, for example, the Crawford County vote revealed a disparity between the rural and urban groups; every township favored John Andrew Shulze while Meadville alone endorsed Andrew Gregg.[41]

The political leaders of Pittsburgh, however, recognized very early the value of cooperation with the countryside. They knew that they could not surrender to country policy, but at the same time were convinced that it could not be ignored. Party principle was either discarded altogether or was spoken of vaguely by the urbanites while they attempted to substitute regional loyalty for party adherence. They urged the election of congressmen and legislators who would promote all three basic interests of the region: agriculture, commerce, and industry.[42] By the contrasting nature of town and country life their mutual problems could not all be resolved, but by 1825 many of the solvable ones had been erased.

REGIONAL ATTITUDES

Differences between town and country were often minimized, however, when relationships with the East were under consideration. Although not everyone in Western Pennsylvania was anxious to cast off Philadelphia's leadership, public opinion was almost unanimous in resenting in one way or another the dominating influence of the seaboard on the region's political and economic life. Since democracy and the doctrine of equality had diffused themselves thoroughly through the minds of the settlers west of the mountains, they could not accept

---

[41] *Crawford Messenger,* October 21, 1823.
[42] *Pittsburgh Gazette,* August 7, 1818.

this inferior role without a struggle. Their opposition to the superiority of the East produced a type of class consciousness and inspired the people at the western end of the state to fight for their understanding of these principles.

With the feeling of frontier democracy spread throughout Western Pennsylvania at this time, the public had no difficulty in sensing the class relationship which placed them below their eastern brethren. Since Pennsylvanians on the coastal side of the mountains represented tradition and convention and those on the other depicted innovation and evolved their own conventions, the two did not always understand each other. Too often, particularly in the minds of the western group, these differences were translated as extreme superiority and inferiority. To them many governmental regulations were merely the "unjust, impolitic, and wicked measures of our Eastern Lawgivers." [43]

At least by self-analysis the Western Pennsylvanian was subject, not sovereign. From experience he had become painfully aware that he represented a small minority of the population, and from this position he readily deduced that the East regarded his ideas and way of life as inferior. In the words of *The Commonwealth* editor, "it has been a custom at the Eastward to censure and burlesque the people of Western Pennsylvania on account of their ignorance." [44]

Out of this insecure attitude came a manifest hostility for the East, especially Philadelphia. The West resented such comments as the one in the Carlisle *Spirit of the Times* which reported William Findlay's proposed tour of that part of the state. This sarcastic article speculated that when Findlay reached Bedford, he would probably

> douse his coach, stockings, and all the other foppery with which he has lately decorated his person; for if the royalists west of the mountains discover that he is in the habit of wearing shoes and stockings and riding in a coach since his election, it is more than probable his popularity will stand on a precarious footing.[45]

This slurring evaluation of western fashions and conduct was frequently personalized. One of the favorite targets of eastern critics was Abner Lacock, a United States senator from Beaver County. In a controversy over the sale of the state house yard in Philadelphia, Lacock had once remarked that he wished the city were burned to the ground.

---

[43] *Monongalia Spectator,* July 20, 1816.

[44] *Commonwealth,* August 6, 1816.

[45] *Spirit of the Times* (Carlisle) quoted in the *Aurora* July 27, 1818.

Although the wish brought no actual damage to Philadelphia, it did touch off an incendiary attack against the senator which also reflected disdain on his section of the state. Editor William Duane of *The Aurora* was quoted as retorting that "the ashes of the ruins [of Philadelphia] would sell for more than the fee simple of the county in which that barbarian resides." [46]

Duane continued to berate the senator from Western Pennsylvania by evaluating his political usefulness to the government. In the editor's opinion Lacock did not possess the humor of Sancho, but was ten times more ridiculous and a source of inexhaustible fun to the senators in their moments of relaxation. *The Aurora* smugly suggested that Lacock was a satisfactory tonic for Federalist leader, Rufus King, who found compensation for his lack of success against the Republicans "by concentrating his contempt on this blockhead." [47]

Such devaluations were taken as personal and regional criticisms by many settlers west of the mountains, but neither they nor the Philadelphia editor realized that his comments were standard parts in a recurring pattern. By one means or another the people with a more advanced way of life normally exhibit their disdain for the less advanced. Just as there had been many in England with a bitter prejudice against all things American, the coastal inhabitants now turned the taunts of an intolerant attitude on their western compatriots.

In spite of the fact that Lacock had many enemies within Western Pennsylvania, even these enemies resented such intolerance as shown by Duane toward their region and abilities. His remarks only engendered a feeling of frustration and insecurity which, in turn, produced a strong hostility toward the East. Although physical violence is the most obvious reaction to frustration, the response in the western counties was more vocal than real. Partly because of distance and partly because of minority consciousness, this hostility was most frequently limited to verbal castigation. Furthermore, since regional affiliation tends to standardize attitudes for group members, those who favored Philadelphia leadership were forced to speak, superficially at least, against the East to avoid criticism and social ostracism. This compulsion to voice one idea while harboring the opposite was likewise a deterrent to violence.

---

[46] *Aurora,* February 28, 1816.
[47] *Ibid.,* August 9, 1816.

The minority feeling of Western Pennsylvania was not new in 1815. It had taken root with the first settlements and had become habitual. Through the years the manifestations of this minority role changed, but the basic problem remained constant. In the Revolutionary Period the threat of Indian uprisings and a British invasion from Canada had caused the greatest alarm; but as 1815 approached, the enemies became more remote, defense grew less important, and the needs of an expanding economy became more acute.

With the rapid influx of population Western Pennsylvania's most pressing need, in the minds of many, was increased federal court facilities because the region found itself in a district where the court sat some 300 miles away in Philadelphia. Thus distance from the East remained almost as much of a conditioning factor as in 1763 and helped to keep the minority feeling alive.

Not only the federal courts, but even the seats of both the state and national governments were far removed from Western Pennsylvania (and distance seems to have a high correlation with fear and suspicion). The western counties of the state believed that their interests were basically different from those of the East, but feared that Congress and the legislature neither understood nor cared to understand. This suspicion manifested itself in numerous unsuccessful efforts to organize the part of Pennsylvania beyond the mountains into a separate state.

By 1815 this proposed solution to the problem had lost most of its support and was replaced with a campaign for judicial revision. To demonstrate the East's lack of interest, the antiquated districting of federal courts still compelled the people of Western Pennsylvania to travel to Philadelphia for justice. Citizens with cases pending before this court were required to make the arduous "expedition" or suffer the inequity rather than defend their claims. If they chose defense, witnesses would possibly have to be subpoenaed from the remotest parts of the state, and counsel would have to be procured from among the unknown barristers of Philadelphia who had no personal interest in the problems of the Western Pennsylvania citizen.[48]

In an estimated nine out of ten disputes the people of the western counties found the difficulties of defense insuperable. "From the absolute impossibility of attending this distant court, the little all of many an honest and worthy man [was] wrested from him." As a result

---

[48] "A Western Citizen," *Mercury*, August 10, 1816.

of the clamor of the citizens and the political efforts of Henry Baldwin,
Congress finally divided Pennsylvania into two judicial districts with
one holding session in Philadelphia and the other in Pittsburgh.[49]

BACKGROUND TO THESE REGIONAL ATTITUDES

Although the division of the judicial district ended this phase of
western frustration, the roots of dissensions ran deep. The generation
living in Western Pennsylvania in 1815 had personally sparred with
the East on numerous occasions and had repeatedly come off second
best. The western counties had opposed both the new federal Constitution of 1787 and the new state constitution of 1790, but both were
adopted over their protests. They objected to the centralizing tendency
of the former and believed that the new state document bestowed
special favor on the eastern commercial interests. In 1791 the region
received a second opportunity to oppose a manifestation of a strongly
centralized government when Congress considered a bill for the establishment of the United States Bank, but the passage of the measure
meant that once again the region's preferences had been shunted aside.

The frustration was transferred from ideas to individuals in 1793
when the seat of Albert Gallatin, the *first* United States senator from
the western counties, was challenged by a group from the eastern part
of Pennsylvania. A petition from York County with 19 signatures
charged that Gallatin had not been a citizen of the nation for the nine
years stipulated in the Constitution when he was elected to office.
Robert Morris of Philadelphia, who was Gallatin's colleague in the
Senate, declined to present the petition and declared his intention to be
perfectly neutral in the growing controversy.[50]

A search of the citizenship records quickly revealed that Gallatin had
taken the oath of citizenship and allegiance to Virginia in October
1785. Thus the required period had not elapsed before his election, and
a test vote was taken in the Senate to determine if Gallatin should be
unseated. The decision was 14 to 12 against the Fayette County resident with Morris seemingly betraying his earlier pledge and voting with
the majority.[51]

---

[49] *Mercury,* August 10, 1816; *Pittsburgh Gazette,* October 6, 1818.
[50] John Austin Stevens, *Albert Gallatin,* Vol. XIII of *American Statesmen,* ed.
John T. Morse (40 vols.; Boston: Houghton Mifflin Co., 1889-1917), p. 62.
[51] *Ibid.,* pp. 63-65.

On the surface at least Western Pennsylvania could not cry "regional discrimination" because the legislature promptly named James Ross of Pittsburgh to fill the vacancy and his credentials were found satisfactory. Ross, however, was a Federalist and a staunch supporter of the strong central government, while Gallatin, a Jeffersonian steeped in Physiocrat philosophy, conformed more closely to the political tenor of the region as a whole.

The citizens of the western counties were not unmindful of the fact that during Gallatin's brief career of a few weeks in the Senate he had supported a resolution urging a reorganization of the Treasury Department which angered Alexander Hamilton. Earlier when the whiskey excise tax had been only a bill under consideration by a congressional committee, Gallatin induced the Pennsylvania state assembly to pass a resolution against it.[52] This stand had likewise antagonized Hamilton, and the people of Western Pennsylvania considered the possibility that Gallatin had been denied the Senate seat more because of his opposition to Hamilton and the supporters of the strong central government, who were located almost exclusively in the East, than because of the citizenship regulations.

Hamilton's resentment of Gallatin is easily understood. From the time the whiskey excise was actually passed into law in 1791 Western Pennsylvania's attitude was closely patterned after Gallatin's resolution. The region became astir with riots, attacks on enforcement officers, and protest meetings. In some of these meetings Gallatin and other prominent political figures of the area took an active part, but their counsel usually favored moderation. In spite of their intentions, participation tended to link them with the extremists.[53] When the Senate unseated Gallatin in February 1794, the violence over the excise was fast reaching its peak, and his ouster only added fuel to the fires of insurrection.

The trials for failure to comply with the tax law were held in the federal court at Philadelphia, inciting the first genuine denunciation of the long journey for justice. The protest was all the more vociferous because the farmer was frequently forced to make the trip when his labors were urgently required on the farm during the planting or harvesting seasons. His opposition eventually produced a modification

---

[52] Raymond Walters, *Alexander James Dallas: Lawyer-Politician-Financier 1759-1817* (Philadelphia: University of Pennsylvania Press, 1943), p. 53.

[53] *Ibid.,* p. 53.

of the law in June 1794, when Congress decreed that trials could be held in the state courts if the violations occurred more than 50 miles from the seat of the United States District Court.[54]

On May 31, 1794, this federal court had issued 65 processes against Western Pennsylvania distillers, but the writs were not served until several weeks after the new law had been approved. Since the processes had been issued under the old law, the violators were still required to trek across the mountains to Philadelphia to stand trial.[55] Such a hollow victory was taken as another eastern taunt and found western frustration resorting to an aggression pattern of violence rather than the verbal castigation which had characterized previous disappointments.

The Whiskey Rebellion that ensued brought many of the grievances of Western Pennsylvania to a focus. The region believed that the whiskey excise was a discriminatory tax which violated the constitutional provision that all excises be applied uniformly throughout the nation. The contention that the tax operated with unequal severity on westerners was based on the difference in the price of whiskey on the opposite sides of the mountains. For example, with whiskey selling at 50 cents per gallon west of the Alleghenies and a dollar on the east coast, a uniform tax was twice as heavy in the West as on the seaboard. The excise not only reduced the salability of this important export of Pennsylvania's western counties; but, in a sense, was also a tax on their currency since whiskey was their principal bartering medium in eastern markets. The federal government further increased the burden with the stipulation that the tax be paid in currency of which the western counties had little—thanks, in their estimation, to Mr. Hamilton's bank.[56]

Although this tax was interpreted as discriminatory, it must be admitted that there was no love for anything called a tax in Western Pennsylvania. The same type of protest was raised when added taxes were necessary to meet the expenses of the War of 1812. In 1815 a letter signed "a poor tax-ridden-afflicted citizen, John F. Quickly" declared that the people were tyrannized as oppressively as the children of Israel in Egypt when they had been forced to make bricks without

---

[54] George P. Schoyer, "James Ross Western Pennsylvania Federalist" (Unpublished Master's thesis, History Dept., University of Pittsburgh, 1947), p. 13.

[55] Ibid.

[56] Walters, Alexander J. Dallas, p. 52; Tinkcom, Republicans and Federalists, p. 92.

straw. "Quickley" charged that he and his neighbors were required to pay more taxes than they had money in order to satisfy the enormous debt which was estimated at $150,000,000. In order to vivify this indebtedness, he reported that:

> My John has calculated it up, and says that all the waggons in the state could hardly carry it, for he says that it would take more than five thousand teams. Then too he says if it was in quarters of dollars, it would, laid side by side, reach 6000 miles.[57]

To this the editor of the *Pittsburgh Gazette* asked: "Are not the feelings and sentiments of the people in this western section of the state, in unison with those of Mr. Quickley?"[58]

Although this tax was designated to meet the extraordinary emergency of war, the people of Western Pennsylvania habitually defaulted in land taxes as well. In 1820 the treasurer of Butler County warned that all lands with unpaid taxes would be put up for sale, and this included some 600 properties. Even such prominent political leaders as Henry Baldwin, John Gilmore, and Moses Sullivan owed on several holdings. Only a small percentage of these claims ran over ten dollars, and of the 51 lots in the borough of Butler on which taxes were due, 39 were in arrears less than one dollar. Probably not an inability to pay, but the idea of taxes kept these people from discharging this obligation.[59] Thus, it would be unfair to the East to charge that the whiskey excise alone, discriminatory though it was, prompted the Whiskey Rebellion.

Western Pennsylvanians were also disturbed by the fact that they were plagued with the busy officialdom of the Washington Administration, intent on collecting this questionable tax while at the same time it was dilatory in adopting measures to resist the Indian menace that had once again flared up. The region further believed that Hamilton intended to be vindictive with his excise legislation because seven of nine delegates from the western counties to the state convention had opposed the Constitution in 1788.[60] The secretary of the treasury was obviously motivated more by political expediency than revenge. He recognized that his plan to extend the power of the central government would get

---

[57] Reprint from *The Gleaner* (Pittsburgh) in the *Pittsburgh Gazette,* June 17, 1815.

[58] *Pittsburgh Gazette,* June 17, 1815.

[59] *The Butler Palladium and Republican Star,* February 12, 1820.

[60] Tinkcom, *Republicans and Federalists,* p. 94f.

little support from Western Pennsylvania, and this tax would not hurt the Federalist Party in the vital areas of its strength.

The western counties also considered the possibility that they were being used as an example. Hamilton's major opposition in these years was stemming from the Jeffersonian South, and he wanted to demonstrate to this area that disobedience to law would be met with force. To accomplish this objective the 70,000 Pennsylvania minority west of the mountains was selected for a sample demonstration, but these settlers resented their role as pawns in the political game between the forces of Hamilton and Jefferson.

Violence seemed to be the only alternative. The Pennsylvania Democratic Society in Philadelphia cautioned the western area against rebellion, but if the "power of reason" failed, the society declared that "the strength of the state" should be exerted.[61]

This suggestion by a Philadelphia faction that force be employed against the western part of the state was a strong indication that the eastern majority would facilitate federal action against the West instead of rising to the defense of their fellow Pennsylvanians. August 2, 1794, President Washington called a conference of state and federal leaders to decide on a course of action. The United States government was represented by the President and his whole cabinet and Pennsylvania by Governor Thomas Mifflin, Chief Justice Thomas McKean of the State Supreme Court, Attorney-General Jared Ingersoll, and Secretary of the Commonwealth Alexander J. Dallas. All of these state representatives were easterners who now sat in judgment on Western Pennsylvania.[62]

According to a law of 1792 the President could not call out the militia unless an associate justice of the Supreme Court of the United States or a district judge had first certified to the inadequacy of the courts to stem opposition to a federal law. Associate Justice James Wilson of Philadelphia reported to the President that in his opinion the groups opposing the laws of the nation in Washington and Allegheny Counties were too powerful to be dealt with by either the marshal or ordinary judicial proceedings.[63]

Dallas, also of Philadelphia, suggested that under the United States

---

[61] Tinkcom, *Republicans and Federalists*, p. 108.

[62] *Ibid.*, p. 96; Walters, *Alexander J. Dallas*, p. 54.

[63] Tinkcom, *Republicans and Federalists*, p. 98.

Constitution the President was empowered to call out the militia to suppress an insurrection while under Pennsylvania law the governor possessed no such power. This was substantially an admission that repressive measures in the western counties were endorsed in the East. In the name of Governor Mifflin, Dallas later declared that the state would give full cooperation to the federal government in carrying out such suppression orders. When they were subsequently issued by President Washington, the action indicated to Western Pennsylvanians the complete disregard for the interests of their region prevalent in the East.[64]

Pennsylvania, as well as Virginia and Maryland, liberally supplied militiamen to Washington's army to march against the whiskey insurrectionists, and the arrival of the army in Western Pennsylvania broke the rebellion. Many arrests were made, but only 20 were taken to Philadelphia for trial. Two were convicted of treason, but even they were later pardoned by the President.

In the midst of the rebellion election time appeared, and Western Pennsylvanians went to the polls as they normally did. State Representative James Kelly of York County challenged the right of assemblymen from Westmoreland, Fayette, Washington, and Allegheny Counties, elected at this time, to take their seats on the contention that the elections in that part of the state had been held during an insurrection and were, therefore, unconstitutional. Kelly's resolution to expel the representatives from the four western counties and thereby deprive one-sixth of Pennsylvania of representation in the assembly passed, 43 to 20. Philadelphia and all the eastern counties with the exception of one vote in Philadelphia County favored expulsion. The Pennsylvania Senate took a similar action against the four senators of these western counties to make the disfranchisement of the region complete. New elections were subsequently held, and all the unseated members, save one who refused to run again, were reseated by the end of February 1795, but the humiliation and the suggestion of illegitimate voting were not to be quickly forgotten.[65]

By the turn of the century the court problem had reentered the picture to complicate the political scene further. Many land titles in the northwestern counties were in dispute, and courts were needed in the

---

[64] Walters, *Alexander J. Dallas,* p. 56.
[65] Tinkcom, *Republicans and Federalists,* pp. 109-111.

immediate area to determine actual ownership. These counties now unsuccessfully championed the fight for an extension of the judicial system. When new counties were established in this period, several were frequently given a common court system, thus requiring some citizens to journey to nearby counties for justice.

This situation had become acute when the Holland Land Company and the Pennsylvania Population Company acquired large tracts of land in Pennsylvania north and west of the Allegheny River in 1792 and 1793, respectively. Almost from the beginning the companies had trouble with squatters on their lands. In Crawford County particularly, the Holland Land Company, composed of Dutch capitalists, further had its time-table for settlement upset by Indian uprisings. In the purchase terms the company had agreed to place a settler on every one of the 400-acre tracts within a two-year period. Furthermore, at least two of every 100 acres in a survey had to be cleared, fenced, and cultivated with a house erected thereon and a family in residence within five years following the first settling. If the company failed to comply with these terms, the Commonwealth could issue new warrants for settlement unless the company had been hindered in its task by the enemies of the United States.[66]

In 1793 the hostility of the Indians forced men to leave their lands for places of safety. When they returned, they often found their cabins in the possession of intruders. This prompted a conflict between the intruder and the warrantee. Other intruders on company lands did not go so far as to take over homes, but simply took possession of the first and best vacant tracts they found and commenced to clear and cultivate the land. These "actual settlers" took up many of the lands claimed by company warrants and incited a keen competition with those who later purchased the lands from the company and attempted to take possession. The companies and their warrantees argued that the Indian menace constituted an enemy of the United States and that they had retarded settlement while the squatters charged that the companies had defaulted in the terms of settlement.[67]

The conflict reached a crisis in 1799 when Tench Coxe, the newly appointed head of the state board of property, not only refused to

---

[66] John E. Reynolds, *French Creek Valley*, pp. 104-106; Ferguson, *Western Pennsylvania Politics*, p. 159.

[67] John E. Reynolds, *French Creek Valley*, pp. 107-109.

allow the Holland Land Company to complete the patenting of its lands, but threatened to revoke the patents it already held and assign them to squatters. The company engaged Alexander J. Dallas to establish its rights through the courts. In the first round of the legal battle, the Supreme Court of Pennsylvania in 1802 held that Indian uprisings had only deferred, but did not excuse the company from meeting the conditions of the original sale. As a result the "actual settlers" could take out warrants for their improved lands and the company was powerless to eject them.[68]

As foreigners the owners of the Holland Land Company were constitutionally entitled to have their lawsuits tried in federal courts, and after appeals the United States Supreme Court finally held in 1805 that Indian hostilities did excuse the non-performance of actual settlement. This verdict in behalf of the company, which reversed the decision of the state courts, only added to the confusion of land ownership and frustrated many farmers in Western Pennsylvania again. The squatters and their supporters could see nothing but gross injustice in the loss of their lands and in the attitude of the federal court, especially since the decision for the Holland Land Company became a pattern for the Pennsylvania Population Company as well.[69]

At one point in the controversy a settler reported that a concerted plan had been laid through three counties to shoot Judge Alexander Addison of the Fifth Judicial District of Pennsylvania, who had even earlier won Western Pennsylvania's disdain with his opposition to the Whiskey Rebellion. Now the land problem constantly required Addison's presence at Meadville, but since the journey was an arduous one, the court held infrequent sessions there. This, in turn, meant delays in dispensing justice and resentment of the judge. The plot on his life, however, was only a part of a grandiose scheme to blow up the land office in Meadville to destroy the county records and to drive off or kill the company agents. The arrival of Harm Jan Huidekoper, as the new agent, poured oil on the troubled waters, but the new representative quickly learned that the Scotch-Irish were always difficult to control and on the frontier they were nigh impossible.[70]

Western settlers resented eastern sympathy for the companies and

[68] Ferguson, *Western Pennsylvania Politics*, p. 183.
[69] *Ibid.*, p. 183f.; Walters, *Alexander J. Dallas*, p. 164.
[70] *Obituary of Harm Jan Huidekoper*, p. 6.

fought to defend themselves against such charges as the one leveled by
The Aurora: The Squatters denounce every man as an enemy and menace them with vengeance if they attempt to gain *possession of their own
lands.*[71]

They sought to ward off such criticism of their conduct by pointing
out that the practice of squatters in Western Pennsylvania conformed
favorably to the method used by the "rich German farmers" in procuring their lands east of the mountains. Surely easterners could not
object because the West was following in their footsteps, and talk of
thievery by western squatters seemed wholly out of place when coming
from eastern mouths. Unlike so many seaboard speculators, the squatters
in the western counties could not be accused of stealing the revolutionary
certificates of orphan children or of running away from militia camps
during the war.[72]

Although this counter-criticism of the East was designed to check
eastern denunciation of the squatters, it in no way alleviated the distress
that threatened the actual settlers following the court decision of 1805.
Their newly-built homes and improved lands seemed doomed in spite
of the fact that companies frequently permitted them to apply to purchase their cleared lands.

Many lacked the necessary capital and the problem remained acute.
In the minds of the settlers in the northwestern counties the wrong
went without redress. Finally the politicians took it up and campaigned
on a platform of obtaining remuneration for the incalculable damage
done to the actual settlers. As late as 1820 George Moore based his
candidacy for an Assembly seat chiefly on a pledge to gain compensation
for the settlers because they had taken possession of these lands with the
understanding that they were vacant. This impression arose from the
prevailing interpretation given to the Act of 1792 and from the encouragement held out to them by the governors, legislature, and the
board of property. In many cases the settlers paid for the lands and were
granted warrants and patents by the state before their ownership was
questioned.[73]

---

[71] "Philander," *Commonwealth,* July 12, 1817.

[72] *Ibid.,* p. 53.

[73] "Address to 'Actual Settlers' of Erie, Crawford, Mercer, Venango, and Warren Counties" printed in *Erie Gazette,* September 30, 1820; George Moore to
Joseph M. Sterrett, dated September 29, 1820, printed in *Erie Gazette,* September 30, 1820.

In spite of an increasing population and a trend toward manufacturing after the War of 1812, the feeling of frustration, engendered by these land disputes and other issues within the lifetime of the minority residing in Pennsylvania's western counties in 1815, continued to grow in intensity. The farmer, merchant, and manufacturer, each using his own experiences as a guide, believed that "a golden age for the West" could be realized if a few more obstacles were overcome. They seemed insurmountable, chiefly because of the failure of the state and national governments to cooperate.

Especially during the war mechanics and manufacturers in the region had come to depend upon industry for a livelihood, but at the same time were forced to watch in anguish as the greatest industrial nation of the world ruthlessly assaulted their modest establishments with Lord Brougham tactics. Merchants, meanwhile, pointed to laws in neighboring states that discriminated against a wholesome trade for them. As the farmer planted his wheat instead of the more exportable cotton, he too was painfully aware of the obstacles to his success; geography and climate debarred him from the rich markets awaiting the seaboard and Mississippi Valley planters.

The feeling of hope and prosperity that shot across the nation following the victory of New Orleans meant little to Western Pennsylvania; in retrospect it was only a flash of light in an otherwise dark night. The region quickly returned to a pattern of frustration and adhered to it through the larger part of the 1815-1825 era. The explanation for this relapse, which will be discussed in the next two chapters, is twofold: an inability to overcome the economic challenges of the decade and the failure to build a political system to fight these and other battles.

III

Confusion in the Social Milieu

*Agriculture, Commerce, and Manufactures—the govern-
ment is wedded to commerce, agriculture pays the piper,
and manufactures "dances in her stocking feet."* [1]

THE background of the people in Western Pennsylvania, influenced by certain economic factors, only partially explains
the region's inferiority and political confusion. Other economic
issues, more peculiar to the era of good feeling and less dependent upon
geography, also conditioned the region's attitudes. Through most of the
decade the interests supporting agriculture, manufacturing, and commerce attempted to crush each other instead of recognizing that the
prosperity of one was unalterably tied to the success of the others.

Conflicting proposals concerning internal improvements, tariffs, and
banking practices divided the region to the point that cooperation at
any level seemed impossible. The notable exception to this pattern of
dissension, of course, was a common resentment of the state's eastern
counties. Economic particularism tightened its grip so securely after
1815 that even the sturdiest political organization would have had
difficulty in maintaining party discipline. Since party lines were not
strictly observed in these years, this economic localism tended only to
minimize party distinctions and promote an area-consciousness.

COMMERCIAL VEINS OF WEALTH

Although Philadelphia had long dominated western commerce, particularly via a trade-lane through Pittsburgh, it now appeared that
Baltimore and New York would assume this leadership because of their
geographic advantages. With the advent of canals and improved turnpikes, the geography of Pennsylvania made Philadelphia's access to the

---

[1] Toast proposed at an Independence Day celebration of the Pittsburgh Independent Blues. *Mercury,* July 10, 1822.

interior the least favorable of all the Atlantic cities of commercial importance.[2] Pennsylvania could boast of no such natural east-west arteries as the Mohawk and Potomac Rivers which made possible the Erie Canal to the north and the National Road and the Chesapeake and Ohio Canal to the south. Not only did the main river systems of Pennsylvania run north and south, but the lofty Alleghenies supplied an additional hazard to westward transportation from Philadelphia. When Ohio proposed to build north-south canals to join the Erie Canal System with the Chesapeake and Ohio, Pennsylvania feared that her day of commerce had passed.

Pittsburgh, in particular, shuddered at the possibility of losing her position as the "Emporium of the West" while Philadelphia was rent with indecision concerning the course that internal improvements should take. Samuel Breck, Mathew Carey, and Zachariah Poulson struggled to arouse Philadelphia from the apathy caused by the indecision, but their efforts produced limited results.

Western trade was diverted from Pennsylvania. The problem of recapturing it grew even more complicated until months and years went by without a positive state-wide program being adopted. Merchants from the western counties watched in utter disgust as their streams of commerce began to dry up.

The principal challenge to Pittsburgh and Philadelphia's commercial leadership in the West came from the National Pike which paralleled the Pennsylvania road across the mountains. This highway began at Cumberland, Maryland, and by 1817 its route was charted as far as Wheeling, Virginia. Since a satisfactory state road already joined Cumberland and Baltimore, this government construction gave the latter city a "window on the West" at Wheeling. The road was 112 miles in length: 24½ miles across Maryland, 75½ through Pennsylvania, and 12 in Virginia. In spite of the extensive piece of road that stretched through Somerset, Fayette, and Washington Counties, there was much opposition to the road from elsewhere in Western Pennsylvania. Pittsburgh merchants complained most bitterly, and the city's *Gazette* became their sounding board.[3]

This criticism reached its peak after Wheeling had officially been

---

[2] Klein, *Pennsylvania Politics*, p. 19f.

[3] Thomas B. Searight, *The Old Pike: A History of the National Road* (Uniontown: Thomas B. Searight, 1894), p. 32.

selected as the crossing point on the Ohio River. Before the federal government could build to this, or any destination for that matter, it had to receive permission from the respective state legislatures to construct the road. Only Pennsylvania made any requests of the federal authorities. While granting unqualified permission, the legislature suggested that the road touch both Uniontown and Washington. No mention was made of Brownsville since it was a foregone conclusion that the highway would cross the Monongahela at that point.[4]

In 1808 Gallatin, who had favored such a highway as early as 1784, urged President Thomas Jefferson to have the road commissioners survey west of Brownsville to both Wheeling and another point on the Ohio. Then the President was to make the final choice between the two routes. Once the road had reached Brownsville by way of Fayette County where Gallatin owned much land, he apparently had no preference for any given destination on the Ohio except to insist that the road cross the adjoining county of Washington which he had represented in Congress for six years.

Not too subtly Gallatin advised the President that Washington County normally gave a 2,000-vote majority to his party. Since this was long before the Wheeling terminus had been decided upon, there was a remote possibility that the road would turn north at Brownsville and meet the Ohio at Pittsburgh. Since 1808 was an election year, Gallatin prevailed upon Jefferson to approve the road through Washington County because indecision could cause the county's political majority to be lost to the opposition.[5]

Gallatin warned that the Jefferson party would lose Pennsylvania if it permitted the 2,000 majority that Washington County could give to slip away. Jefferson deplored this political pressure employed by the Pennsylvanians to influence him, but nevertheless ordered a survey of a route through the county and borough of Washington. He made no formal commitment to sanction such a course, but stated that deflections from the most direct route to the Ohio would be approved when they would benefit certain towns and better accommodate travelers.[6]

---

[4] Searight, *Old Pike,* p. 36f,; Archer B. Hulbert, *The Cumberland Road* (Cleveland: The Arthur H. Clark Co., 1904), p. 54.

[5] Albert Gallatin to Thomas Jefferson, July 27, 1808. Henry Adams (ed.), *The Writings of Albert Gallatin* (Philadelphia: J. B. Lippincott & Co., 1879), I, 395.

[6] Thomas Jefferson to Albert Gallatin, August 6, 1808. Paul L. Ford (ed.), *The Works of Thomas Jefferson* (New York: G. P. Putnam's Sons, 1904), V, 333.

After the road was eventually approved to Washington, the contest for the location of the Ohio River terminus reached its final stages with Wheeling and Steubenville as the principal contenders. James Ross and Henry Baldwin of Pittsburgh had realized the near impossibility of having the road pass through their city because of the avowed objectives: shortness and an Ohio River destination where navigation was reasonably satisfactory in all seasons.

They seized the opportunity presented by the War of 1812 to begin the erection of a woolen mill at Steubenville in partnership with Bazaleel Wells and Samuel Patterson. Since theirs was the first woolen mill west of the mountains, Steubenville was called to public attention, and the area became the goal of many emigrants from the East. Ross, a large landowner in the Steubenville area, annually auctioned off land on liberal terms in order to populate the town and countryside with mechanics and farmers and thereby increase the pressure for that terminus to the National Road. Meanwhile, the landholders at Wheeling, in anticipation of having the highway come to their borough, held their lots at such high prices that few could afford to buy. Wells and Ross were property owners in Washington County and stood to profit from a main communication line through or near their holdings. Also the possibility that the road would go to Steubenville caused the Pittsburghers, Baldwin and Ross, to raise no protest to the by-passing of their home city.[7]

The fact that Ross and Wells were avowed Federalists may have influenced the Republican administration to favor Wheeling, but on the positive side of the scale Henry Clay, a tower of political strength, threw his support behind the Wheeling route. Although Clay defended his choice on the basis of efficiency, there were rumors that he had been swayed by the charms of Lydia Shepherd. Since Clay was always attracted to women, it was inevitable that tales of sexual irregularities would be spread abroad by his opponents, and the decision to direct the road to Wheeling gave them a chord on which to harp.[8]

Lydia's husband, Colonel Moses Shepherd, was a large landholder

[7] Catherine B. Smith, "The Terminus of the Cumberland Road on the Ohio River" (Unpublished Master's thesis, History Dept., University of Pittsburgh, 1951), pp. 17, 21, 24, 27.

[8] George Dangerfield, The Era of Good Feelings (New York: Harcourt, Brace & Co., 1952), p. 10; Philip D. Jordan, The National Road (New York: Bobbs-Merrill Co., 1948), p. 114.

in the Wheeling area, and his mansion at the forks of Wheeling Creek was a favorite stopping point for travelers, including congressmen and senators. The dark-eyed Lydia, a frequent visitor to the nation's capital, developed a keen interest in national affairs. Her ability to discuss them with remarkable insight captivated Clay, and on his travels to and from Kentucky he generally arranged to be a guest at the Shepherd mansion house. Since his visits frequently coincided with the business trips of the colonel, the gossip was soon flourishing. As the story eventually spread, Pittsburghers wondered if their prosperity had actually been placed in jeopardy because of the nation's best interest or because of the sparkling eyes of the woman at Wheeling Creek.[9]

This toll-free highway stirred Pittsburgh's jealousy of not only Wheeling, but also the areas of Pennsylvania that profited from the road. This resentment reached its peak in 1818, the year that the war-stimulated prosperity collapsed. Many war-born factories closed their doors, and unemployment mounted rapidly. This dire outlook was supplemented by an unusual drought which extended the customary low water period beyond September into November. By the middle of the latter month the editor of the *Pittsburgh Gazette* counted 30 large keelboats, beside the flat-bottoms, loaded with goods for Kentucky merchants, anchored in the Monongahela River because of the low water.[10] The Steubenville *Western Herald* estimated the value of this cargo marooned at Pittsburgh to be $3,000,000. At the same time the editor predicted that unless the river between Pittsburgh and Steubenville were dredged to permit the passage of 50-ton vessels in all seasons of the year, Pittsburgh would be replaced by Wheeling as the depot for western merchandise.[11]

The low water also placed a burden on the Pittsburgh proprietors of the large fleet of keelboats and barges that operated on the western waterways. While waiting for the river to rise, they were forced to pay between 15 and 30 dollars per day in wages to idle boatmen or run the risk of losing them. The economy of Pittsburgh was further crippled by the diminishing carrying-trade which was being siphoned off by the

[9] Smith, "Terminus of the Cumberland Road," p. 65.

[10] *Pittsburgh Gazette,* November 17, 1818; F. Frank Crall, "A Half Century of Rivalry between Pittsburgh and Wheeling," *The Western Pennsylvania Historical Magazine,* XIII (1930), 240.

[11] *The Western Herald* (Steubenville), November 7, 1818, quoted in *Poulson's Advertiser,* November 20, 1818.

Cumberland Road. This loss to the city was estimated at $100,000 annually, and James Stevenson reported to the state legislature that the federal turnpike produced a $600,000 vacuum in Pennsylvania's economy every year.[12]

Pittsburgh was more upset at this financial loss than any other part of the state. The city looked about to find the culprits that caused the disaster and unearthed two, the people of Philadelphia and those of Ohio. In the minds of Pittsburghers, Ohioans endorsed the new turnpike with its Wheeling terminus in order to make themselves successful highwaymen. They had accumulated financial obligations at the "Emporium of the West" without any intention of meeting them. The new highway conveniently shifted their commercial dependence from Pittsburgh and permitted them to escape their old creditors in favor of exploiting the more liberal laws of indebtedness in Virginia.[13]

The complaint against Philadelphia was completely different, apathy rather than aggression. In regard to the competition among coastal cities for the domination of western trade, the Philadelphia attitude was succinctly expressed by William Duane when he said, "there is room enough . . . for us all." An eastern merchant was also quoted as saying that it was "much better for us to trust Baltimore, than the whole country west of the mountains." [14] Rather than attempt to compete with the Erie Canal and the National Road, Philadelphia passively accepted their advantages and because of her proximity to Baltimore was content simply to trade with the West through that port.

The western counties decried this reaction. They foolishly hoped to arouse Philadelphia to the sponsorship of state improvements to combat the Cumberland Road by hurling a combination of derogatory criticism and forthright admonitions at eastern policies. Led by the *Pittsburgh Gazette*, they charged that the understanding of eastern counties on the subject of improvements was limited to township roads and their geographical knowledge was bounded by the Alleghenies on the west. The editor wanted the people of Philadelphia to recognize that the problem involved more than the interests of Wheeling and Pittsburgh; they could not continue to shrug their shoulders and say calmly: "Let

---

[12] *Pittsburgh Gazette*, November 17, 1818; *Mercury*, February 14, 1821; March 20, 1822.

[13] "Fair Play," *Pittsburgh Gazette*, October 12, 1819.

[14] *Aurora*, July 3, 1815; *Pittsburgh Gazette*, March 23, 1818.

the western gentry fight it out themselves; it is nothing to us: our Academy of fine arts cannot be affected by the contest." [15]

Pittsburghers attempted to shock Philadelphia further by hammering at the theme that the Cumberland Road was a greater threat to the eastern part of the state than to the western because the latter's future was not as dependent upon transmontane trade. With the growing efficiency of steam navigation on the Mississippi and Ohio, Pittsburgh argued that she was in a position to turn her back on the Atlantic seaboard (but certainly gave no evidence of demonstrating it). Actually downstream commerce was recognized as a poor foundation for transmontane politics. While superficially exhibiting concern for Philadelphia's future, Pittsburgh was at the same time admonishing the eastern metropolis that her conduct exhibited alarming parallels to the rotten borough of old Sarum. She warned that, unless changes were made, Cato's *delenda est Chartago* would be modified to *delanda est Philadelphia*.[16]

Pittsburgh's jealousy of the areas profiting from the toll-free road was prompted by the feeling that they had done nothing to deserve such federal assistance. Pittsburghers understood and appreciated thoroughly their own struggle to haul commodities over the mountains against such obstacles as adverse weather, poorly-graded roads, wagon accidents, and damaged cargoes. After such exertions the government stepped in to help an area that displayed less initiative and faced fewer geographic hazards. There seemed to be no justice, moral or political. The sceptre of wealth and influence was presented as a gift to the people of Wheeling who simply sat around stroking their chins with a disgusting air of self-complacency.[17]

Brownsville, the first point where the National Road reached navigable western waters, was regarded as another undeserving, but nevertheless rewarded, Pittsburgh rival. Even before the highway was completed to Wheeling, Brownsville developed a narrow concept of state improvements. Aware that a high percentage of the cargoes destined for the West could be embarked there if the Monongahela were navigable in all seasons, Fayette County legislators became preoccupied with bills to improve navigation on the rivers.[18]

[15] *Pittsburgh Gazette,* November 5, 1819; May 1, 1820.
[16] *Ibid.,* June 30, 1818.
[17] *Ibid.,* September 17, 1819.
[18] *American Telegraph,* May 1, 1816.

When the people of Washington became conscious of their potential through the "wonderful magic of the Cumberland Road," they exhibited a similar particularism. Landlords gleefully considered the prospect of selling their property at $5,000 or $6,000 per lot. In anticipation of a 25 per cent increase in the sale price of their local products as well, the road was lauded as an evidence of good national feeling. On the other hand, Pittsburgh's anticipated depression and subsequent denunciation of the road as "a lavish and wanton expenditure of the public money" was branded a "local jealousy." While Pittsburgh insisted that Pennsylvania was paying for the stick to break its commercial back, Washington accepted the turnpike as the only necessary tangible proof of national growth and prosperity.[19]

Obviously Pittsburgh's major condemnation for the state's lag in internal improvements was aimed at Philadelphia, and her criticism was not without foundation. Zachariah Poulson, the Philadelphia publisher, agreed that his city was rich in means, but poor in spirit where patriotic exertions in behalf of state improvements were concerned. He pointed out that the inhabitants had been faithful and liberal contributors to roads in the immediate vicinity of their city, but that they did little to support any more distant state works. Cognizant that continued high transportation costs would incite a "manifest prejudice" against Philadelphia, the editor solicited the city to throw off its lethargy.[20]

Even this warning was an understatement since half the selling price of western flour at both Baltimore and Philadelphia in this decade after the War of 1812 went to pay the carrying charges. On the Ohio flour brought $4.00 per barrel and $8.75 in the East while Indian corn sold for a mere 25 cents per bushel at the former point in 1815 and $1.20 in Baltimore.[21]

The alpha and omega of Pittsburgh transportation demands upon Philadelphia to remedy this situation was an improved, toll-free turnpike between the two cities. Through their spokesman, Samuel Breck, many Philadelphians opposed the improvement of the existing southern road because of its nearness to the Maryland line. Its location enabled the citizens of Baltimore to form connecting roads and enter into com-

---

[19] *Washington Examiner,* September 7, 1818; "Memorandum of a Tour into Ohio" quoted in the *Pittsburgh Gazette,* February 5, 1819.

[20] *Poulson's Advertiser,* May 17, 1817.

[21] *Western Herald* quoted in the *Commonwealth,* October 28, 1815.

petition with Philadelphia for the inland trade of Pennsylvania. There were those in Western Pennsylvania who agreed with Breck's opposition to the southern road, but who arrived at their conclusion for an entirely different reason. Nevertheless, it smacked of the same particularism. The group insisted that the absence of a turnpike across the center of Pennsylvania showed that the legislature had neglected the more northerly counties, and that this was the time to rectify the error with an advantage for all. Produce from such a northern road would go to Philadelphia alone, and the eastern and western parts of the state would be more closely united.[22]

Although Breck and his eastern cohorts opposed large expenditures on the southern turnpike across Pennsylvania, they did not object to internal improvements in theory. In keeping with the theme of national feeling Breck proposed a grandiose transcontinental waterway tying the Delaware, Susquehanna, Juniata, Kiskiminetas, Allegheny, Ohio, Missouri, and Columbia Rivers together with miraculous lifts over the Allegheny and Rocky Mountains. The plan, with no practical meaning for America of this period, seemed to be the work of a visionary, but embodied three new improvement features for the Pennsylvania discussion: a more northerly route across the state, involvement in a general scheme of improvements, and the medium of water.[23]

Breck's "fanciful naval communication" hopelessly divided public opinion and retarded the development of a practical means of retaining Pennsylvania's valuable commerce for several years. The proposal was quickly recognized as absurd, but support for the first legs of the project was stirred up. Philadelphians sponsored the idea of a canal system from southeastern Pennsylvania to Lake Erie in the northwest corner, and they courted the endorsement of the southwestern counties with the announcement that the system would join the Allegheny.

The possibility that the project would become a reality aroused much rivalry among the state's middle counties. McKean County knew that the best route from the Susquehanna to the Allegheny was via Pine Creek, emptying into the Allegheny at Coudersport. Both Centre and Clearfield Counties claimed that they controlled the most accessible approaches to the West, but they were not to be outdone by an Arm-

---

[22] The Westmoreland Republican (Greensburg), October 24, 1818; Mercury, October 29, 1819.

[23] Statesman, November 28, 1818.

strong authority who voiced his local preferences. He suggested four possible channels by which the canal system could reach the Allegheny: by Red Bank Creek, Mahoning Creek, Crooked Creek, or the Kiskiminetas River—all in Armstrong County.[24]

Pittsburgh and the southwestern counties were not interested in the fact that the proposed canal system would place Erie 100 miles nearer Philadelphia than New York. They saw only that it would enhance Philadelphia's commercial opportunities with the interior counties while their own position would be weakened. Such a water route would extend the distance between Philadelphia and Pittsburgh by several hundred miles over the length of the southern turnpike. Pittsburghers in particular agitated for something more practical and less expensive than "digging canals through mountains and melting down rocks." [25]

The editor of *The Genius of the Lakes* in Erie supported this contention and predicted that only a turnpike direct from Philadelphia to Pittsburgh could save Pennsylvania trade from the ruinous competition of the Cumberland Road. In explaining the state's failure to undertake such a project, however, he agreed with eastern authorities and placed the blame on a glaring weakness in the policy of the southwestern counties. The Pittsburgh area wanted exclusive patronage for its road instead of making a vigorous effort to connect it with a general scheme of improvements embodying the whole state. The people of Washington, Greene, and Fayette Counties, meanwhile, felt secure with the Cumberland Road. Their legislators simply refused to support western measures, such as improved navigation on the Ohio and a toll-free highway across the mountains, which would aid the Pittsburgh area.[26]

HOME SECURITY THROUGH HOMESPUNS

From the beginning of this decade in 1815 there were individuals, groups, and editors in Pittsburgh who argued that Western Pennsylvania should refrain from further entreaties toward Philadelphia for cooperation. As years passed without any significant improvements in transportation, this idea gained more and more adherents, both in the

---

[24] *Aurora,* July 14, 1815; *Statesman,* May 22, 1819.

[25] *Pittsburgh Gazette,* July 31, 1818; *Democratic Press,* March 1, 1825.

[26] *The Genius of the Lakes* (Erie) quoted in the *Statesman,* November 28, 1818; *Pittsburgh Gazette,* November 23, 1819.

city and beyond. Supporters of the idea urged the region to forget state programs and adopt a policy of self-sufficiency which, after all, was "the germ of eventual greatness."

The seeds of this proposed independence had germinated in the period between the Embargo Act of 1808 and the Treaty of Ghent in 1814. In those years manufacturing indelibly planted its mark on the American economy and left one of its clearest impressions in Western Pennsylvania. As early as 1810 a combination of seven of these "frontier" counties [27] exceeded the industrial output of such states as New Hampshire, Vermont, Rhode Island, and New Jersey.

The factories which gave rise to this self-reliant spirit were not built with any patriotic motive, but with the intent of personal emolument. The establishment of these industries for private advantage, however, did not detract from their benefit to the region, but the high prices of their products, caused by wartime inflation, inefficiency, the need for reinvestment capital, and occasionally sheer greed, antagonized many local consumers. Their resentment turned every request for the protection of domestic manufactures into a pitched battle during this era of good feeling.

The anti-manufacturing element denounced the high costs as simply the result of a lack of competition and through its representatives voted "no" on all tariff proposals. These antagonists failed to consider the just and unavoidable causes of temporary high prices. They ignored the war and the fact that in areas like Western Pennsylvania industry could only be expanded by a reinvestment of whatever profits could be obtained since there was no other money available. [28]

Such conditions afforded an added compulsion to the natural inclination of selling at the highest prices the market would conveniently bring. Perhaps, too, the opponents deliberately closed their eyes to all justification of protection for domestic manufactures because "they sighed for the silks and fine muslins, the tea and the coffee, from which all but the very wealthy had been deprived" during the war. [29]

Although handicapped by the public's desire for such foreign luxuries,

---

[27] These counties were Allegheny, Greene, Fayette, Westmoreland, Washington, Beaver, and Butler.

[28] *Aurora*, October 12, 1814; *Mercury*, October 21, 1815; Louis C. Hunter, "Financial Problems of the Early Pittsburgh Iron Manufacturers," *Journal of Economic and Business History*, II (1930), 524.

[29] Sharpless, *Pennsylvania History*, p. 271.

western industry was pushed forward by a more powerful set of forces. Aside from the transportation difficulties which encouraged local production, the area west of the mountains was favorably disposed to manufacturing because it was relatively free of the long traditions of commerce that characterized the conservative East. Too many men in the coastal cities regarded an appeal to their own labor and resources to supply their manufacturing needs as economic folly. They doubted their ability to compete with experienced Britain and feared that Britain might interpret such activity as an act of hostility.

The entrenchment of this commercial attitude and economic subservience did not meet with approval in the western counties. Impatience of restraint and belief in their own abilities dominated the thinking of young western entrepreneurs. The invigorating spirit of their industrial vision was well expressed by their leader in the field of glass, James O'Hara, who triumphantly recorded in his notes: "today we made the first glass bottle at a cost of $30,000." [30]

These entrepreneurs and their supporters in Pittsburgh desired, not only to break Britain's maritime monopoly, but also to be economically independent of the East as far as possible.[31] In June 1816, when the federal government abruptly repealed the double duties imposed on all imports during the war, the realization of their ambition was threatened. The government believed that repeal would simply return the nation's economy to conditions as they had been when war came in 1812.

This reasoning was faulty because the Napoleonic Wars ended almost simultaneously with our War of 1812. The entire European picture was altered. Immense armies were disbanded, and thousands of soldiers returned to their labors in the field, or the workshop, or on the merchant vessel. This disarmament, not only curtailed our market and carrier trade, but also produced great quantities of food staples and manufactured goods to compete with our own. The federal government did not recognize that a complete change in economic policy was necessary to avoid disaster and refused to heed the warning of the *Pittsburgh Gazette*:

---

[30] James O'Hara to James Morrison, June 24, 1805. Box 48, Denny-O'Hara Papers; Wilson, *History of Pittsburg*, p. 997.

[31] *Niles' Register*, May 28, 1814 (VI, 207); Killikelly, *History of Pittsburgh*, p. 129.

We are no longer a neutral nation busied in gathering the harvest of European conflicts. The state of the world is changed, and our Domestic policy must be adapted to the permanent relations of peace.[32]

Congress was not swayed by such advice and responded only with the ineffectual and partisan Tariff of 1816 which afforded less protection than the wartime double duties. The benefits of this limited protection, moreover, were not equally distributed; manufacturers of cotton and woolen textiles, who were concentrated largely in coastal areas, were accorded greater protection than Western Pennsylvania's producers of iron and glass. Two years later the disparity on iron was corrected, but glass protection was negligible for years in spite of Pittsburgh protests. The nation's duty on foreign glass was less than the export bounty paid by the British government. In fact, the entire cost of landing British glass in the United States, including the American duty, was covered by the reimbursements and manipulations of the British government.[33]

Although the tariff did not become a national political issue until 1824, it attained that distinction in Pittsburgh with this discrimination of 1816. Economically as well, the birth of protection was in the western rather than the eastern counties of Pennsylvania and was pushed forward most militantly by the iron industry which had been snubbed by this original protective tariff measure. The strength of protectionism in Western Pennsylvania was also due to the fact that industry was a necessity, not just another business enterprise. In the eastern part of the state, on the other hand, the commercial element overshadowed the manufacturers and fought to import as much European goods, duty-free, as judiciously possible.[34]

Western Pennsylvania demanded that the American people and the government exhibit the same faith in the manufacturer in peacetime that he had shown the government in wartime.

Our manufacturers are as much entitled to what they ask for as the crippled soldier who claims his pittance of a pension. *They*, too, were allured into the service; were induced to put every thing at hazard by the language of the constituted authorities. On the faith of that language they put forth their

---

[32] *Pittsburgh Gazette,* October 26, 1819.

[33] *Mercury,* October 28, 1823; William J. Bining, "The Glass Industry of Western Pennsylvania, 1797-1860" (Unpublished Master's thesis, History Dept., University of Pittsburgh, 1936), p. 49.

[34] Frank W. Stonecipher, "Pittsburgh and the Nineteenth Century Tariffs," *The Western Pennsylvania Historical Magazine,* XXXI (1948), 84.

strength to render the country *independent of Great Britain;* and now, when they are broken down by that power, when their nerves are cut by something more powerful than an English broadsword, they are entitled to ask the means of pouring balm upon those wounds, and causing them once again to heal.[35]

The disruption of prosperity in 1818 caused the people of Pittsburgh to look back to "the good old days" of 1812-1815 when a high tariff (temporary double duties) and prosperity reigned. They came to regard these two as synonymous, but a more academic appraisal would have attributed the prosperity to a wartime economy. Depression times, however, are not primarily periods of sound thought and scientific judgment, but of emotional and impulsive behavior. The people were perplexed and anxious to grasp at any panacea. The protective tariff seemed destined to become their credo; even the apathetic farmers slowly identified their prosperity with the success of industry.[36]

Amid this political and economic unrest the name of Henry Baldwin surged to the foreground as the Moses who could lead Western Pennsylvania out of the wilderness of troubled times. Born in New Haven, Connecticut, in 1780, Baldwin moved to Pittsburgh in 1799 and through the first 40 years of the 19th Century was frequently toasted as the "Pride of Pittsburgh" and the "Idol of Pennsylvania." By profession he was a lawyer, but rose to prominence through his newspaper activities and interest in local Democratic-Republican politics.

After 17 years of public service to his community, Baldwin was elected to Congress in 1816. The manufacturing interests of Pittsburgh had seen the double duties removed that very summer and immediately responded by sending a representative to Congress who would agitate for a higher tariff to save their factories from possible collapse. Baldwin was more than a political front for these manufacturers; he was actually one of them. He held a financial interest in at least three rolling mills of Western Pennsylvania of which the Union Rolling Mill of Pittsburgh was the largest and most expensive of its kind in the whole western country.[37]

Since the Pittsburgh industrial interests were not able to control the more numerous agrarian element in the surrounding parts of Allegheny

---

[35] "Hamilton," *Pittsburgh Gazette,* October 6, 1818.

[36] Arthur C. Bining, "The Rise of Manufacture in Western Pennsylvania," *The Western Pennsylvania Historical Magazine,* XVI (1933), 242.

[37] M. Flavia Taylor, "The Political and Civic Career of Henry Baldwin 1799-1830," *The Western Pennsylvania Historical Magazine,* XXIV (1941), 45.

and Butler Counties, Baldwin was not the choice of the regular Democratic-Republican ticket, but of the Independent Republicans and Federalists. In spite of an anti-manufacturing attitude in rural areas, the task of organizing opposition to Baldwin was an awkward one because his popularity and lengthy Democratic affiliation were well-known, even among the farmers.

Thus Baldwin's opponents could not be too vociferous without endangering their county and township tickets as well. This forced them into an indirect campaign, and oftentimes they were even induced to pay him left-handed compliments. For example, in explaining Baldwin's support, the editor of *The Commonwealth* declared that many lawyers, a class in general disrepute among the farmers, had a personal interest in wishing to send him to Congress. According to the editor, they stood ready to destroy their party to aid their selfish ambitions. Since they were unable to compete with Baldwin at the bar of justice and were unable to equal his high standards, they rejoiced at the thought of having him absent from the city for five months each year on Congressional business.[38]

As the result of a substantial victory, Baldwin took his seat in Congress in December 1817, at a time when the ill effects of the Tariff of 1816 were being felt. He was assigned to the Committee on Commerce and Manufactures where for the next four and a half years he was inordinately active in an effort to promote the welfare of his constituents. It did not follow, however, that his untiring activity would produce the desired results. The 15th and 16th Congresses (1817-1821) were in no mood to discuss the tariff problem extensively, but gave precedence to the questions involving Florida and Missouri.

In these years Congress became bogged down with the problems of admitting Missouri as a free or slave state and of censuring Andrew Jackson for his conduct in Florida. The demands of Western Pennsylvania, a charter section of the Union, were shelved while the Congressmen worried about a territory that desired to become a state and about a mismanaged Spanish possession. Pittsburgh particularly was discouraged that Congress consumed so much time in evaluating the report of the military committee dealing with Jackson's demeanor in Florida, but had done nothing to relieve the plight of her manufacturers. Again the busy officialdom of the federal government seemed, to the Pennsyl-

[38] *Commonwealth,* August 27, 1816.

vanians west of the mountains, to be preoccupied with a secondary issue while one essential to their vital needs went unattended. Both the *Mercury* and the *Statesman* voiced their impatience and denounced the discussion of Jackson's conduct as a waste of time "worse than useless." [39]

Although the *Statesman* was disturbed by these lengthy deliberations, it echoed the ideas of its principal political endorsee, United States Senator Abner Lacock of Beaver who insisted that Jackson was in error.

The good old republican doctrine about "standing armies" and "military usurptions," appears to be getting out of fashion; and the decision of the house would lead one to believe that the constitution and laws may be violated with impunity by any fellow who can contrive to get a pair of epaulets stuck on his shoulders.[40]

This argument, plus Lacock's position as chairman of the Senate committee to investigate Jackson, was unable to obscure Western Pennsylvania's genuine feelings. The public in other parts of the nation was given the true picture through the speeches of Pittsburgh Congressman Henry Baldwin, who spoke out strongly in defense of the general and who made it clear that vindication would clear the floor more quickly for the consideration of vital legislation.

Lacock, on the other hand, desired a detailed investigation, largely with the idea of attracting attention to himself since his Senate term was about to expire in 1819. He seemed to regard this as his opportunity to gain publicity, but the cause he championed at this point was in disrepute in the western part of Pennsylvania. Furthermore, he had already developed many enemies in the East, killing any chances he had for reappointment.

Even before this Jackson controversy finally passed from the lips of men locked in Congressional debate, the question of admitting Missouri took priority over all other issues. In February 1820, Henry Baldwin reported three bills to aid manufacturers, but before any action on them could be initiated, the House went into the committee of the whole to debate the Missouri problem. Fearing that another round of excessive wrangling would ensue over the introduction of this decidedly partisan topic, the *Pittsburgh Gazette* quipped:

---

[39] *Mercury*, February 5, 1819; *Statesman*, February 20, 1819; M. Flavia Taylor, "The Political and Civic Career of Henry Baldwin 1799-1830" (Unpublished Master's thesis, History Dept., University of Pittsburgh, 1940), p. 64.

[40] *Statesman*, February 20, 1819.

We cannot help on this occasion wishing that those men who pretend to be so anxious about manufactures in our different legislatures would exert themselves on this subject with the same spirit which they display on the Missouri question.[41]

Once the House took up the Missouri debate, Baldwin seemed only desirous of concluding it as quickly as possible so that the attention of the group might be called back to his manufacturing measures. He declared his willingness to admit Missouri in any form that had been considered. Thus, free from any extreme interpretation of the slavery issue in Missouri, he became the most valuable co-adjutor of Henry Clay in achieving a compromise.[42]

This failure of Congress to provide tariff relief produced a new wave of memorials and demands from industrial communities throughout the nation. So many petitions on the subject of manufactures greeted the House of Representatives when it convened in 1819 that a special committee was required to report them. The Committee on Commerce and Manufactures was replaced by two committees, one on commerce and the other on manufactures, with Henry Baldwin appropriately assigned as chairman of the latter. The new alignment in itself brought no relief, but did increase the volume of the manufacturers' sounding board and raised the hopes of Western Pennsylvania, and other areas seeking higher tariff, for positive action during the session.

Baldwin christened his new appointment by presenting a petition from the inhabitants of the western counties of Pennsylvania, praying that measures be immediately adopted for the security and encouragement of the nation's manufacturing interests. His committee proposed an upward revision of the tariff which planned to increase the duties on nearly all articles manufactured in Pennsylvania from 20 to 100 per cent. The bill passed the House with Western Pennsylvania representatives supporting it unanimously, but by a majority of one vote the Senate decided to defer discussion to the next session in favor of debate on Missouri.[43]

In the next session, however, the tariff suffered a severe setback; Baldwin was unable to bring the issue onto the floor of the House for

---

[41] *Pittsburgh Gazette,* January 11, 1820.

[42] Charles F. Adams (ed.), *Memoirs of John Quincy Adams, comprising Portions of His Diary from 1795 to 1848* (Philadelphia: J. B. Lippincott & Co., 1875), V, 210f.

[43] *Annals of Congress,* 16th Cong., 1st Sess., I, 710, 737.

consideration. In complete disgust Pittsburgh denounced the legislators for their "idle, frivolous debate" and attacked both Congress and the President for not recommending a single act during the entire session to restore the country to prosperity.[44]

Numerous organizations sprang up to rescue industrial development from oblivion. Though not political in nature, they inevitably came into either direct or indirect contact with politics. The Pittsburgh Manufacturing Association, for example, was set up to facilitate the exchange of commodities; it supplied raw materials and agricultural produce to the mechanic and manufactured articles to the farmer and country merchant. About this same time various counties also organized societies for the promotion of domestic manufactures, frequently in conjunction with ones for the encouragement of agriculture.

These organizations publicized and promoted the cause of protectionism, and their members often ran for political office with the knowledge that they could count on the support of their fellow-members to elect them. Other politicians undoubtedly discovered that an endorsement of protection would win the support of these various blocs because a higher tariff would work toward the realization of their goals. Once these groups were organized, they had a political potential which was finally exercised in 1824. Thus almost a decade after agitation for protection had begun, the objective was in sight.

WESTERN PENNSYLVANIA VS. ITSELF

This victory for protectionism in 1824 was an uphill battle; before it was achieved Western Pennsylvania was rent with confusion. Although both politicians and the general public talked continuously on the subject, their bombastic utterances were full of words, but empty of understanding. One observer pointed out that domestic manufactures were "in every body's mouth—but not on every one's back" and suggested that "less talk and more action, would look better." [45]

More action was difficult because the term "domestic manufactures" had come to have many different connotations to its endorsers, some of whom were often denouncing what other sponsors were advocating. The most general meaning ascribed to the term included all home and

---

[44] *Mercury*, March 14, 1821.
[45] *Greensburg Gazette* quoted in the *Mercury*, August 27, 1819.

factory processed goods of the nation, but to men of limited vision it implied the manufacture of only the raw materials of their immediate vicinity, such as the raw wool of Washington County. To others domestic manufacture was taken literally and denoted only textile production in the individual homes, and then there were those who championed "the greatest and most important of manufactures, agriculture." The 71 head of cattle produced at the "manufactory of R. S. Reed, Esq., of Erie county" were praised by a writer in the *Crawford Messenger* as the *"kind of manufacture* suited to the *interests of this section of the country."* [46]

This picture was further blurred when a group of Allegheny County citizens met to discuss an association to promote the whole domestic economy. Attorney Charles Shaler was selected chairman, and industrialist Alexander McClurg was chosen secretary. The group, calling themselves the "practical farmers" of the county, decided to draft a memorial to both houses of the United States Congress. Their petition was drawn up by a trio of farmers as practical as Shaler and McClurg: Walter Forward, Harmar Denny, and Richard Biddle, who were writing to tell Congress that protection was of national importance. They were certain of this decision because they were impartial farmers with "no particular or direct ax to grind on the tariff question." [47]

Not only had these men cast themselves in a false role, but also their assumption that impartiality and wisdom were synonymous terms was fallacious. Through the use of such a cloak politicians and manufacturers attempted to masquerade as farmers while some farmers in equal desperation depicted themselves as the basic manufacturers.

The farmer was the center of much of this chaos. To him agriculture, performed in a pure, healthy atmosphere, was the natural, moral, and most American of economic pursuits. Manufacturing, on the other hand, nursed horrible physical and moral evils. Workers, including children beginning work at a tender age without moral or literary education, were continuously confined to sedentary employment without knowing "the love of rustic liberty." Many farmers became convinced that it was their duty to thwart the manufacturer who was endeavoring "to seduce the American youth into the servile drudgery of looms and

---

[46] "Agricola," *Crawford Messenger,* January 16, 1818; "Domestic," *Crawford Messenger,* March 25, 1823.

[47] *Pittsburgh Gazette,* February 8, 15, 1820.

spinning jennies." The farmer further cultivated the seeds planted by the merchants when he observed that, unlike himself, the factory hand did not reap the whole benefit of his labor. Instead, he received a low wage while the manufacturer fattened "on the *poverty* of those who perform the labour." [48]

Since many workmen were jammed together in the larger factories, the farmer reasoned that they were automatically given to low, debauched conversation during their tedious hours of labor. Because of this suspected weekday routine the factory worker was not an habitual churchgoer, but regarded Sunday as a day of jubilee, a day of freedom from the walls of the factory to be celebrated by dissipation and profanity. [49]

To protect people from such a life was looked upon as the farmer's moral duty. Of course, he was better able to perform that duty after having been exposed to the doctrine of John Taylor of Virginia who held that every dollar paid as duty or bounty to encourage manufacture was a dollar robbed from the pockets of the farmer and planter. Although this argument ignored the fact that the accumulated profits of all merchants through whose hands an imported article passed and the cost of employing a collector were paid by the consumer, the farmer of Western Pennsylvania at first threw his support to the merchant. Those of the northwest counties, in particular, insisted that nature had destined the United States as an agricultural nation and had determined free trade to be her true policy. [50]

The endorsers of domestic manufactures attempted to discredit this thesis that agriculture and commerce were natural partners in trade. They pointed out that there was nothing new in the principle of governments affording protection to industries in their infancy. Enlightened

---

[48] "Agricola," *Crawford Messenger*, January 16, 1818; "Moderation," *Crawford Messenger*, April 1, 1823.

[49] "Economicus," *Pittsburgh Gazette*, July 16, September 24, and October 5, 1819.

[50] Mathew Carey, *The New Olive Branch: or an Attempt to Establish an Identity of Interest between Agriculture, Manufactures, and Commerce* (2d ed.; Philadelphia: M. Carey & Sons, 1821), p. 297; *Speeches of Henry Baldwin, Esq. in the House of Representatives on the Bills Reported by Him as Chairman of the Committee of Manufactures* (Pittsburgh: R. Patterson & Lambdin Printers, 1820), p. 9.

governments had always subscribed to the practice and industry always responded by rewarding the nation with prosperity.[51]

According to their argument, the prosperity of Pittsburgh manufacturing interests, prior to the depression of 1818, had increased the value of every farm within a 40-mile radius of the city because of the added demands for agricultural products. The farmers of Western Pennsylvania were asked to consider this proof that their best market was at home, but in order to keep the market healthy, they were warned that they must buy home manufactures. These purchases were required to put money in the hands of the industrial workers who, in turn, had need of farm products. As further evidence of the comparative importance of domestic manufactures, a *Mercury* writer statistically proved that the glass industry alone had "given employment and support to more people than all the retail merchants of Pittsburgh." [52]

Although merchants did not like to admit it, the high prices they charged for products brought over the mountains were prompted, in part, by the limited purchasing power of western dollars in the East. The people of the western counties had observed the comparative prosperity of the Atlantic cities and attributed their success simply to the establishment of banks.

Anxious to participate in the apparent advantages offered by these institutions, the western counties erroneously concluded that the establishment of banks would in itself increase the region's wealth and that the promise to pay money was money. A bank came to be regarded, not as an instrument by which surplus wealth could be loaned to industrious citizens, but "as a mint in which money could be coined at pleasure for those who did not possess it before." [53] Under such delusive impressions many banks sprang up in Western Pennsylvania, holding out inducements to the farmer, merchant, manufacturer, and mechanic alike.

In an effort to offset the instability of these banks, the East responded with an unfavorable discount rate on western paper. From the end of the War of 1812 to late 1818 the discount on Western Pennsylvania paper varied between three and seven per cent in Baltimore and Phila-

---

[51] Walter Lowrie's Report on Manufactures to the Pennsylvania Senate on February 19, 1817, in Pennsylvania, *Senate Journal,* XXVII, 251-255.

[52] *Ibid.;* "A Pittsburgher," *Mercury,* July 18, 1817.

[53] Holdsworth, *Financing an Empire,* I. 313f.

delphia, but in the depression years that followed, it fluctuated between 10 and 30 per cent. John M. Snowden of the *Mercury* deplored the fact that the Bank of Pittsburgh with $100,000 in specie in its vaults was forced to pay a seven per cent discount in Philadelphia while the notes of the Bank of the Schuylkill, with only $7,000 in specie, were received at par. Using a seven per cent exchange rate, he attempted to compute the cost of this discounting system to Pittsburgh and concluded that the city alone was annually "taxed" $100,000 "to satisfy the avarice of eastern cormorants." [54]

Snowden was not so shortsighted as to ignore Western Pennsylvania's part in this unhealthy financial situation. He declared that Presidents Jefferson, Madison, and Monroe had all encouraged the purchase of domestic manufactures while Lord Castlereagh and Lord Brougham, on the other hand, had said to destroy them. Unfortunately too many people in the western counties followed the dictates of the Britishers. Only through their lavish purchases of "British gew-gaws," French trinkets, and India silks from the eastern merchants did the transmontane settlers become so deeply involved in the monetary exchange.[55]

The disastrous effects of the discount system and of British imports were felt almost immediately following the War of 1812, and Western Pennsylvania was quick to seize upon the Second Bank of the United States, established by Congress in 1816, as their instrument of relief. Western Pennsylvanians believed that a national bank would abolish the hated monetary exchanges, increase the general circulating medium, and provide the means to discharge their eastern indebtedness without onerous sacrifices.

In the interest of strengthening their financial structure, the citizens of Pittsburgh held a public meeting in December 1816, and resolved to make application to the president and directors of the Bank of the United States for the establishment of a branch bank at Pittsburgh. Among the signers of the petition were John M. Snowden, George Allison, William Hays, John Darragh, and Thomas Cromwell, all directors of the Bank of Pittsburgh. Certainly in the minds of these men the Bank of the United States was above suspicion; there was no thought that it would compete with their bank instead of cooperating

---

[54] *Mercury,* July 25, 1817.

[55] *Ibid.,* August 8, 1817; November 20, 1818.

with it, but like the general public they soon realized their tragic mistake.[56]

The branch was established in 1817, and in the short space of months westerners learned the "awful truth." The Bank of the United States did not relieve their financial difficulties, but tended only to force the weaker banks out of existence. Communities, remote from Pittsburgh and accustomed to banking facilities, were now destitute. The branch made a practice of collecting specie from local banks and merchants in the western counties and dutifully remitting it to the "dear mother in Philadelphia."

As this pattern took form, hatred of the national institution mounted. The following year the *Pittsburgh Gazette* reported that the whole western country was confronted with general bankruptcy and placed the responsibility for the crisis on the national bank.[57] Although the depression was not that simple, the Bank of the United States was established at an unpropitious moment and conducted itself in an unseemly manner to gain the plaudits of the West.

In 1820 the same bank was again the subject of a public meeting in Pittsburgh. On this occasion a memorial, in the form of a letter written by Charles Shaler, was adopted and sent to bank president Langdon Cheves. Shaler charged that the stockholders of this institution had joined with the commercial element of the nation in a union that was intended "as an engine to destroy the manufacturing interests of the west." He denounced the refusal of the bank to aid manufacturers as a deliberate attempt to doom Pittsburgh as a vassal of the commercial cities. The directors of the institution were further reproved for their growing wealth while the families of mechanics and manufacturers in Pittsburgh suffered in misery because of their failure to get loans from the Bank of the United States. Cheves was told that Pittsburgh had relied upon her banks to aid her manufacturing establishments, but that his "branch here had been so conducted, as not only to refuse its aid to minor manufacturers and mechanics, but likewise so as to render it necessary for other institutions to curtail their discounts, and thereby destroy the prosperity of the place." [58]

---

[56] John Newton Boucher, *A Century and a Half of Pittsburg and Her People* (Chicago: Lewis Publishing Co., 1908), II, 69.

[57] *Mercury*, August 21, 1818; July 30, 1819; *Pittsburgh Gazette*, September 15, 1818.

[58] *Mercury*, February 19, 1819; *Statesman*, March 20, 1819.

This banking crisis became a source of irritation to everyone in Pittsburgh, including those who knew nothing about the problems of finance and who had no direct affiliation with industry. An unidentified Pittsburgh editor wrote to William Duane, pointing out that even the mails were being held up because of the money problem. The postmaster-general had instructed the Pittsburgh postmaster to accept nothing in payment for letters except silver or what would be received upon deposit at the Bank of the United States. The poorer people of Pittsburgh were unable to procure this kind of money, and the editor painted a plausible picture of a laborer going to the mail window to ask if there were any letters for him:

> One is held up by the clerk—probably from the old country—from a father, a mother, or a loving friend. He eagerly stretches forth his hand with that kind of money which he has received for his labor, it is refused, and he is obliged to turn mournfully from the window, unsatisfied, after having held in his hands the paper that contained the news from those "he held most dear." [59]

Every experience of this sort spoke volumes against the Bank of the United States and aroused the emotions of all with a feeling of bitterness. Even the unintelligent who never mastered the multiplication tables or the second reader and who knew nothing about the principle of printing press money or discount rates could denounce such regulations with a sense of understanding and a degree of finality. Even when recovery began in 1822, no kindly feeling toward the bank developed; antagonists simply became less outspoken. The problems of the exchange rate and of British imports never offered such a serious challenge again, but when Clay and Jackson revived the issue of the Bank of the United States a decade later, Western Pennsylvania distrust and bitterness were still prevalent and reasserted themselves vigorously.

The Bank of Pennsylvania in Philadelphia, like the Bank of the United States, was severely criticized in the West. It was accused of circulating falsehoods concerning western banks in order to depreciate their paper and thereby raise the cost to the people of Western Pennsylvania on every article imported from the eastern market. Similar charges were hurled against the developing urban economy of Pittsburgh by the region around the city. When banks within a 100-mile radius exhibited a willingness to loan money, Pittsburghers crowded around like leeches for accommodations. As the maturity dates on their

---

[59] *Aurora,* October 29, 1819.

loans approached, they were accused of taking every means in their power to injure the credit of the bank that had accommodated them so that they could buy up the notes of that bank, necessary for payment, under par.[60]

All of these brokers, but particularly those of the East, were denounced as "maggots who gnaw at the heart of every man's mercantile credit." Their greatest crime was defined as the conversion of bank paper, which had been intended as a circulating medium, into a type of merchandise. In a manner befitting business speculators, they bought up western paper at a considerable discount and then demanded the face value in specie from the western banking institutions concerned. The specie so acquired was used to buy a fresh supply of western paper at a reduced rate. This paper was, in turn, exchanged for more specie to keep the cycle moving and to keep western finances on the brink of disaster.[61]

Although western newspapers villified eastern banks for saving western paper until they could present large blocs of it for specie, westerners did the very same thing to each other. The practice was partly deliberate and partly dictated by the region's poor means of communication. Rather than journey a hundred or more miles to a given bank each month, there was a tendency on the part of merchants, bankers, and manufacturers to accumulate paper on that bank for four or five months before demanding payment.

Such delays often produced crises as David Redick of the borough of Washington discovered in 1818 when he appeared at the bank of New Salem, Ohio, to demand a considerable sum of specie for notes on that bank. The cashier refused to comply with his request either because he did not have the specie or more likely because its loss would have undermined whatever stability his bank had. The covetousness of both Redick and the cashier for the gold led to a scuffle in which Redick was stabbed to death.[62]

The details of the case are relatively unimportant, but the incident itself symbolizes the confusion and distrust engendered by the nation's financial structure. All paper was regarded with suspicion, and gold

---

[60] *Commonwealth,* January 6, 1817; *Western Herald,* April 11, 1817.

[61] "Caleb Cowhide" to "Oliver Homespun," *Statesman,* September 14, 1819; *Genius of Liberty,* October 10, 1818.

[62] *Greensburg Register* quoted in *Democratic Press,* August 21, 1818.

was so scarce that banks became reluctant to honor their own paper by accepting it freely for gold.

The most deplorable conditions of Western Pennsylvania were found in Fayette County's two unincorporated banks of New Salem and Perryopolis. In 1817 John Sparks, a retail merchant who had accepted a large number of notes on the New Salem Bank in payment for goods, submitted the notes to the cashier with a request, not for specie, but for notes on *any* chartered bank. The request was denied, and Sparks was forced to sell his New Salem notes at a 15 per cent discount to get chartered bank currency. A stockholder in the Perryopolis Bank exhibited an even greater lack of integrity when he refused the notes of his own bank in payment for a neighbor's debt. Since a Pennsylvania law of 1814 had decreed that neither banks nor persons with claims against unchartered banks could prosecute them, it might at first seem strange that in Fayette County, where two chartered banks were open for business, there would be any support at all for unincorporated institutions. Poor transportation facilities and the urgent need for currency afford the only necessary explanation to understand the willingness of the people to gamble on the soundness and integrity of such banks as New Salem and Perryopolis.[63]

In an adjoining county the solvency of the Bank of Washington was challenged more on the basis of politics than finance, but nevertheless the charges tended to destroy public confidence in the banking system. William Sample who was feuding with the Washington Club was chiefly responsible for this attack which began in 1818. Although he testified to the soundness of the bank's notes, Sample contradicted himself in his anxiety to slander the bank's president and cashier. He declared that they were guilty of "criminal neglect" for suspending specie payments. Basing his conclusion on the fact that the Bank of Washington and the Club at one time had a common executive, Thomas H. Baird, he insisted that the bank was a mere political tool. When Baird tried to quell all fears of insolvency by pointing out that he would auction off his $75,000 worth of property before he would let the bank fail, Sample countered with the suggestion that Baird must have exploited the depositors of the bank to have acquired such valuable land because he did not think it possible for him to have gained it honestly.[64]

---

[63] *Greensburg Gazette,* January 18, 1817; *Mercury,* February 15, 1817.
[64] *Reporter,* February 2, and September 28, 1818.

This political attack on Baird, as well as David Acheson and other directors of the Bank of Washington, undoubtedly helped to undermine the value of the bank's paper. John Grayson of the *Examiner* further reported that Sample had actually conducted a personal campaign against the bank directors in Greene County. The county's depositors were so bestirred that they plodded through rain and mire to the bank to demand their savings. Prompt payment was made to indicate that the bank was solvent, and Grayson explained that specie payments had been suspended, not because of an inability to pay, but because similar action had been taken by banks in Ohio, Indiana, Kentucky, and the other parts of Pennsylvania.[65]

Sample continued to prophesy doom for the Bank of Washington unless the stockholders would elect a new board of directors. He charged that without reform the bank's stock would soon fail to bring 50 cents on the dollar. As the bank's paper depreciated in value because of this political maneuvering and the engulfing general depression, the quarrel between the directors and the stockholders was brought into the open with the directors being accused of playing Midas in reverse—by turning "gold into rags." Finally at the expense of the stockholders and depositors, Sample overthrew the banking institution of his political opponents. Failure to meet dividend payments for the year ending November 1819 caused the bank's charter to become null and void; the stockholders voted to close the affairs of the bank as soon as possible.[66]

Because of the general distrust of paper currency, based on either political or economic conditions, many Pittsburgh banks and merchants forced the farmers and merchants of the country areas around the city to sell their local bank paper at a discount. Pittsburghers refused to accept all bank paper except that drawn on Pittsburgh, Philadelphia, New York, or Baltimore banks in payment for debts due them. Residents of the countryside who had obligations to meet in Pittsburgh were required to sell the paper of their country banks to a broker at a discount ranging from two to ten per cent in exchange for acceptable paper. The country paper, which the rural merchant or farmer had been obliged to sell at a discount, was bought by persons who purchased country produce with it at par. In this way the countryside was "shaved"

[65] *Examiner,* September 21, 1818.
[66] *Reporter,* August 30, and December 6, 1819.

in all its transactions "with the *honorabl*—and *honest* city of Pittsburgh." [67]

The farmers of the outlying districts were encouraged to retaliate to these banking practices of Pittsburgh by refusing to accept any paper in payment for their produce except that of Pittsburgh banks or of their own country banks. They hoped that this would prevent Pittsburgh from "pawning off" depreciated paper on them and from "filling her pockets" at the expense of the farmers. This proposal for the conduct of trade between the countryside and Pittsburgh creditors was exactly the same prescription as that offered by the editor of the *Gazette* for trade relations between the debtor areas west of the mountains and their "Atlantic enemies." His naive suggestion urged that all those carrying produce to the seaboard refuse to accept payment in anything but specie. Then, if western bankers would offer these merchants a premium for this specie, it could be placed in their bank vaults to increase the value of the region's circulating paper.[68]

Needless to say, these schemes to revitalize the financial structure of Western Pennsylvania did not succeed. Continued disappointments in attempting to trade agricultural products to the East disgusted many throughout the region. Commerce, they charged, had ceased to be a stimulus to the productive labor of the state, had become diseased, and was threatening to communicate the infection to the citizens at large. Farm products were rotting in the granaries, and Pittsburghers at least traced their difficulties to those who opposed domestic manufacturing in the western counties by urging them to rely solely on their agricultural production and to import their industrial needs from the East.

Pittsburgh wanted to consolidate the region by establishing a community of interest among the farmer, manufacturer, and merchant within Western Pennsylvania. The farmer, meanwhile, had come to harbor the same resentments against Pittsburgh that characterized the whole region's attitude toward Philadelphia and the East. Suspicions of his city neighbor's motives did not begin to fade until the farmer considered changes to prevent a reoccurrence of the depression.

The clash was partly that of an urban industrial economy against a rural agrarian one although this distinction was to be more sharply drawn in later years. Certainly the regional differences were more

---

[67] *Reporter*, March 16, 1818.
[68] *Ibid.; Pittsburgh Gazette*, February 25, 1817.

pronounced and took precedence at this time. With the complaints against Philadelphia more obvious than those against Pittsburgh, it was more convenient to attack the eastern metropolis, especially when Pittsburghers were in the foreground leading the charge.

IV

The Battle Lines

*The Reformers of Penna.—Give them a loaf and a fish a
piece, and you will hear no more about reform.*[1]

SINCE the war with Britain ended in a flourish of victory in 1815,
Western Pennsylvania was temporarily unmindful of her frustra-
tions and inferiority. Like the other parts of the nation, the western counties believed that an era of good feeling had dawned. They temporarily accepted the American System in nearly all its aspects; they
clamored for internal improvements, acquiesced in the establishment of
the Bank of the United States, and accepted the Tariff of 1816 with
mixed emotions.[2] Politically the people of the region appeared to be in
general agreement since only the Republican Party was able to retain its
strength beyond the war years. Federalist factions remained, but their
vigor contributed more to confusion and uncertainty than to spirited
party contests and an understanding of current problems.

This pattern was indicative of the national trend reflected in the
presidential elections of 1816 and 1820. These contests maintained the
status quo, but are conspicuous in the stream of national development
for the absence of the normal party conflict surrounding presidential
races. A superficial evaluation would suggest that the whole nation was
in accord with the election and re-election of James Monroe, especially
since in 1820 only one vote separated him from being the unanimous
choice of the Electoral College, a distinction held only by George
Washington.

Although these facts are correct, there is a fallacy in their obvious
interpretation. A detailed observation of the political scene would not
reveal agreement, but total disagreement. The status quo was maintained for two interrelated reasons: a growing interest in politics at the

---

[1]Toast proposed at an Independence Day celebration in Harrisburg and quoted
in the *Statesman,* July 19, 1820.

[2] Ferguson, *Western Pennsylvania Politics,* p. 233.

state and local levels at the expense of the federal, and a rampant factionalism with overtones of regionalism. Indeed there were so many factions, even within the Republican Party, that not one of them was strong enough to offer a serious threat to the group in power.

It is misleading even to apply the term "party" to most of the political alignments of this decade since permanence and organization were lacking. Every issue produced a shift in the political arrangement, and it became impossible to create even a lasting county organization, much less a state machine. Independent candidates by the score entered contests against "regular tickets"; and about a year later, to demonstrate the poor party discipline, these individuals could return to the fold to endorse the "regular ticket" and perhaps even be a candidate on it.[3]

To the alarm of the disciples of party politics, this practice was thoroughly diffused into the political life of Pennsylvania's western counties during the era of good feeling. Since nearly everyone had come to regard himself as a Republican of some sort, party adherence did not play a prominent role in the selection of public officials. Personal qualities instead tipped the scale for or against the candidates.[4] Furthermore, because Western Pennsylvania was a sparsely settled region, the inhabitants were more likely to know their candidates personally than those of densely settled areas where the people experienced contacts with so many that they assumed a more impersonal and businesslike attitude. The region, therefore, was fertile ground for this brand of politics which emphasized personal and local attributes.

This political pattern was possible only because of a relaxing of the party reigns at the national level. Although a definitive study of the decline of national party strength is beyond the scope of this research, a few clues to the collapse of the Federalist and Democratic-Republican Parties are necessary to explain the confusion in Western Pennsylvania.

After Hamilton and Jefferson had dramatized rival doctrines, the line was firmly established. It began to crack and then to splinter when the two parties interchanged several of their ideas. The Republicans crossed the line with a series of enactments indicative of a strong central authority; the purchase of Louisiana, the Embargo Act, the seizure of West Florida, and the imposition of a direct tax were reminiscent of

---

[3] Klein, *Pennsylvania Politics,* p. 71.
[4] George Thornton Fleming, *History of Pittsburgh and Environs* (New York: American Historical Society, Inc., 1922), II, 110f.

Federalist theory. In 1811 Albert Gallatin of Fayette County further contributed to this apparent contradiction of Republican policy when he tried mightily to swing the party behind the United States Bank. He almost succeeded through his own efforts, but required an assist from the strains of war to complete the task of restoring the Hamiltonian institution in 1816. Likewise, the responsibility for the first protective tariff must be placed on Republican shoulders since the Federalists were too few to carry any measure in 1816.[5]

This Republican policy of a new nationalized democracy, purged of most of its impractical theories, had definitely matured by 1815. Some Republicans accepted the political ideas taken over from their political enemies while others rebelled, wishing to return to the "pure" philosophy preached so widely by Jefferson before 1801. Federalists, meanwhile, applauded this usurpation of their principles and hailed it as a complete triumph for the nation "over French philosophy and democratic whimsies and theories." [6]

Even while they were absorbing political defeats, the Federalists of Western Pennsylvania saw an omen of good feeling in this trend; to many party feeling was no longer necessary since the federal government had, in general, accepted the principles of Hamilton and Washington for which they had been contending. Of course, too, the belief still prevailed in many circles that parties were unnecessary and even undesirable agencies in carrying on the functions of government. Such believers seized this opportunity to agree with many Federalists that party strife was no longer practicable.[7] The *Pittsburgh Gazette* editorializes its approval:

> Our political adversaries find, after all, that commerce is better than embargo, and peace preferable to war. It has cost us, to be sure, some few millions expended in philosophical experiments, to bring our *Republican* brethren to concur in our opinion—[8]

---

[5] Kendric C. Babcock, *The Rise of American Nationality, 1811-1819,* Vol. XIII of *The American Nation: A History,* ed. Albert B. Hart (28 vols.; New York: Harper & Bros., 1904-1918), p. 195; William O. Lynch, *Fifty Years of Party Warfare 1789-1837* (Indianapolis: Bobbs-Merrill Co., 1931), p. 247f.

[6] *Pittsburgh Gazette,* September 3, 1816.

[7] *Ibid.;* Homer C. Hockett, *Western Influences on Political Parties to 1825: An Essay in Historical Interpretation* (Columbus: Ohio State University, 1917), p. 82.

[8] *Pittsburgh Gazette,* September 3, 1816.

The Federalist Party, on the other hand, had begun its decline with the passage of the Alien and Sedition Acts which the Republicans abhorred. This opposition argued that only the individual states had the power to determine the constitutionality of federal legislation and that failure to comply with a state's interpretation was justification for secession. In 1811 the parties reversed their positions; the Federalists threatened secession because the Republicans were about to admit a part of the Louisiana Purchase as a state without the consent of all the original states. Later, in 1814, the Federalists reasserted their concept of states' rights in the form of the Hartford Convention, and this fiasco completed the decline of their party as an instrument of national power.[9] Ironically, the collapse came at a time when many of the economic interests for which the party had been contending were beginning to rise to a place of prominence. With Federalism discredited these interests were forced to turn elsewhere for political leadership.

In most areas where the war met at least mild approval, the Federalist Party, by such a name, was dead. A writer in Harrisburg estimated that the prejudice was so deeply rooted that only a miracle could give the Federalists, as a party, control of politics in Pennsylvania again. He lamented that citizens of the Federalist stripe were required to shoulder their full share of public burdens, but at the same time were shut off from the honors in the gift of the state.[10]

Pittsburgh's *Gazette* agreed. The editor suggested that the hackneyed watchwords of party be either abolished or altered. "An honest, but uninformed yeomanry have too long had their fears kept alive by the designing demagogues of what is called the republican party." He encouraged the Federalists to denounce the "tedious essays, clothed in pompous diction," to restore public confidence, and to remove the groundless notions that the Republicans had practiced the principle of a weak central government.[11]

Since the Republicans had confiscated many Federalist principles, certain members of the latter party were content to accept dissolution. Rather than ask their constituents to vote for a party associated with a secession movement in the midst of a great national triumph, these

---

[9] Babcock, *Rise of American Nationality,* p. 195.
[10] No. 11 in the "Letters on Pennsylvania Politics" dated Harrisburg, March 25, 1817, and quoted in the *Aurora,* April 22, 1817.
[11] *Pittsburgh Gazette,* June 10, 1815, and September 6, 1816.

men were inclined to follow their principles into the Republican ranks. Other Federalists wanted to fight their way back into power under the old banner, but they were not agreed on a common course to be pursued in attaining this goal. Since this marked the first instance of an American political party out of national power and attempting to recapture control, there was no precedent to draw upon; the party became even more schismatic. After several false starts, the Federalists of Western Pennsylvania, concentrated largely in the Pittsburgh area, permanently divorced themselves from New England Federalism and devised a new type of alignment to accomplish their objectives. Regional loyalty was substituted for party loyalty. This task was not too difficult since the extensive patronage enjoyed by the governor of the state caused every region to become afflicted with an anxiety to have one of its own men chosen governor.[12]

Before taking refuge in regional allegiance, John I. Scull, the editor of the *Pittsburgh Gazette* and a faction leader, tried to persuade the party to remain aloof from party contests and endorse no candidates until the prejudices against Federalism would wear away. He encouraged the party to "let mere politics sleep for a while" and give the Republicans a little more rope.[13] Anticipating a complete breakdown on the Republican front which would cause the public to clamor for a return of Federalist control, Scull editorialized, early in the gubernatorial race of 1817, for a Federalist boycott of the election.

Of what consequence is it to the federalists whether Heister or Findlay is made Governor? Do the federalists expect to gain any thing from either of them? If they do they will be woefully disappointed—and they will be equally disappointed if they expect any change of policy. It is as easy for the Leopard to change his spots or the Ethiope his skin, as for a democratic officer in Pennsylvania to act independently. It is to be hoped therefore that the federal party will not disgrace itself by becoming the catspaw of either. Let us vote for a federal candidate or not at all; and let Duane, Binns, Lieb, Sutherland, Heister and Findlay fight it out among themselves.[14]

This naive understanding of the political exercise that is necessary to keep a party healthy was not long practiced by the editor before he recognized his folly. Quickly he altered his position and joined another Federalist school, a group that favored cooperation with the Independent Republicans who, generally speaking, were those out of office

---

[12] Klein, *Pennsylvania Politics,* p. 25.
[13] *Pittsburgh Gazette,* February 7, 1817, and July 3, 1818.
[14] *Ibid.,* June 10, 1817.

struggling to get in. Their objective was similar to that of the Federalists, and they intended to accomplish it with vigorous campaigns stressing regional and local interests.[15]

In Western Pennsylvania Editor David MacLean championed this faction of cooperative Federalists. He argued that the Federalists should not place a member of their party in nomination for the governorship because such a move would only assure victory for the unscrupulous caucus or "in" candidate, William Findlay. As the financial facts of Findlay's political career were revealed during the campaign, the Pittsburgh Federalists, under Scull's leadership, acquiesced. The editor announced his willingness to meet the opponents halfway—to nominate the most intelligent and judicious men for office, providing, of course, that it could be arranged in a manner that would reflect honorably on both parties.[16]

Although MacLean, and later Scull, of the Federalists endorsed this course, there were also Democratic-Republican roots to this proposal of cooperation. In 1816 the Democratic-Republicans had agreed to discuss a fusion ticket for offices in the city of Pittsburgh, but the negotiations broke down.[17] An Independent faction parted company with the Republican leadership over the situation and joined the Federalists in insisting that party labels meant nothing. With the roots of personal politics thus laid in both parties, the floodgates to political confusion were opened.

The apparent amalgamation which brought Federalists to the support of Hiester in 1817 was denounced as a base conspiracy of Federalists and Old School Independents by the Washington *Reporter*. The editor charged that under a preconceived plan the Old School had nominated the candidate with the Federalists showing an indifference at first, but finally falling in line to support him with all their strength. His accusation asserted that the Federalists were aware of their inability to carry an election, but they recognized that a candidate who had *once* belonged to the Republican Party and who made sweeping campaign promises was a good choice to hoist the party back to power.[18]

---

[15] Harry E. Houtz, "Abner Lacock" (Unpublished Master's thesis, History Dept., University of Pittsburgh, 1937), p. 56.

[16] *Greensburg Gazette,* May 3, and September 6, 1817; *Pittsburgh Gazette,* July 18, 1817.

[17] *Commonwealth,* June 25, 1816.

[18] *Reporter,* September 22, 1817.

This inference of secret cooperation on the Hiester candidacy was unfounded, as was the suspicion that the Federalists took part in it because of a "divide and conquer" plot against the Republicans. Actually they were too disunited as a party to gain agreement on any program. Politics in Western Pennsylvania throughout this decade was more a matter of opportunism of the moment than party or even faction continuity. The Washington editor was attempting to establish continuity where none existed. By the late summer of 1817 practically all Federalist politicians had abandoned any thought of restoring the party as a unit to power. Their cooperation with the Independents in several elections was a series of personal choices which were prompted either by a belief in Old Schoolism or more likely by a desire for an assist in gaining power personally.

In previous years Federalist power had been especially potent in Allegheny, Washington, and Westmoreland Counties; and by casting their lot with disgruntled Republicans, these Federalists now made the Independent alignment a formidable foe for the Delegate or Regular Republican organization. Elsewhere in Western Pennsylvania dissatisfied Republicans exhibited no such organization and were forced to take refuge in fusion or double tickets on which they had no identity separate from that of a Delegate candidate, except their personal popularity.

As the Independents and Federalists closed ranks under the banner of the former, the Pittsburgh *Statesman* joined the Washington *Reporter* in leading the assault on the Federalist tactics. An editorial warned that "they are worse than foreign foes. Though you may put them down in one shape, they rise in another, proteus-like, assuming every color & every form." [19]

This coalition, which angered the *Statesman,* was stressed by the *Pittsburgh Gazette* during the 1818 campaign when the Federalist Party set up no candidate in opposition to Henry Baldwin, an Independent who was running for Congress. The *Gazette* shrewdly suggested that the Federalist Party had not capitulated, but had accepted the Independent candidate in exchange for full support of its new platform of regional allegiance. The editor declared that the Federalists had "sacrificed old party sentiments" in order to ensure the services of a man so profoundly concerned with the needs of Western Pennsylvania. [20]

---

[19] *Statesman,* August 22, 1818.

[20] *Pittsburgh Gazette,* September 11, 1818.

Earlier in the campaign another writer in the *Gazette* had condemned the Delegate Republicans for nominating a candidate to oppose Baldwin. He insisted that the Federalist Party, "seeing that republican talents had become the desire of the people" had acquiesced, and he called upon the Delegate group to make a similar sacrifice for sectional good. Without the election of Baldwin and support for domestic manufactures, he charged that "this part of the country, town property, and country property must go down." [21] With this election the congressional district composed of Allegheny and Butler Counties had reached a crossroads; which was to be superior, party or sectional allegiance?

Baldwin's victory demonstrated conclusively that the Federalist idea was paramount. In spite of this vote, Western Pennsylvania manifestations of regionalism were generally ignored by the federal government, and the area concentrated on state and local action to satisfy its demands. After witnessing the failure of Congress to act in behalf of the region, "A North-West Pennsylvanian" condemned a plan to prime the economic pump solely because it depended on congressional action. Experience, he insisted, had taught that "we shall have to look at home for the theatre of action." [22]

The *Statesman* strove mightily to weaken this Federalist-Independent coalition and to debunk the Federalist claim that the party had acted in the interest of political good feeling. An article signed "Laocoon" charged that during the War of 1812 the "Feds" had groaned with each United States victory and chuckled at her reverses. Actually this conduct was not inspired by any love for England, but only by the hope that the war would be disastrous enough to overthrow the Republican administration and cause a revolution in party power. The Federalists were depicted as a party that would have acceded to the destruction of a few American cities if such a catastrophe would have aided them to purchase the reigns of government. Unsuccessful in having the war achieve their objective, the "Feds," according to "Laocoon," decided on a new approach; with an air of patriotism they dramatically pleaded that party spirit be set aside in favor of political unity. [23]

Skeptical Delegate Republicans condemned this "good feelings slang" which cried peace when there was no peace and talked of harmony and unanimity when neither was intended or practiced. They observed that

---

[21] *Pittsburgh Gazette,* August 11, 1818.
[22] *Crawford Messenger,* February 25, 1823.
[23] "Laocoon," *Statesman,* September 28, 1819.

in states and districts where the Federalists held a majority, there was neither good feeling nor a union of parties. Where they controlled a majority of the voters, there was no suggestion to divide the political loaf, but where they were in the minority, they were willing to unite with Republicans.[24]

Although the Federalists of Western Pennsylvania obviously talked the language of good feeling as a front for party weakness, they had no monopoly on this stratagem. Independent Republicans also found it useful.

The *Westmoreland Republican* likened these tactics to the guise of a fox in one of Aesop's fables. After prowling all night for food and finding none, the fox caught sight of a flock of fowls roosting in the trees of the barnyard. He altered his strategy and sought his food through deception. He tricked the fowls by telling them that universal friendship and good feeling between the furred and feathered tribes had been proclaimed and invited them to come down and rejoice with him. Just as a wise old cock cautioned the hens and pullets against a hasty acceptance of this news, the editor warned that the Federalist concept of politics was like the assertions of the fox. He predicted that when Federalists "cannot *coax* the democrats down from their *roosts,* they will abandon their notions of 'good feeling' and resort to their old ground again." [25]

This suggestion that the Federalist Party was to be feared by Republicans as a fox by the fowls of the barnyard was as groundless as the "divide and conquer" charge made by the Washington *Reporter.* Not Federalist strength, but weakness, spelled trouble for the Republicans. Under a two-party system the disappearance, or appreciable weakening, of one party will almost inevitably lead to the weakening of the second party. Since both Independent and Delegate candidates claimed to be adherents to the Republican Party, the issue of orthodoxy arose to plague the leaders struggling for Republican unity. In contests between members of the same party, one of the best political weapons is the creation of doubt as to the party loyalty of one's opponent. Much name calling and many personal scandals were substituted for legitimate party campaigns.

---

[24] *Western Herald* quoted in *Statesman,* September 5, 1818; *Statesman,* June 27, 1818.

[25] *Westmoreland Republican,* August 22, 1818.

Since the differences between these two major Republican factions were not sharply drawn, only a few general distinctions can be set forth. For the most part throughout this decade in Western Pennsylvania, the Delegate Republicans were in power and campaigned in the language of a moderate Jeffersonian agrarianism. The Independents, editorially maligned under many flags by the Delegate group, [26] were out of power; and in the western counties they exhibited a stronger trend toward regionalism and spoke out more boldly in behalf of a spirit of good feeling.

This group represented the growing urban industrialism which kept alive the spirit of Federalism at a time when the physical structure of Federalist authority was in ruin. The Independents wooed and won Federalist support for their cause, but their success in this endeavor prompted the *Statesman* to vent its disdain chiefly on the Federalists. Their leadership was likened unto an old maid with a waning hope of marriage and a willingness to accept "any thing white in the shape of a man," [27] but in spite of such criticism the Federalist-Independent coalition made noticeable gains throughout the larger counties in the southern part of the region.

In other counties where the Independents were not strong enough to formulate election tickets of their own, individual Republican politicians accepted their principal thesis and campaigned on the basis of local needs. Thus the Independents led the way in dramatizing issues that were not national, but local—issues that were peculiar to certain counties or economic interests. Some counties and interests sponsored aids to commerce; some solicited encouragement for manufacturing, while others wanted a greater volume of money for circulation or improvements to roads, rivers, and harbors. These demands overlapped and conflicted with each other, producing as many combinations as numerically possible to encourage their advancement or to thwart their adoption. In effect, the attitudes developed by every county on each of these issues conditioned the local character of political alignments, and these alignments, in turn, caused the people of the Western Pennsylvania region to look inward instead of outward during the decade.

---

[26] *Democratic Press,* April 14, 1817, published a list of the most common synonyms used to denote Pennsylvania's Independents: Old School, Old Tories, Old Federalists, Peace-party men, Anti-embargoists, Blue Lights, Hartford Conventionists, English Agents, Boston Stampers, and English Guineas.

[27] "Laocoon," *Statesman,* September 28, 1819.

OFFICE HOLDERS AND HUNTERS

Generally, when politicians campaigned for office in this decade, they rested their case on one of the economic issues, namely the bank, tariff, or internal improvements, but in varying degrees Western Pennsylvania politicians also questioned the election machinery. In Pittsburgh where urban industrialism was exhibiting its political strength under the banner of the Independent Republicans and attempting to reach at least the bottom rung of the office-holding ladder, the attack was vigorously pressed. Nearby boroughs of considerable Independent strength also challenged current nominating methods. The entire nominating system from the election of township and county officials to the choice of a President of the United States was under fire in counties where urban and agrarian competition for control was keen.

At the local level the delegate system of candidate selection which had developed many features in common with the state and national caucus was denounced as undemocratic. This delegate method had been created several decades earlier when Republican Party spirit ran high and success in combating the Federalists depended upon union. No sooner had the delegate system achieved complete ascendancy over factionalism, however, than the machinery began to break down. It was diverted into an instrument to advance the aspirations of office seekers. Although this mode of nominating candidates had performed an essential service to the Republican Party while Federalism was strong, it contained the seeds of Republican destruction because areas were now frequently left with only one ticket on election day. The people enjoyed only the empty right of depositing ballots in boxes.[28]

Triumph over Federalism spelled the decline of party spirit and the drifting away of popular attention from civic responsibilities. Political control fell to the personally ambitious. If one of these office hunters wanted a particular post, the task of accomplishment was simple according to a writer in the *Mercury*. He satirized the corruption of the political machinery from one end to the other by demonstrating first how a perverted committee of vigilance could advertise in an obscure newspaper for a short time, or perhaps by handbills privately circulated, that an election of delegates was to be held. The election would take place although

---

[28] *Reporter*, August 5, 1816; *Mercury*, October 26, 1816.

the people know little or nothing of all this—two or three of our cronies in different townships, hold these elections and return if possible one of themselves as a delegate. Our delegates meet—we make a great noise about republicanism—protest against caucussing—talk much about democracy and the rights of the people—and then pompously announce to the public that *the delegates chosen by the democratic republicans of the different townships* have formed a ticket to be run at the election—and woe be to the man who dares to question our authority. He cannot be a republican, he must be a most terrible federalist, or something worse. By this happy management we save the people an immensity of trouble. . . .

Well, our candidates caucus again at the seat of government. They in their turn, nominate a governor or a president, which becomes equally binding on all the people to choose, under pain of excommunication from the true political church; and thus by the delightful play of this beautiful piece of political mechanism, the wheels of government move on in unobstructed harmony.[29]

Alert committees of vigilance recognized the wisdom of this satire and pointed out to Republican electors that the party was in danger of becoming the tool of a conniving few. Delegate adherents brushed aside this possibility with the comment that they were simply continuing a precedent of long standing. Many people in Western Pennsylvania, however, were no longer willing to be deceived by the assertion that the Federalist Party was still a threat to Republican principle. Times had changed with the Federalist collapse, but the Delegate group showed no desire to keep in step by modifying its practices. Instead, these "caucusites" sought to straitjacket the times into their system by deluding the public into believing that the issues were basically the same as they had been 15 or 20 years before. Their effort achieved partial success because many of the same politicians remained in the limelight although under new banners and in behalf of new issues.

The conditions made the people of Western Pennsylvania painfully aware that, when a democracy grows in size, the task of electing officials is rendered more complex, especially the presentation of candidates to the public for an examination of their qualifications before a conclusive vote. The system seemed to operate with greatest facility when party spirit was kept aggressive by the existence of two contending parties. During the decade of good feeling, however, areas were frequently embarrassed on election day by the appearance of only one ticket, and elections tended to decline into hollow ceremonies.

When more than two tickets were offered to the public, they usually

---

[29] "A Caucusite," *Mercury*, August 24, 1816.

resulted from a breakdown in the two-party pattern. Pressure on the majority party was occasionally so relaxed that it schismatized into numerous splinter parties while the minority retained its unanimity and ultimately achieved victory. This type of "scrub race" was repugnant to the fundamental principle of elections, but in spite of such possible pitfalls nominations were essential. Unless they were made, half the people would have been candidates. The "scrub race" would not only have sunk to the lowest depths possible, but at the same time would have violated the principle that an interchange of ideas among the people results in the most satisfactory compromise of inconsistent opinions.[30]

Nominations, therefore, had to begin somewhere—either at mass meetings of all the voters or through delegations. In Western Pennsylvania of 1815 the latter appeared more feasible, and the Delegate leaders defended it as true republicanism and practical democracy. In the absence of Federalist power the Independent opposition, on the other hand, predicted that the system would ultimately be the instrument of the interested few.

The supporters of this local caucus, as the delegate system was stigmatized, fortified themselves against the charge that the township meetings selecting the delegates were sparsely attended by pointing out that this condition was not the fault of the system, but of the people. They further denied that the system imposed a type of "mental bondage" on party members by insisting that there is a point in all political affairs at which controversy obviously must cease and action commence in order to accomplish anything.

The proper time for discussion, they argued, was before the caucus or delegate meeting, not afterward. These sympathizers insisted that widespread opinion was sought and encouraged before action was initiated just as a general would consult his experienced officers before an engagement on which the fate of his country depended. On the other hand, however, who could forgive the soldier who introduced insubordination into the ranks and lost a victory because he did not have the virtue to suppress a personal opinion? [31]

The most absurd application of this caucus principle was suggested during the 1815 election of a state senator from Allegheny, Beaver,

---

[30] "Laocoon," *Statesman*, September 14, 1819.

[31] *Commonwealth*, April 17, 1816.

Butler, and Armstrong Counties. Ephraim Pentland of Allegheny and Samuel Power of Beaver were the candidates. Since Allegheny County had 5,518 taxable inhabitants and the other three only a total of 5,343, a writer in the *Mercury* charged that Pentland should have been automatically elected. Because Pentland had been nominated by a majority of the total Republican voters of the district, namely the electors of Allegheny County, the writer reasoned that he should occupy the senate seat. In other words the decision of a majority of the electors of the majority area (Allegheny County), or approximately 18 men, was tantamount to the election of a senator to serve 10,861 voters.[32] This extreme Delegate position, needless to say, did not have the endorsement of Editor John M. Snowden who was the leading advocate of both caucus and delegate reform in Western Pennsylvania.

Politicians who agreed with Snowden were generally those out of power struggling to get in by advocating the advancement of democracy through "rotation in office." In earlier years this had been the cry of the Delegate sponsors throughout the state. From 1805 to 1808 they were attempting to unseat Governor Thomas McKean in favor of Simon Snyder and eventually succeeded. They retained political dominance under Snyder and William Findlay until the election of 1820, but in the meantime the old principle of "rotation in office" had slipped from their minds.[33]

The dilemma of being out of power was more impelling than party or faction affiliation in determining delegate or anti-delegate sympathies. In Western Pennsylvania during the decade of good feeling the coalition of Federalists and Independents formed the backbone of the anti-delegate, anti-caucus strength, but in Lancaster County, where the Federalists predominated, nothing but the delegate system was tolerated. The *Lancaster Weekly Journal* declared in 1818 that the desirable objectives of party unanimity and organization could be achieved only through a reconciliation of the conflicting interests of opposing candidates at delegation meetings. Two years previously, however, the *Journal* had denounced the Republican caucus that nominated James Monroe for the presidency as was characteristic of a party out of power.[34]

---

[32] "An Elector," *Mercury,* October 7, 1815.

[33] *Beaver Gazette* quoted in *Aurora,* May 20, 1818.

[34] *Lancaster Weekly Journal* quoted in *Statesman,* September 14, 1819.

This apparent contradiction was the result of many editors, politicians, and public-spirited citizens developing more emotion than understanding concerning the threat to the democratic machinery offered by the caucus and delegate systems. Some understood that it was good politics to cast their opponents in the role of enemies to democracy, but many really believed that the basic issue was the salvation of democracy itself and never recognized any relationship between the caucus and delegate concepts—often endorsing one and condemning the other.

Committees of vigilance particularly attempted to repress the possible iniquities of the delegate system. In the northwestern counties this was comparatively simple; without any effort to delimit the number, all the candidates for a given office were lumped together on a single ticket and voted for on a personal basis without reference to party or faction allegiance. The more densely populated southwestern counties could not resolve their personal and group differences so easily.

When the township committees of vigilance and a majority of the citizens in Washington County advised their delegates to nominate eight candidates instead of the customary four for the four assembly seats in 1819, the delegation defied the recommendation.[35]

The opponents of the Delegate or Patent ticket seized the opportunity to capitalize on this refutation of the expressed will of the people in the various townships. They called a second meeting and with much fanfare nominated a second ticket of four, but two of the candidates were common to both slates. This meant only a partial fulfillment of the popular request for eight nominees, but that was of little consequence since the second meeting was no more concerned with democratic principle than the first. Both were manipulated by political factions vying for control. The factional nature of the second meeting was attested by the composition of the committee appointed to defend its candidates. Alexander Murdoch, George Baird, and David Acheson of the Washington Club were prominent members of this committee which attacked the Delegate group for ignoring the recommendations of the public and the committees of vigilance. Their partial ticket, however, betrayed their sincerity. They talked the language of expressing the will of the people, but actually they were resorting to the technique of hoisting two Club members to power on the coattails of the established

[35] *Examiner,* September 13, 1819.

group. Their efforts were in vain, and the election proved a complete success for the original Delegate slate.[36]

This was a typical outcome of clashes between the two. Although the anti-delegate group fought earnestly, the Delegate ticket was repeatedly victorious in all western counties except Allegheny where the two divided the spoils. The near-solid front of the delegation was demonstrated by the effectiveness of the group in the state legislature during this decade. From 1815 through 1825 the speaker of the assembly was a Western Pennsylvanian in 10 out of 11 years, and from 1817 to 1825 the speaker of the senate was also from the western counties.

In the lower house Rees Hill of Greene County occupied the speaker's chair for three sessions and Joseph Lawrence of Washington for four while William Davidson of Fayette, John Gilmore of Butler, and Joseph Ritner of Washington enjoyed single terms of one year each. Only in 1824 when Joel B. Sutherland of Philadelphia County was elected over Ritner did the distinction of speaker fall to an easterner. The shift came after Lawrence, who had dominated the Washington County delegation for at least five years dropped out of the assembly. Ritner, who was Sutherland's opponent, had apparently not yet gained a reputation among the legislators.[37]

All these western speakers came from counties that either had no Independent opposition or successfully overcame it year after year. Since the strength of the two forces was more evenly matched east of the mountains, both eastern schools of thought were willing to endorse a western speaker over their local rivals. This attitude was more important than homogeneity among western delegates in explaining how the minority west of the Alleghenies succeeded in monopolizing this administrative post in the assembly. Actually in the speakership contest of 1820 the western counties had three competing candidates, but still retained control of the office.[38]

Almost to the last detail this pattern of western speakers was duplicated in the state senate. Isaac Weaver, representing Greene and Washington Counties, was elected speaker during the 1816-1817 session when John Tod resigned to enter private business and held the post

---

[36] *Examiner,* September 27, and October 18, 1819.

[37] Pennsylvania, *House Journal* (1824-1825), p. 5f.

[38] *Ibid.* (1820-1821), pp. 5-7.

until he, in turn, resigned in March 1820. William Marks of Allegheny County, who had successfully outmaneuvered Baldwin, Forward, and other anti-delegate leaders by being a candidate on both tickets, was rewarded with the speakership and retained the office until 1825 when he entered the United States Senate.[39]

This almost unbroken control of the legislature's high offices was only a superficial victory for the people of Western Pennsylvania. Their representatives could not agree among themselves on state programs to stabilize the monetary system or to encourage domestic manufacturing, nor could they harmonize their views concerning a priority rating for internal improvements. The eastern counties had recognized that it was the better part of discretion to vote with the western representatives in organizing the legislature, but saw no advantage in supporting partisan western proposals. By agreeing on that, rival eastern factions kept Western Pennsylvania's legislative minority suppressed.

STATE AND NATIONAL CAUCUSING

The caucus nomination of James Monroe in 1816 by the slim margin of 11 congressmen stirred an anti-caucus tempest in many parts of the nation. Hitting Western Pennsylvania with all its fury, the storm raged out of control until 1824. Aware that a Republican caucus nomination for the presidency was almost equivalent to election, the public was startled more by what the caucus had almost done than by its actual results. The people approved of Monroe, but shuddered at his scant majority over William Harris Crawford who nearly became the party standard-bearer under the caucus system. The circumstances caused them *"to damn the dice, but spare the player."* [40]

Pennsylvanians were especially dissatisfied with the system because their congressmen had voted for Monroe in the belief that the Virginia members would, in turn, endorse the state's governor, Simon Snyder, for the second position on the ticket. When the choice fell to Daniel D. Tompkins of New York by a wide margin, they were willing to vent their anger on the system.

The caucus was condemned as an unconstitutional attempt to perpetuate the aristocracy in office and undermine the rights of free men.

---

[39] Pennsylvania, *Senate Journal,* XXVII, 51; XXX, 517.

[40] *Greensburg Gazette,* June 22, 1816; Klein, *Pennsylvania Politics,* pp. 56-57, 77-78.

The editor of the Brownsville *American Telegraph* declared that the senators and representatives had exceeded their delegated powers. He insisted that, if the public wanted a caucus nomination to be binding on all party members, the people should be spared their trip to the polls merely to add a stamp of approval, and Congress should be given the constitutional power to appoint the President and Vice-President.[41]

This general attitude, that perhaps the control of the government was slipping from the hands of the people, encouraged more extensive newspaper and public discussions concerning the character of all persons running for office. Many in Western Pennsylvania responded with the cry of "rotation in office" and developed a determination not to be controlled by an aristocratic political clique.

In Pennsylvania the national and state operations of the caucus were linked together. The legislature nominated the 25 electors for the presidency in 1816, and these electors, in turn, recommended a Harrisburg convention to nominate a gubernatorial candidate for the 1817 election. This proposed conclave was held with 44 members of the assembly and 69 other delegates in attendance. William Findlay was nominated for governor to the disgust of many who charged that the legislature had been converted into an elective, as well as a legislative body, a condition not contemplated by the state constitution. When the convention denounced all opposition to Findlay as enemies to the Republican cause, it met with widespread criticism and was arraigned as a caucus, partial and ruinous to the rights of free suffrage. Its antagonists countered with a convention of their own at Carlisle which the Findlayites termed a "contemptible burlesque" and a slight refinement of the Hartford type. With the contending forces thus referring to their own nominating groups as conventions and to their opponents' as caucuses, it was obvious that the one term was unpopular while the other was fast becoming the generic expression for democratic action.[42]

The caucus had been condemned partly because of the failure of the Independents and Federalists to wrest control of the governorship from the Snyder-Findlay machine. Under the state constitution of 1790 the

---

[41] *Greensburg Gazette,* February 24, and March 30, 1816; *American Telegraph,* April 3, and July 3, 1816; *Pittsburgh Gazette,* October 18, 1816.
[42] *Pittsburgh Gazette,* August 5, 1817; *Mercury,* August 15, 1817; *Commonwealth,* August 16, 1817.

governor had acquired extensive appointive powers which permitted him to dispense patronage effectively in every county of the state, and the Snyder-Findlay group well understood the political value of these powers.

Other factions found it difficult to overcome this advantage and capture control of the political machinery, so they decided instead to attack it, especially the legislative caucus. They pictured the executive looking to the representative (a caucus member in disguise) for repeated nominations which were paramount to elections while the representative, in turn, looked to the governor for patronage and political endorsement. According to the anti-caucus politicians and editors, the rights of the people were sacrificed and the interests of the state forgotten in this disgraceful scramble for votes on the one hand and offices on the other.[43]

When the caucusites realized that they were losing public support, they skillfully pointed out that the right of nomination had never been assumed by the members of the legislature, but had been imposed upon them by their political friends. Because of transportation and communication hazards, it had been difficult to find delegates with both sufficient knowledge of the candidates and a willingness to leave their work and homes to attend a convention at Harrisburg. The best alternative to secure the nomination of candidates for state-wide elective office had appeared to be the legislative caucus, but now that system was in disrepute.[44]

In order to cover their retreat toward the end of the decade, the caucusites emphasized that the present legislature offered a strong bulwark against corruption and intrigue in making nominations, but agreed that less responsible men could at some future time take over the legislature. Since this was possible, they believed that the best time to raise the barriers against corruption was under such a wholesome administration as that of Findlay and proposed to hold a *convention* of delegates somewhere other than the state capital. Thus Findlay, who had been nominated by a group in Harrisburg in 1817, was renominated by the same group in Lewistown in 1820. This shift, however, was

---

[43] *Mercury,* October 26, 1816; Higginbotham, *Keystone in the Democratic Arch,* p. 304.

[44] *Westmoreland Republican,* October 1, 1819; Myers, "Committees of Correspondence in Western Pennsylvania as the Forerunners of Party Organization" (Unpublished Master's thesis, History Dept., University of Pittsburgh, 1949) p. 52.

unable to offset the damaging propaganda of the anti-caucus faction which had charged that the convention was really a caucus, dominated by the legislature and the governor.

In 1823 the Delegate Republican members of the legislature resolved that the delegates from the various counties should return to Harrisburg for their gubernatorial convention. Every county and district was directed to send delegates, but if any should fail to fulfill this request, the Delegate Republican senators and assemblymen from the particular district were entitled to convention seats. This half convention—half caucus, often known as the "mixed caucus," still met formidable opposition. The anti-caucusites claimed that since each district paid the expenses of its delegates, the general tendency would be to permit the legislators, particularly those of distant counties, to become convention delegates.[45]

The Pennsylvania Delegate Convention which met in Harrisburg on March 4, 1824, was the first to produce no serious repercussions in Western Pennsylvania; all important factions were overjoyed at the convention's unanimous choice of Andrew Jackson and John C. Calhoun for the presidency and vice-presidency, respectively. On the other hand, the dying gasp of the caucus system in Pennsylvania was demonstrated by the action of the state's supporters of William H. Crawford who was the choice of the congressional caucus for the presidency. His endorsers met *in convention* at Harrisburg to approve his nomination. Their intention was to give a stamp of approval for the caucas method of nominating a President and Vice-President, and to identify their candidate, indirectly at least, with the popular convention system.

The sweeping acclaim given the Pennsylvania state convention that nominated Jackson was an important cornerstone in the development of the national convention system. The state convention technique in Pennsylvania had undoubtedly evolved from the local convention or delegate system for nominating county and inter-county tickets. The unfolding of this growth process was obscured in the western counties during the decade of good feeling because the delegate system became intertwined with the state and national caucus.

The delegate system itself was a thoroughly democratic device, but frequently its manipulators were unscrupulous although this distinction was seldom considered in the heat of political campaigns. Unfortunately

[45] *Mercury,* January 28, 1823; Myers, "Committees of Correspondence," p. 75.

the system found itself in the midst of a political tug-of-war between the Independents and Regular Republicans under the guidance of Henry Baldwin and Abner Lacock, respectively. In 1816 the regular Delegate slate had proposed Walter Lowrie, who was serving his second term as state senator, for the congressional seat allotted to Allegheny and Butler Counties, but the selection was dramatically challenged by another Republican faction. This opposition could not be taken lightly. The caliber of the Independents' candidate, Henry Baldwin, who was obviously the more personally popular nominee because of his newspaper and legal career, indicated a genuine party crisis.

In their campaign the Baldwinites immediately attacked the election machinery. They pointed out that everyone in the district recognized Baldwin's abilities, but not all were willing to acknowledge them on election day because he was not the caucus or Delegate nominee. Continued reliance on the delegate system was branded as folly. It had succumbed to the connivance of a few men who called themselves the delegates of the Republican citizens and preferred Lowrie for their own selfish purposes, but the Baldwin school reminded the voters that the Constitution and the laws of the state guaranteed them the right to choose their own candidates. Voters were informed that with a clear democratic conscience they could bolt the Delegate ranks to support the man whose abilities they admired and respected. The *Pittsburgh Gazette* denounced those who thought that Baldwin would reflect honor on his district and acquit himself well, but opposed him because "I must support my party." [46]

This election in 1816 marked the beginning of sectional endorsement over party alignment, and in Western Pennsylvania this sectional emphasis was quickly translated to mean encouragement for domestic manufacturing. Delegate leaders were accused of keeping industry from enjoying a golden age; Pittsburgh wealth and population were curtailed because the local caucus leaders had not been willing to sponsor men of tariff convictions for Congress. Manufacturers claimed that they would endorse the sectional ticket headed by Baldwin in order to salvage their businesses. Farmers in the western counties, Allegheny and Butler particularly, were also urged to support this sectional party out of self-interest. When manufacturing flourished during the war,

---

[46] "A Democratic Republican," *Mercury,* August 24, 1816; *Pittsburgh Gazette,* September 4, 1818.

farm land sold at 50 dollars per acre, but when manufacturing was permitted to languish, the value of the same lands slumped to 30 dollars per acre. The mechanic was likewise encouraged to support this Independent ticket in order to increase employment and raise wages to the level necessary for him to procure his weekly needs from the farmer and merchant. With every part of Western Pennsylvania society in a position to gain from the Independent ticket the Baldwin leaders concluded that this was no time to stand on party prejudice; it was the time to push sectional advancement.[47]

Baldwin defeated Lowrie in 1816 with three-fourths of his 800 majority coming from the city of Pittsburgh, the hub of industrial, anti-Delegate sentiment. In the two years of his first congressional term Baldwin lived up to the expectations of his constituents. On the positive side he was credited with establishing cordial relations among the friends of domestic manufacture by increasing the import duty on glass and with procuring a District Court of the United States to hold sessions at Pittsburgh. The new court saved local citizens the ruinous expenses of lawsuits in Philadelphia and permitted "western people to decide western causes." Baldwin's opposition to the odious compensation law and his vote against the appropriation of additional funds for the National Road which by-passed Pittsburgh also won the plaudits of many citizens in Allegheny and Butler Counties.[48]

This popular record stirred United States Senator Abner Lacock of Beaver County to throw his political weight against Baldwin's candidacy for re-election in 1818. On the ballot Baldwin's oponent was Samuel Douglas who had successfully carried the Delegate banner in the assembly races of 1816 and 1817, but in reality Lacock controlled him like a puppet on a string.

Douglas was content to be "the tool and the machine of such a political demagogue as the sovereign of Beaver." Since Lacock's term as senator was due to expire in 1819, he had visions of moving to Harrisburg as governor. After Findlay's gubernatorial victory in 1817, Lacock's ambition appeared to have a good chance for success. Politically he was a "near friend & house-mate" to Snyder and Findlay whose

---

[47] "A Democratic Republican," *Mercury*, August 24, 1816; *Pittsburgh Gazette*, September 4, 1818.

[48] *Commonwealth*, October 22, 1816; *Pittsburgh Gazette*, September 22, 1818; *Mercury*, October 9, 1818.

Delegate organization controlled the state's highest office. Believing that the next Delegate candidate for governor would come from Western Pennsylvania, Lacock, a "cringing" office seeker, wanted to be that nominee. If he could retain the Delegate voting strength in the western counties, he had reason to believe that the Snyder-Findlay machine would reward him, but Baldwin and the Independents imperiled his scheme.[49]

In order to repulse the surge of Baldwin and dominate Western Pennsylvania politics, Lacock was forced to intervene in the political welfare of Allegheny and Butler Counties in 1818. This action antagonized the individualistic spirit of many inhabitants who believed that they were capable of electing a congressman without outside assistance. His major attack weapon was *The Statesman,* a new journal launched in 1818 under the direction of Lacock's son-in-law, Ephraim Pentland. Lacock used this paper to make himself the off-stage manager of the campaign and was suspected at times of being an editorial contributor under the non de plume of "Hannibal." [50]

In its editorial columns *The Statesman* attacked Baldwin's voting record in Congress. First of all, the journal dismissed the possibility that Baldwin possessed the character of a statesman because of his vote against increased funds for the Cumberland Road. Editorials assailed his pettiness in refusing to promote harmony and advance the interest of people in other parts of the Union simply because the road did not run through his own hometown.

Aware of his investments in the region's industries, Baldwin's critics argued that this brand of self-interest also motivated his program of protectionism. Since 25 cents of every dollar paid for domestic manufactured goods by the mechanic and farmer reportedly enabled Baldwin and other producers to compete with foreigners in our market, they were denounced as leeches on the body politic. Of course, the Independents countercharged that the "unpatriotic opposition" was working mightily to prevent the nation from declaring its independence from foreign maritime monopoly.[51]

The Patentees also encouraged the constituents to consider the fact

---

[49] *Pittsburgh Gazette,* September 29, October 9, 1818; Adams, *Memoirs,* IV, 408; Jonathan Roberts Memoirs, I, 133. (Bound photostats of the original)

[50] *Pittsburgh Gazette,* September 29, and October 6, 1818.

[51] *Statesman,* October 3, 1818.

that Baldwin was a member of "a kind of amphibious, half-horse, half-alligator party" that flopped from Republican to Federalist ideas and back again as the opportunity of the moment demanded. In their determination to place politics on a regional basis, the Independents, on the other hand, attempted to blot out Baldwin's loyalty to the Republican Party in previous years. They falsely declared that he had never leagued himself with any party, but stood always for principle, opposing Republicans in many instances and Federalists in more. He was depicted as an honorable democratic citizen—acting according to the dictates of his own judgment and in the interests of his own section. As forcefully as possible, he urged Congress to save property values by encouraging domestic production and to share with Pittsburgh some of the favors the government had showered on the city's rivals.[52]

Baldwin was more successful than Douglas in convincing the public that he was not the leader of a faction and that faction could not lead him. In the minds of many voters, the latter was handicapped by his alliance with Lacock, a self-styled politician whose character was basically honest, but not above reproach, especially if an irregularity would permit him to continue to feast at the public trough. This reputation accompanied him to Pittsburgh, Philadelphia, and even into the United States Senate. At the end of his senatorial term John Quincy Adams predicted that Lacock "will before long get into some office where he may intrigue with members of Congress." [53]

Aside from being a member of the Snyder-Findlay machine and its spokesman in the western counties from its humble beginning in 1805, Lacock had little to recommend him for the Senate seat he had acquired in 1813. Uneducated, indiscreet, and not a particularly good speaker, he was the politician who seemed to do everything wrong. His defense of the National Road, together with his opposition to buying at the mercy of domestic manufacturers during peacetime at wartime prices, ended Lacock's popularity in Pittsburgh and much of Allegheny County. He achieved a similar distinction elsewhere in Western Pennsylvania as a result of two endorsements in 1816, one in favor of the hated compensation law and the other in favor of the Bank of the United States.

---

[52] *Statesman,* October 19, 1818; "Self-Interest," *Mercury,* September 11, 1818; "An Old Mechanic," *Mercury,* September 18, 1818.

[53] *Monongalia Spectator* quoted in the *Mercury,* August 28, 1818; Roberts Memoirs, I, 132; Adams, *Memoirs,* IV, 408.

After temporarily condoning the bank, the region drastically altered its opinions two years later when a depression set in. Resentment spread to politicians like Lacock who had supported the establishment of the bank and weakened his prestige throughout the western counties.

For all practical purposes this sequence of events ended Lacock's opportunity to become the state's first citizen since he had earlier riled the eastern counties against him. In 1814 he had sneered at President Madison's suggestion that Alexander J. Dallas replace Gallatin who had resigned as secretary of the treasury—"a mere Philadelphia lawyer" was beyond consideration. The President switched his preference to George W. Campbell of Tennessee who was confirmed, but unqualified for the assignment. Within months it was obvious that the treasury department needed a firmer hand at the helm. Now willing to consent to the appointment of Dallas after the financial situation had become unbearable, Lacock pompously announced: "Tell Doctor Madison that we are now willing to submit to his Philadelphia lawyer for the head of the treasury. The public patient is so very sick that we must swallow anything the doctor prescribes, however nauseous the bolus." [54]

Baldwin's victory over Douglas in 1818 was a clear indication that Lacock had passed the crest of his political power. In the last months of his senate term, however, he fought to stem the tide, but instead caused it to flow out more rapidly. As chairman of the Senate committee to investigate Jackson's behavior in Florida, Lacock sought to reclaim his prestige by boldly recommending a courtmartial for this brash display of militarism.

Like his other political causes, this one "boomeranged." His courtmartial proposal came at a time when Jackson was becoming a political idol in Pennsylvania, especially throughout the western counties. When Jackson became an active presidential aspirant in 1824, Lacock sealed his doom. By supporting Crawford he not only condemned the man who was personally popular throughout the state, but at the same time upheld the unpopular caucus system; all perished together.

In this struggle between Lacock and the caucus on the one hand and Baldwin and the Independents on the other, the delegate system was temporarily discredited. Branded the local instrument of the caucus fathers, the delegate system was suspected of fostering the policies of

---

[54] Quoted in Walters, *Alexander J. Dallas,* p. 187.

its manipulators. Although the two groups nominated candidates by identical methods, they were made to appear vastly different.

The Independents held the advantage with their endorsement of tariff protection for industrial development, recognized as the wave of the future for the Pittsburgh area. As more and more people realized that their destinies were linked to manufacturing, the movement to suppress Delegate opposition grew. The Regular Republicans were properly identified with the state and national caucus, but voters were also induced to believe that the caucus principle was the same as the delegate system of nomination on the county level. This interpretation by Independents in the Pittsburgh area spread directly through four counties since Allegheny, Beaver, Butler and Armstrong composed one senatorial district and the Independent ticket sought support in all four against the Delegate slate.

Other counties did not enjoy the same interest in manufactures and saw little relationship between the caucus and the county delegate system. There the Independent ticket was viewed as a possible resurgence of Federalism, and these Delegate-dominated counties braced themselves against such infiltration.

The chaos was not transformed into order until the various economic groups, namely the merchant, farmer, manufacturer, and mechanic, recognized that they were all members of the same economic family and defined their political interests more accurately. An almost unanimous decision in the western counties both to support a protectionist program and to endorse Jackson for the presidency lifted the cloud from the delegate system which was then permitted to grow to state and national proportions. Designated a convention at these levels, it became an integral part of the election machinery before another decade passed.

PART TWO

The Weapons of Battle

V

Newspapers and Their Editors

The Liberty of the Press—It develops the recess of the palace, and carries light within the confines of the cottage.[1]

HISTORIANS of a generation ago were prone to minimize the importance of newspapers in their research endeavors. They sought causation in the scientifically-proven fact and in the unique events of the period under study. Newspapers were important only insofar as they assisted in the development of these ends.

More recently social psychology has introduced the idea that public opinion and the typical occurrences in society are pivotal factors in explaining causation. In studying the dynamic effects of a policy on social groups, it is frequently as important to know what the people of that time thought the policy was as to know what it actually was. Although some discrepancy between a policy and the public understanding of it is inevitable, the newspapers of the early 19th Century tended to promote a divergence, especially in the area west of the mountains where the editors were literally all leaders of political cliques or crusaders for a cause.[2]

From the standpoint of travel time, the people of Western Pennsylvania in the decade from 1815 to 1825 were farther removed from communication with their state government than any other area in the nation. They were forced to rely heavily on a few editors with limited means and decided preferences for their reports on governmental activity. Although this was not the only raw material from which western attitudes and patterns of action were formulated, the narrow views and prejudices of newspaper editors represent the best available source of public opinion in this period. Therefore, no study of Western Pennsylvania is worthy of the name of history if the newspaper accounts are not thoroughly investigated and evaluated.

---

[1] Toast proposed at an Independence Day celebration in Crawford County. *Crawford Messenger,* July 9, 1819.

[2] Miller, *Genesis of Western Culture,* p. 76.

Popular concept of the press varied radically. The pendulum swung from the frontier isolationist who had no interest in government at all and no thought for life beyond his own county to the citizen who regarded the newspaper as a public instrument through which he could present his personal political and economic theories uninhibited. The general tendency was strongly inclined toward the second extreme, but the isolationist was certainly not extinct. A Venango farmer revealed this attitude when discussing the subject of newspapers with a traveler in a tippling house.

> About these Meadville newspapers, all I ever knew or heard is, that I heard our squire say that he once took them a *whole quarter of a year,* and that they cost him as much as would buy a gallon of whiskey, and they never did him as much good as to drink a gill—for they were filled with a mess of sober stuff, and politics that he knew nothing about, and told about people and things all over the world, which our squire said was enough to make a man crazy to think of.[3]

The other extreme is well depicted by Jacob Herrington of Mercer who was a combination editor and politician. So firmly did he believe that all articles in good taste, whether the editor agreed with them or not, should be published, that his *Western Press* printed condemnations of himself when submitted in articles by his political opponents. Herrington actually appeared upset when two such political rivals, Aaron Hackney and David McKnight, charged that he had refused to print one of their items. He quickly pointed out that he had already set his type when the article was presented for publication, but pledged himself to publish it in his next issue.[4]

Such a concept of a lone county editor's function was shared by many in Beaver County. There James and Andrew Logan of the *Beaver Gazette* had the only press in the county. In 1817 the brothers decided to endorse Joseph Hiester for governor, but the advocates of his opponent, William Findlay, demanded that they adopt the role of independent editors and print the speeches and material favorable to both. The Logans suggested that they publish an "extra sheet" for the Findlayites, who demanded such control over the new edition that they could attack the editorials of the regular *Gazette* and expose the editors' arguments. Unlike Herrington, the Logans refused to permit their ideas

---

[3] "Yeoman," *Crawford Messenger,* January 28, 1820.
[4] Jacob Herrington to Thomas Atkinson, printed in *Crawford Messenger,* October 7, 1815.

to be criticized in their own press, and the Findlay faction had to turn to *The Commonwealth* in Pittsburgh to get sympathetic accounts of their candidate.[5]

Many people possessed the idea that the newspapers in a sense belonged to them to use as the occasion dictated. They believed that since they were subscribers, the editor had an obligation to insert their epistles and queries.[6] Under such pseudonyms as Clodhopper, E. Pluribus Unum, Oliver Homespun, Civis, Domesticus, and Caleb Cowhide much discussion took place in the local journals.

These articles were often indicative of the intensity of issues, but frequently they represented only the intensity of personalities. One letter might set off a flurry of replies or counter-charges which, in turn, would necessitate rebuttals by the originator. Through a weekly's editorial columns, Clodhopper might feud with Domesticus, and the two would monopolize several full columns of each issue for months before both would exhaust their vocabularies. These letters, as well as the editor's own comments, were fashionably dotted with statistics; they seemed more authentic that way. Of course, no one paid any attention to the source of the statistics, but that was of little consequence because they played no part in the writer's interpretation. Generally, the statistics were devised to substantiate what he had already concluded.

Western editors welcomed this participation and were thankful for the contributions. When articles were refused, it was generally done in the name of good taste or party harmony. Editors were particularly grateful for letters from local residents who were traveling elsewhere in the state, and these travelers, who received much satisfaction in knowing that their impressions written to the editor today would be published next week, responded copiously. They actually curtailed their personal letters and advised their correspondents to see the letters to the local editor for a "general view of the business going on." [7] Letters from legislators who were attending a legislative session were of particular significance because of the keen interest in local projects and proposals. This local consciousness is clearly demonstrated by the greater newspaper space given to local candidates and issues by the Pittsburgh weeklies than by the daily *Aurora* in Philadelphia.

[5] *Commonwealth,* August 29, 1817.

[6] *Western Herald,* July 6, 1815.

[7] Patrick Farrelly to William McArthur, February 8, 1812. Patrick Farrelly Letters in the Crawford County Historical Society.

Editors printed much material without a thought concerning its accuracy. They assumed the attitude that, if a person took offense at comments in an article, he could not come back on the editor except to demand the name of the writer of the offensive material.[8] Editors like Richard Hill of Warren's *Conewango Emigrant* pulled out all the stops and published anything for money. According to his critics, no matter how abusive a communication was, if accompanied by a dollar, Hill published it. Characteristically he ran an advertisement submitted by Naper Tandy which announced the opening of a tannery where he stood ready to tan all kinds of hides, "especially carrotty-colored hides from Hibernia's Isle." [9]

Needless to say, these literary gems from the subscribers did not constitute the chief source of copy for the Western Pennsylvania editor; that was afforded by the bundles of newspapers that came with every mail. Delay in the mail service, particularly from Philadelphia and Harrisburg, often meant delay in the publication of the western weeklies. The editors were dependent on this supply for all their eastern and foreign news, for government legislation and proclamations, for political speeches and messages, and for the varied literary filler that was used to round out the remaining columns. Newspapers came to the western editor on an exchange basis, but undoubtedly the exchange was more essential to the westerner than to the editor across the mountains.

In 1819 during the depression the eastern publishers threatened this source of news with higher costs or extinction. They proposed that the exchange of newspapers would not be continued without payment by the western editors of the difference in the price of the papers. To the *Pittsburgh Gazette* this was the crowning insult by Philadelphia in the hour of Western Pennsylvania's tribulations; just as bank paper had fallen below par in the East, now newspapers also fell below par.[10]

The fact that eastern publishers contemplated this change in policy and that westerners regarded it as burdensome indicates that journalism was not a lucrative profession. As one approached the frontier, he recognized that the editor's career grew less and less remunerative in

---

[8] Thomas Atkinson, *To the Democratic Republican Citizens of Crawford County*, October 9, 1823. Bound with the *Crawford Messenger* for the period 1818-1821 in the Crawford County Historical Society.

[9] Schenck, *Warren County*, p. 279.

[10] *Pittsburgh Gazette*, August 13, 1819.

terms of dollars and cents. The limited purchasing power of the people and the high price of newspaper materials produced few subscribers and advertisers. They, in turn, paid so little in cash that the task of meeting expenses was often too much for the printer.

Thomas Patton of Uniontown's *Genius of Liberty* pointed out that during six months in 1823 he had received only two dollars from his subscribers and advertisers and that during the three years of his direction the *Genius of Liberty* had not received enough from the subscribers and advertisers to pay the cost of the paper on which it was printed.[11] In lieu of money editors were happy to accept such items as tallow, bacon, beef, pork, grains, rags, flax, linen, iron, feathers, and wood ashes at the market price. As a postscript to such a plan of barter, Thomas Atkinson once added that he needed a few quarts of good clover seed and was quite willing to have someone dispose of his newspaper debt by providing it.[12]

The financial plight of the Western Pennsylvania journalists was dramatically demonstrated by the newspaper failures in the decade 1815 to 1825. At the beginning of this period the western end of the state had 13 papers spread over nine of the 15 counties, with only Allegheny having as many as three. Within ten years the number had doubled, and all the counties save Jefferson operated at least one press of its own. Although 13 new journals were functioning successfully by 1825, the decade also witnessed 17 fatalities, meaning that nearly 60 per cent of the new presses were forced to close their doors, generally within two years after opening them.

Of the 13 newspapers in 1815 a dozen were still operating independently in 1825. The pioneer of this group was the *Pittsburgh Gazette,* founded by John Scull in 1786 when Pittsburgh was little more than a village. On the *Gazette's* thirtieth anniversary, this Federalist publisher turned the editorship over to his son, John I. Scull, who sold a half interest to Morgan Neville in 1818.[13]

By the time of these changes the Federalist Party had collapsed in most areas, and the term itself was in disrepute. The younger Scull and

---

[11] James A. Hadden, *A History of Uniontown, the County Seat of Fayette County, Pennsylvania* (Uniontown: James A. Hadden, 1913), p. 459.

[12] *Ibid.; Crawford Messenger,* January 30, 1818, and October 28, 1823.

[13] J. Cutler Andrews, *Pittsburgh's Post-Gazette* (Boston: Chapman & Grimes, 1936), pp. 55-60.

Neville, however, were able to prevent their press from meeting the same end as the party it had endorsed. Neville, on whom most of the editorial burden fell, was chiefly responsible for the new editorial policy based on sectional allegiance. It stressed encouragement to domestic manufactures and internal improvements and tied "men of talents" to these principles. In this manner these editors very cleverly shifted the emphasis from men to principles and kept functioning. Of course, this transition was costly, as were the panic years from 1818 to 1822, but the firm foundation on which this paper had been built permitted it to weather the storms. The same is true of the other journals in existence by 1815; in their formative years they had no competition while those founded in the decade of good feeling had to face established rivals, and often did so unsuccessfully.[14]

EDITORS PLAY POLITICS

Since newspapers were seldom profitable enterprises west of the mountains, editors, of necessity, allied themselves with other occupations. Almost inevitably this meant direct or indirect implication with politics. Some sought lucrative contracts for government printing, others entered politics and used their journals to sing their own praises while a third group desired to profit from the spoils of office and sought to be the beneficiaries of such political appointments as alderman or prothonotary. Still others had no avocation, but were simply men with a cause, professional crusaders for a political faction or proponents of a social or economic program.

In an effort to replenish newspaper deficits, editors would accept printing of all kinds, but the most rewarding financially were contracts to print the laws of the state and federal governments. Such grants were often indispensable to the success of western editors; new journals were often started with the prospect of getting a government contract to replace the losses of newspaper publication. In 1817 Henry Eddy reversed the procedure and wrote to the state department announcing that he had established at Pittsburgh a paper called the *Swallow*, similar in form and contents to *Niles' Weekly Register*. Eddy declared that the *Swallow* had an extensive circulation and that he would like to have a

---

[14] Andrews, *Pittsburgh's Post-Gazette*, pp. 55-60; *Pittsburgh Gazette*, March 30, 1820.

grant to print federal laws.[15] This, however, is the only known reference to the *Swallow* and suggests that Eddy was attempting to get a government contract first and only then establish his paper.

This attempted fraud also suggests strongly the intrigue of Abner Lacock, then United States senator from Pennsylvania. Lacock, who had married Hannah Eddy, was a staunch supporter of Henry Clay rather than John Quincy Adams, who was then in the state department. In view of Lacock's more definable political exploits, one might infer that Eddy was merely the senator's pawn to gain a concession from his political opponents. This possibility appears much clearer when one observes that the next year Lacock's son-in-law Ephraim Pentland reorganized *The Commonwealth* into a Lacock sounding board which was thereafter called *The Statesman*.

In 1821, with Adams still in the state department, James S. Stevenson, a member of the Pennsylvania Assembly, delivered a letter to the secretary from Charles Shaler who urged that *The Statesman* be re-appointed to print the laws of the United States. Adams replied that it was a standing rule to re-appoint a publisher unless some objection was raised by a delegation from the state involved. Stevenson pointed out that Congressman Henry Baldwin might recommend a change, but that a majority of party members in Western Pennsylvania would be adverse to it. He continued by saying that Baldwin was out of favor with the party, especially on state issues.[16]

As further proof of an editor's great concern for government printing, Senator William Findlay called on Adams on January 4, 1825, also in behalf of *The Statesman*. The senator explained that Editor Pentland feared that he would lose his contract to print the laws since he had favored Crawford for the presidency. Undoubtedly mindful that the choice of Presidents still rested with the House of Representatives as a result of the electoral split in 1824, and well aware that astute politics called for the courting of the enemy, Adams assured Findlay that he had already sent the commission of re-appointment to *The Statesman*.[17]

---

[15] Brigham, *History and Bibliography of American Newspapers*, II, 967, cites Eddy's letter, dated November 27, 1817, and which is filed with the collection of State Department Papers in the National Archives.

[16] Adams, *Memoirs*, V, 394.

[17] *Ibid.*, VI, 459.

Even among the editors who received government patronage in the form of contracts to print the laws were many who desired additional political plums. Because of the governor's extensive appointive powers, unscrupulous editors regarded appointments to political office as a just price for a favorable press. Other more honorable editors were also rewarded with offices, especially for support in previous campaigns. Partly through this power to appoint a printer or two to lucrative offices in every county and partly through his own official position, the governor was able to give his own tonic to public opinion.[18]

The offices to which editors were most frequently appointed were prothonotary, justice of the peace, clerk of the county courts, and county register and recorder. Some, like James Logan of Beaver's *Western Argus* and affiliated journals, served in all these capacities.[19] The real meaning of the governor's control through the appointment of editors was further demonstrated by the pattern in four adjoining southwestern Pennsylvania counties. In Allegheny, Fayette, Washington, and West-moreland newspaper editors or newspaper sponsors were appointed prothonotaries by Governor William Findlay. Ephraim Pentland and William Sample of Allegheny and Washington, respectively, were the rewarded editors while the brother of Frederick A. Wise of the *West-moreland Republican* and John S. Clair, principal endorser of Union-town's *Genius of Liberty,* were commissioned in the other counties.[20]

In order to evaluate the prestige that a governor may build for him-self through these appointments, one need only consider the case of William Findlay "who was *elected out* of the office of governor" in 1820 and who had been "convicted of mal-practices in the office of treasurer of this state." He so ingratiated himself with the state legisla-tors and their political friends through such grass roots instruments as local editors that immediately upon being turned out of the office of governor he was selected to represent the state in the United States Senate.[21]

In Allegheny County Pentland, who had been first appointed pro-thonotary by Governor Simon Snyder in 1809, was recommissioned by

---

[18] *New York Columbian* quoted in *Mercury,* August 8, 1817.
[19] Francis S. Reader, *History of the Newspapers of Beaver County, Pennsylvania* (New Brighton, Pennsylvania: F. S. Reader & Son, 1905), p. 16.
[20] *Western Register* (Brownsville) quoted in the *Aurora,* August 17, 1820.
[21] *Aurora,* December 10, 1821.

Findlay and served continuously until 1821. The original appointment appears to be the editor's reward for his support of Snyder when dissension in the Democratic-Republican ranks of Pennsylvania developed in 1805. That year Pentland had organized *The Commonwealth* and endorsed the radical Republican cause against the *Pittsburgh Gazette* and *The Tree of Liberty* which constituted a Federalist-Republican coalition and successfully carried Thomas McKean into the governor's seat.

While the *Gazette* represented the Federalist part of the coalition, *The Tree of Liberty* sponsored a Republican faction. John Israel was the nominal editor and publisher of the latter paper, but Pentland believed it to be under the influence of the triumvirate of Henry Baldwin, Tarleton Bates, and Walter Forward. According to his suspicions, Baldwin and Bates supplied the money and Forward the editorial work.

Pentland's resentment of the power of these conservative Republicans caused him to establish his rival journal which espoused the cause of Snyder who was eventually victorious in 1808. The governor's reward came the following year. Paradoxically, Pentland had been formerly employed on the staff of the conservative *Aurora* in Philadelphia before coming to Western Pennsylvania to promote the radical Republican faction.

During his editorship of *The Commonwealth* from 1805 to 1810, his career showed the indiscretions of youth and brought disgrace to his name. As the result of a newspaper quarrel, Bates applied the cowhide to Pentland. Thomas Stewart carried the latter's challenge of a duel to Bates, but because of the verbal exchange that ensued Bates dueled with Stewart and was killed. Pentland revealed his bitter hatred with the editorial comment that he would not "engross the columns of his paper with remarks on the private character of Mr. Bates because that already appears to the public in colors as dark as the skin of his mistress." [22]

In 1810 Pentland left the newspaper field to give attention to his law practice and political offices. *The Commonwealth* passed under the direction of Benjamin Brown who had been associated with other Western Pennsylvania papers, namely the Washington *Reporter* and a journalistic experiment at Williamsport (Monongahela). Pentland re-

---

[22] Charles Dahlinger, *Pittsburgh: A Sketch of Its Early Social Life* (New York: G. P. Putnam's Sons, 1916), p. 149.

gained control of *The Commonwealth* in 1818 in time to close its doors and start another weekly, *The Statesman*. He could no longer be branded a radical; instead he reverted to a pattern of conservatism, the type advocated by his father-in-law, Abner Lacock, who had been a regular contributor to the columns of *The Commonwealth*.

Editorial comment, however, was subject to abrupt changes in this period, and newspaper rivalry was frequently propelled into an overnight bitterness due to the governor's policy in appointing editors to political office. When editors proved somewhat unruly to the administration, the governor could generally pacify them with appointments. In the gubernatorial election year of 1817, Governor Snyder pulled the editors of the *Juniata Gazette, Huntingdon Republican,* and *Dowingtown Republican* into line with commissions as justices of the peace.[23]

In cases of more vehement opposition, the governor had two alternatives: to ride out the tide of denunciation or to buy out the obnoxious editor. In 1822 Governor Joseph Hiester adopted the former course when Robert Fee of Brownsville's *Western Register* desired an appointment, but failed to have his petition viewed favorably. Fee, humorously known to his opponents as "Fee Simple," quickly made the discovery upon the rejection of his request that Hiester was "a very ignorant old blockhead of a Dutchman and very unfit to be Governour of the State." All anti-Hiester papers copied these sage remarks with becoming zeal, but the governor did not purchase the editor's friendship.[24]

The Snyder-Findlay machine, on the other hand, pursued the alternate course in an earlier scuffle with a rebellious editor. John McFarland of the Chambersburg *Democratic Republican,* who later founded the *Allegheny Democrat* in Pittsburgh, was bought out by the Franklin County politicians who took over his publication.[25] Editor David MacLean of the *Greensburg Gazette* suggested sarcastically that he would not be surprised if the editor of the *Beaver Gazette* would be offered the same attractive price for his printing establishment as that tendered McFarland since he has endorsed Hiester in preference to Findlay.[26]

In communities where two or more journals were published, bitter rivalry could flare up over the appointment of one of the editors to

[23] *Greensburg Gazette,* June 28, 1817.

[24] *Ibid.,* April 19, 1822.

[25] *Aurora,* May 23, 1817.

[26] *Greensburg Gazette,* June 28, 1817.

political office. In the borough of Washington the commissioning of William Sample, editor of *The Reporter,* as prothonotary by Governor Findlay in 1819 occasioned a long-standing quarrel with the *Washington Examiner.* This feud produced repercussions throughout the state as the anti-Findlay papers carried reprints of the *Examiner's* charges of bargain and sale of offices in the running battle.

The Reporter had been established in 1808 as the Democratic-Republican voice of the county, but nine years later John Grayson was persuaded to forsake a career of journalism in Baltimore for one in Washington. In the prospectus of his *Examiner,* Grayson declared that he recognized only two parties in the state and nation, the Federalist and the Republican Parties, and pointed out that he had been the painful witness of a conspiracy tending to prostrate the Republican Party in Pennsylvania. Seeing the need for a barrier against this intrigue and believing neutrality to be criminal in 1817, Grayson established his paper. The prospectus also endorsed principles and not men, but in the same paragraph praised Findlay as a gubernatorial candidate without so much as a passing reference to his talents.[27]

More than a year later when Grayson was explaining the circumstances which had brought him to the Washington scene, he pointed out that he had corresponded with a gentleman in Washington whom he failed to identify. He outlined his ideas and prospectus to this mysterious resident, presumably George Baird or a member of his political family. The unnamed contact worked the prospectus into its final form and presented it to the public under the editor's name. Grayson submitted to this procedure because he believed that local issues should be mentioned in the prospectus although he knew nothing of them in Washington.[28]

This admission suggests strongly that the *Examiner's* policy was controlled by someone other than the editor, especially since the paper's major interest was to be attention to local affairs. This is borne out by the fact that the *Examiner* and the *Reporter* both supported Findlay for governor that year, but the former was urban in sympathy with a strong support from the business classes while the *Reporter* talked the political and economic language of the farmer of the countryside.

In the campaign Grayson commented that "we are supporting the

[27] *Examiner,* May 28, 1817.
[28] *Ibid.,* September 7, 1818.

same cause which the 'Reporter' professes to advocate" and attempted to sow seeds of doubt as to the *Reporter's* real purpose. The *Reporter* insisted that the *Examiner* was employed by the "hated Bairds" to promote their personal objectives and denounced Grayson as a Federalist because he had ventured into the *Reporter's* domain and established a so-called Republican newspaper. Grayson countered the attack with the claim that he wished to maintain the unity of the Republican Party by checking the rudeness of Sample's "shallow brain and malignant heart" in libeling certain gentlemen of the Republican Party.[29]

With the same ease that they slandered each other, these editors denounced the candidacy of Hiester for governor. Both pointed out that in the battle of Brandywine Hiester ran off and was almost shot in the back by his superior.[30] After Findlay's victory Grayson attempted to show that Sample would have been just as satisfied with a Hiester triumph and to demonstrate by such indirection that the *Examiner* was the *real* friend of Findlay in Washington County.

A more fundamental split between the two came in the spring of 1819 when Grayson commented that a report was circulating to the effect that on his last trip to Harrisburg Sample had purchased the office of prothonotary. He doubted its authenticity because he did not think that Findlay would venture to insult the free and independent people of Washington by bartering for Sample's press. A week later, however, he had to admit the rumor as fact. The Findlay administration immediately fell from the *Examiner's* conception of the "high ground" that should be maintained by a chief magistrate.[31]

John M. Snowden of the Pittsburgh *Mercury* defended the appointment while John Binns of Philadelphia's *Democratic Press* was an outspoken opponent. Such concern tended to give this local incident statewide significance. Binns labeled Findlay's action as a betrayal because he had promised to make no appointments without an expression of public sentiment on the subject. The Philadelphian further charged that Findlay had no testimony of the people's wishes and had acted without their suspecting what was coming to pass. For Binns to condemn Findlay was as much a contradiction of his campaign editorials as was the *Examiner's* denunciation. He, therefore, leveled his attack, not at Find-

---

[29] *Examiner,* June 18, 1817; *Mercury,* June 13, 1817.
[30] *Mercury,* June 13, 1817.
[31] *Examiner,* May 19, 24, 1819.

lay directly, but at the "desperate intriguers" who influenced the governor and charged that they judged it necessary to have fiery thorough-going corruptionists in the various counties to propagate the art of "corruptionizing" without regard for the wishes of the people.[32] By 1820 the *Examiner* had discovered Hiester's "glorious revolutionary service" and boomed him as Findlay's replacement.[33]

Since Sample's appointment was not only to the position of prothonotary of the court of common pleas, but also to the positions of clerk of the quarter sessions, clerk of the orphan's court, and clerk of the court of oyer and terminer, he resigned as editor of the *Reporter*.[34] His place was taken by Samuel Workman, a brother-in-law who conducted the journal until 1821 when Sample returned to his old post. After his brief stint as editor Workman launched a political career of his own which carried him from the position of county treasurer in 1822 through that of sheriff to the Pennsylvania Assembly where he served from 1827 to 1830.[35]

Sample, after a brief interruption of holding office through appointment, was returned to the position of prothonotary and allied posts in 1823 and remained there until 1830. Throughout the years of Workman and Sample's ventures into politics the *Examiner's* repetitious denunciations of the *Reporter* as "The Family Paper" of "Sample, Workman and Co." resounded over the state.[36]

Other Western Pennsylvania editors were likewise frequent recipients of political appointments. In Armstrong County Frederick Rohrer of the Kittanning *Columbian and Farmers' and Mechanics' Advertiser* was listed among the county's registers and recorders, clerks of the various courts, and justices of the peace.[37] Maurice Bredin, who edited the Butler *Repository* with his brother John, served first in elective capacities on the Butler borough council and as county commissioner, but he also joined the ranks of the appointed editors, serving four years as register and recorder and many more as justice of the peace.[38]

---

[32] *Democratic Press*, August 13, 1819.

[33] *Examiner*, August 14, 1820.

[34] *Reporter*, May 31, 1819.

[35] Pennsylvania, *House Journal* (1827-1828), I, 4; (1828-1829), I, 4; (1829-1830), I, 5.

[36] *Examiner*, June 7, 1823.

[37] Robert Walter Smith, *History of Armstrong County, Pennsylvania* (Chicago: Waterman, Watkins & Co., 1883), pp. 35-36, 599.

[38] Robert C. Brown (ed.), *History of Butler County, Pennsylvania* ... (Chicago: R. C. Brown & Co., 1895), p. 691.

In Beaver County another brother combination, James and Andrew Logan, conducted numerous newspapers before they found a satisfactory formula for success. These men generally opposed the county's leading political figure, Abner Lacock, and possessed the ability to throw their opposition into confusion with pungent and persuasive ridicule. James, who was the more ambitious of the two politically, served on the Beaver borough council for twelve years, but also held such gubernatorial appointments as clerk of the various courts, justice of the peace, and prothonotary over the years from 1814 to 1836.[39]

While many editors awaited the patronage of governors, others became active campaigners and sought elective office. Thomas Atkinson of the *Crawford Weekly Messenger* was such a man. His importance, however, does not stem from his career as county commissioner or as burgess of Meadville or as state assemblyman, although he held all of these posts.[40] Atkinson is noted instead for the broad scope of his editorial perspective, which presents one of the best comprehensive understandings of Western Pennsylvania in this period, and for his deep sense of civic responsibility.

Born in Cumberland, Pennsylvania, July 11, 1781, Atkinson came to Meadville in 1804 and launched his newspaper career the following year. This *Crawford Messenger,* except for a brief interruption of 18 months, remained under his supervision until four years before his death in 1837.[41] This pioneering effort in journalism in the area north and west of the Allegheny was first printed on a hand press which had been employed many years before by Benjamin Franklin and which, according to legend, had been used to print continental money as well. The type had been brought by boat from Pittsburgh, and for several years the paper stock had been carried from the same depot by pack horse.[42]

In 1819, however, Atkinson and William Magaw built the first

---

[39] Reader, *Newspapers of Beaver County,* pp. 16-18.

[40] Pennsylvania, *House Journal* (1827-1828), I, 5; Robert C. Brown, *History of Crawford County* . . . (Chicago: Warner, Beers & Co., 1885), pp. 312, 314, 444.

[41] Notes from the Reynolds Collection in the possession of James R. Shryock, Meadville.

[42] John E. Reynolds, *French Creek Valley,* p. 122; Joseph Riesenman, *History of Northwestern Pennsylvania* (New York: Lewis Historical Publishing Co., 1943), II, 712.

paper mill in northwestern Pennsylvania. After a brief period Atkinson became the sole proprietor; progress was rapid, and he began exporting large quantities of white and straw paper by boat.[43] Success with this paper mill and printing shop caused him to suspend publication of the the *Weekly Messenger* in 1821; he saw an opportunity to turn his talents toward the remedy of a serious educational problem in his part of the state. Books for schools and seminaries could be procured only from distant centers and the type of currency required to purchase them was possessed by less than ten per cent of the people in the community. Thus upon realizing the basic requirements of his region, Atkinson gave up the *Messenger* to devote his labor and attention to the printing of the urgently needed books for the western counties.[44]

His civic ingenuity, moreover, was not limited to the realm of education although he was among Meadville's citizen group that successfully petitioned the legislature for a college charter. Along with such notables as Roger and Timothy Alden, Patrick Farrelly, John Reynolds, and Jesse Moore, Atkinson was one of the original trustees appointed by the legislature for the newly authorized Allegheny College. He was also active in organizing the Protestant Episcopal Church of Meadville and in forming such improvement enterprises as the Mercer & Meadville and the Susquehanna & Waterford Turnpike Companies. When the editor was not bending his energies in the direction of these activities, he was busy with the North Western Bank of Pennsylvania or political committees of correspondence or the Meadville Society for the Encouragement of Domestic Manufactures and the Useful Arts which he served as secretary.[45]

Atkinson also found time to offer his services to the farmers of the surrounding country who depended primarily on their cattle to supply the articles of comfort to their families, as well as to meet the maintenance costs of their farms. Generally, farmers were forced to dispose of their cattle in order to discharge the debts previously contracted with

---

[43] William Reynolds, "Water Street and the Residents of Olden Time," p. 9. MS in Reynolds Collection of Mr. Shryock.

[44] "William Reynolds' Scrapbook" II, 100, in Crawford County Historical Society; *Crawford Messenger*, February 6, 1821.

[45] William Reynolds, "Public Enterprises of the Early Citizens," p. 9 f.; "The Olden Town," p. 11; "Incidents and Notations, 1788-1816 of Northwestern Pennsylvania," p. 11; MSS in Reynolds Collection of Mr. Shryock.

a merchant. If they were fortunate enough to receive cash payment, it was frequently in a currency that was worthless outside the county. In either case the advantage lay with the merchant, and Atkinson sought to establish a more equitable exchange. He estimated that the cattle driven out of Crawford County in one season to be valued at $800 or $900, and according to his mathematics, only about $500 of this money paid by the merchants could be used to pay debts beyond the limits of the county.[46]

To correct this abuse, he proposed to open a registry at his office in the spring of the following year for the benefit of both prospective purchasers and the farmers with cattle for sale. Under the plan the farmer would sign the register stating his township, and the number of head of cattle available for market, along with their age and weight. Then the cattle dealers, who had previously approved Atkinson's scheme, would apply at this "cattle bureau" set up at the newspaper office where they could get systematic information about the cattle for sale.

In this way it was hoped that the farmer would dispose of every hoof for sale at a fair price. Thus the farmer would be aided by payment in cash, in a currency suitable for general circulation. Although this plan did have an advantage for the editor of permitting him to keep his finger on the economic pulse of the nation through direct contact with both the farmer and the merchant, it was primarily a public service freely offered by Northwestern Pennsylvania's journalist of greatest vision and sense of progress.

The same section of the state produced two other outstanding politicians among the ranks of the newspaper editors, Jacob Herrington of Mercer and Moses Sullivan of Butler. They did not exhibit the same civic-mindedness that characterized Atkinson, but they proved no less successful at the ballot box. After publishing a paper in opposition to the *Crawford Messenger* for two years, Herrington moved to Mercer in 1811 and established the *Western Press*.[47] After another two years he entered politics as a member of the Pennsylvania Assembly from Mercer and Venango counties. In the eight years between 1813 and 1821, he was elected on six occasions to represent his district in the

[46] *Crawford Messenger,* September 17, 1822.
[47] J. G. White, *A Twentieth Century History of Mercer County, Pennsylvania* (Chicago: Lewis Publishing Co., 1909), I, 217.

Assembly,[48] and then he spent the next four years in the upper house of the legislature.[49]

While Herrington was a member of the Assembly, Henry Hurst of his senatorial district presented a petition from Herrington, a soldier of the American Revolution, stating his services and suffering. The records revealed that Herrington had been honorably discharged and was entitled to a state pension. A bill was then proposed granting him an annuity for life; it passed both the Senate and Assembly with Herrington having an opportunity to assist in voting himself a pension. Governor Snyder signed the measure in 1817;[50] to have done otherwise would have probably meant increased opposition to the administration on two fronts; in the legislature in the persons of Hurst and Herrington and in the editorial columns of the *Western Press*.

While this pension afforded Herrington a total of three politically-allied sources of income, Moses Sullivan, on the other hand, had to be content with two, newspaper "profits" and political office. He operated the *Butler Sentinel* with his brother John who was commissioned prothonotary and clerk of the several courts of Butler County by the governor. Add to this the three terms of Moses in the Assembly from 1822 to 1825 and a term in the state senate (1825-1829), and this newspaper family reveals a picture of more than nominal influence in state politics.[51]

The journalistic career of John M. Snowden was likewise intertwined with politics, but he did not attempt to mix the two extensively at any one time. A native of Philadelphia, Snowden first edited a Chambersburg paper in 1798, but then moved across the mountains to Greensburg where he established a republican journal, the *Farmers' Register*. This he sold in 1808 when he entered the state assembly to represent Westmoreland County. After one year his legislative career was at an end; he moved to Pittsburgh and re-entered the newspaper field with the purchase of the *Mercury*, which he published while con-

---

[48] Pennsylvania, *House Journal*. All sessions from 1813 through 1820, except those beginning in 1817 and 1819, carried the name of Jacob Herrington on the assembly roster.

[49] Pennsylvania, *Senate Journal*, XXXII, 3.

[50] *Ibid.*, XXVII, 75, 189, 226, 365.

[51] Pennsylvania, *House Journal*, for the sessions 1822-1823, 1823-1824, and 1824-1825, carried the name of Moses Sullivan on its rolls; Pennsylvania, *Senate Journal*, XXXVII, 4; Brown, *History of Butler County*, p. 676 f.

ducting a law practice and attending to his political job as alderman.[52]

The *Mercury* represents a creditable job of unbiased reporting except on the subject of tariff protection for American manufactures and on caucus procedures; on both the editor was a devout disciple of Independent philosophy. Generally, his approach was not bitter, even when his ideas and candidates were doomed to failure. In 1825 Snowden returned to the political arena when appointed mayor of the city of Pittsburgh, and he served in that capacity for three years before he became an associate judge of the county court.[53]

CHANGES IN NEWSPAPER TRENDS

Throughout most of the decade 1815 to 1825 local and state themes constituted the broadest range of the editor's considerations. At times papers were established on the basis of journalistic zeal and then assisted through commissions to print government laws, but more often such enterprises were undertaken with other objectives in mind: the hope of political appointment for the editor and his friends or the establishment of a propaganda organ for a local political faction. Failure to realize these objectives brought collapse to more than half the 30 journals founded in Western Pennsylvania in this period. Of the 13 successfully established, five sprang up in 1824 and 1825. A preliminary examination would attribute this development to the natural growth of the region, but only one of the five, the *Conewango Emigrant* at Warren, was started in an area not already serviced by a local newspaper. A more detailed study of this spurt in newspaper expansion reveals the embryonic growth of a new idea in regard to government. Political focus was gradually shifting from the state and local levels to the national.

In these years the change brought forth a great anxiety over the man that should represent the nation in the White House. Many candidates came forward, but the western counties of Pennsylvania decided at an early date that Andrew Jackson was their choice. In Pittsburgh, where

---

[52] "Observer," *Examiner,* August 6, 1817; Pennsylvania, *House Journal* (1808-1809), p. 4; George D. Albert (ed.), *History of the County of Westmoreland, Pennsylvania, with Biographical Sketches* . . . (Philadelphia: L. H. Everts & Co., 1882), p. 279.

[53] John Newton Boucher, *History of Westmoreland County, Pennsylvania* (New York: Lewis Publishing Co., 1906), I, 324.

three long-established newspapers had devoted their editorial abilities to informing and arousing the public on chiefly state and local problems and had sought solutions on the same levels, John McFarland established his *Allegheny Democrat* in 1824 with the express purpose of promoting the candidacy of Jackson.

McFarland, though penniless upon arrival in Pittsburgh, was not poor in newspaper experience; he had edited at least three Eastern Pennsylvania weeklies before moving west. The first of these was the *Democratic Republican* at Chambersburg where he discovered that he was arrayed against "nests of hornets." According to his own confession, he opposed a Franklin County commissioner who was a member of the William Findlay political clique. This stand brought the ire of a prothonotary, a judge, a brigadier-general, a coroner, a commissioner, and many justices of the peace upon him because Franklin County possessed a simulated aristocracy of family interests which sacrificed public interest to family combinations. Instead of parties the county had these family combinations which caucused among themselves as party leaders would normally do.[54]

These were the "nests of hornets" McFarland opposed, and they pooled their financial resources to buy him out for $500 more than he had paid for the *Democratic Republican*. The Findlayites, however, charged that this was not an accurate representation of McFarland's position. They pointed out that he had earlier been a staunch supporter of Findlay; only after he had applied for and had been denied the office of county treasurer, did he conduct his militant campaign against the office-holding group.[55]

After these "treasury interests" had purchased his Chambersburg paper in the spring of 1817, McFarland immediately established the Shippensburg *Spirit of the Times*. In his first number on Independence Day of the same year, McFarland admitted that his career in Chambersburg had been largely devoted to supporting "the office holders and their *corrupt practices against the people*," but in this new enterprise he pledged himself

> to support the *people against office holders, right against might,* and endeavor to assist in breaking that *chain of no-ability* which is fast gathering strength through age and a long continuance in power . . .[56]

---

[54] John McFarland to William Duane, May 28, 1817, printed in the *Aurora*, June 2, 1817; *Aurora*, May 23, 1817.

[55] *American Telegraph*, August 20, 1817.

[56] *Aurora*, July 8, 1817.

By this time it was apparent that the Scotch-Irish editor was off on a stormy journalistic career. After a brief fling with the *Spirit of the Times* he moved to the Carlisle *Republican* and was quickly attacked by enemies far and near. A Uniontown editor censured McFarland for the dictatorial methods he employed in imposing his ideas on the public, particularly his epithets of opposition to Governor Findlay's administration.[57]

This distant criticism hardly disturbed McFarland, but the battles with his journalistic confreres in Carlisle doomed his *Republican* to a short life. He denounced the editors of his competitor journals as "sots and drunkards" who operated "more scurrilous and abusive" papers than existed in other towns. According to his own evaluation of the situation, McFarland believed that his anti-Findlay campaign was simply an expression of public opinion which his rivals wished to thwart with licentiousness and abuse of his private character. An appeal to the public produced only apathy and increased McFarland's indignation. He decided to give up in an ungrateful town where a premium was placed on the "greatest blackguard of a printer." [58]

In March 1824 after a nebulous career of more than two years, McFarland again ventured onto the journalistic scene with the publication of the Harrisburg *Commonwealth*. Not content in this role, he was easily persuaded two months later by Edward Patchell to establish the *Allegheny Democrat* at Pittsburgh and sing the praises of Jackson to the western counties. This offer came as a welcome opportunity to sever his relationship with a string of newspaper failures in four eastern towns. He was inspired, not only by the change in locale and the romance of the Jackson cause, but also by the prospects of an eager and sympathetic constituency in Pittsburgh. Patchell and his Jackson cohorts gave assistance to this new venture both in editorial material and in monetary contributions for the establishment of the new press.[59]

Although McFarland had physically removed himself from his eastern difficulties, they left their imprint on his personality. As a result of his turbulent career in the East, he developed a complex that made him the

[57] *The Genius of Liberty,* February 22, 1820.

[58] *Mercury,* October 24, 1821.

[59] Edward Patchell to Andrew Jackson, August 7, 1824. John Spencer Bassett (ed.), *Correspondence of Andrew Jackson* (Washington: Carnegie Institute, 1927), III, 264; *Allegheny Democrat,* August 3, 1824.

protector of all that was just and upright. He assumed a crusading spirit in his newspaper battles with his opponents who to him were personifications of evil. In the *Allegheny Democrat* he took the position that Jackson represented the "good life" and until his death three years later was his leading advocate in Pittsburgh.[60]

With this new enterprise, the Western Pennsylvania phase of increased attention to the national government was launched. Interest in state and local politics remained strong for many years, however, because the governor's appointive powers were not curbed until the new Pennsylvania constitution of 1838. Newspapers and their editors had not only contributed greatly to the local and state emphasis of this decade, but with the *Allegheny Democrat* as their guide at the end of the period, they were preparing to give leadership in the next era as well.

---

[60] James A. Kehl, "The *Allegheny Democrat* 1824-1836: The Biography of a Political Journal" (Unpublished Master's thesis, History Dept., University of Pittsburgh, 1947), p. 4.

VI

The Committee System

Republicanism—Mr. Adams said it meant any thing or nothing—and patent democrats are employed in experiments to prove it.[1]

EDITORS and their financial sponsors found the newspaper a most effective weapon for political control, but the committee system afforded men of more varied backgrounds a valuable instrument through which they also could exercise political influence. Manufacturers, doctors, lawyers, bankers, farmers, and many others recognized that membership on committees of correspondence or committees of vigilance provided a strategic advantage for making their political preferences known.

Many authorities have failed to make any distinction between these two types of committees. They have more or less disregarded the term "committee of vigilance" and have used "committee of correspondence" in a generic sense. More accurately, however, especially when applied to Western Pennsylvania in the decade 1815 to 1825, the latter term only denotes committees on the county and inter-county level. It was the intermediate political instrument between the state or nationwide convention on the one hand and the committees of vigilance, which functioned at the township level, on the other.

In the period under discussion the political machinery of the committee system was generally set in motion through a county meeting. Either this meeting was provided for in the minutes of an earlier one held by the same organization or was called by a group of individuals intent upon promoting popular support for a particular program. In either event the meeting selected a committee of correspondence which, in turn, was responsible for the formation of committees of vigilance. Occasionally, however, party or faction leaders quarreled among them-

---

[1] Toast proposed at an Independence Day celebration in Philadelphia. *Aurora.* July 7, 1817.

selves and instead of consulting the public, appointed their own committees to carry the fight to the people. Because of these several possibilities for implementing the committee system, parallel committees often
sprang up, even at a time when a great majority of the people in Western Pennsylvania nominally saluted the same political party.

The pattern of action that followed this beginning was a modification
of the original form of the committees of correspondence which date
back to the turbulent period prior to the American Revolution. Then
they were the forerunners of party organization instead of the pivotal
part of it as in the decade of good feeling. Because of poor transportation and communication in frontier sections both in colonial days and
even after the Revolution, the belief that people's rights were in
jeopardy there gained wide acceptance. Groups began putting their
collective thoughts and proposals in letter form and exchanged them
with each other.[2]

This belief by the people in rural areas that their rights were at
stake caused their committees of correspondence to develop an almost
crusading spirit. By the second decade of the 19th Century, they had
assumed a powerful political position as well. They organized and expanded with the idea of permanency and firmly believed that they were
keeping their fingers on the pulse of government and were retaining the
government of the people for the people.

COUNTY ORGANIZATION

When a public meeting at the county level was called, its function
varied, but was generally intended to serve one of three purposes: (1)
the organization of a party slate for a coming election, (2) the selection
of delegates to a convention, or (3) the consideration of a plan of action
to relieve an irritating situation. The working of the system in the
case of the first two major purposes was more or less standardized, but
the last had no set pattern. The initial public meeting, when called in
response to either the problem of political organization or the selection
of delegates, was most frequently county-wide in invitation although
boroughs and the city of Pittsburgh did, on occasion, hold their own
meetings.

---

[2] James M. Myers, "Committees of Correspondence," pp. 3, 57.

In the course of a county meeting the topic for discussion was presented to those assembled and a committee of correspondence and committees of vigilance for every township were selected. The primary function of the committee of correspondence, which almost invariably numbered between four and ten members, was to write an address to the people of the county and have it published in the local newspapers. This address set forth the problem discussed and the decisions reached at this preliminary meeting as to the means to be employed in seeking a solution.

The committees of vigilance, on the other hand, had the responsibility of setting the time and place of township meetings to consider the problem further. To these grass root gatherings the committees would verbally explain the nature of the previous county meeting just as the committee of correspondence had done in its address published in the local journals. The committees of vigilance, therefore, were limited almost completely to face-to-face contacts while much of the activity of the committee of correspondence constituted publishing addresses and the exchange of information with other counties or even states as was true of a Pittsburgh Jackson committee in 1824.

After a township discussed the problem presented by the committee of vigilance, it would select and instruct generally two conferees to a second or delegate county meeting. This county convention, as it was sometimes called, would then choose the party slate or appoint the county's delegates according to the demands of the situation. This second meeting would also select its own committees of correspondence and vigilance, which may or may not coincide with the earlier committees, to conduct the business at hand. In the case of well-organized political groups this was the point at which the committees of correspondence and vigilance for the ensuing year were chosen. Certain names appeared year after year on the committees—indicating the interest and influence of those individuals in local politics. Some never aspired to be campaigners in their own right; but others, such as James S. Craft, Algernon S. T. Mountain, and Robert J. Walker used this door as their entree to politics.

The committee of correspondence appointed at such a meeting was the county steering committee. In addresses and official releases to newspapers the committee would not only popularize the action of the delegate meeting, but would also give the public and private background of the candidates they endorsed and demonstrate their fitness for office when elections were involved. Committee members often found their position an excellent channel for calling public attention to themselves and their own ideas. In instances where two or more counties endorsed one candidate for the legislature or for Congress, the county's committee of correspondence or a fraction thereof always met with similar bodies from the other counties to make the final choice of candidate.

Inter-county politics experienced a particularly keen rivalry over the posts in the Pennsylvania Senate and in the United States Congress. As late as 1823 only Fayette and Westmoreland of the counties in Western Pennsylvania elected their own state senators without forced cooperation with at least one other county; in fact, as many as six counties had had to agree on a single senatorial candidate at that time.[3] The compromises and political trading necessary to arrange a ticket under these conditions prompted a lively competition among the counties and made committee members pivotal figures whether or not they desired to be.

In these contests between the committees of correspondence from the various counties each group believed that the candidate should be chosen from its constituency; this was true in the large and small counties alike. The former argued on the basis of their population while the latter, frequently isolated, insisted that no "outsider" understood their needs. The small counties, curiously enough, came off the victors on many occasions. In the battle for the assembly seat from Crawford and Venango Counties in 1824 there were three nominees, Thomas Atkinson and Timothy Alden of Crawford and Samuel Hays of Venango. The election returns in Crawford County gave Atkinson 632 votes, Alden 488, and Hays 188, but the over-all totals for the two counties credited Hays with 773 to Atkinson's 721 and Alden's 596. Thus the sparsely settled county, by splitting the vote of its larger neighbor, was able to send Hays to Harrisburg and attain a type of political dominance.[4]

The smaller counties possessed another effective weapon which the Indiana committee of correspondence employed against Westmoreland in 1822. Richard Coulter of Westmoreland had been nominated by the Independent Republicans of his county to represent the district of Westmoreland and Indiana in the Congress of the United States. In Indiana,

---

[3] Pennsylvania, *Senate Journal* XXXIV (1823-1824), 4f.
[4] *Crawford Messenger,* October 16, 1824.

the smaller of the two counties, the Independent Republicans selected Alexander W. Foster, also of Westmoreland, as their choice to go to the nation's capital. In an election under these conditions the Westmoreland Independent Republican vote was destined to be split between the two, but the Indiana faction endorsed only Foster. A Foster victory under these circumstances would have placed him under obligation to the Indiana group, and to ignore this position, as few politicians did, would have ended his congressional career with one term. Through this system of divide and conquer, Indiana was able to force its choice on the larger county. The Westmoreland committee saw the effectiveness of this political trick and induced Coulter to withdraw his name from candidacy.[5]

In these inter-county contests between committees of correspondence there was a wide acceptance of the idea that the nominations should be passed around. This argument was especially popular among the groups that had not recently elected an official at a given political level. In 1825 the Erie County committee of correspondence argued that it had a legitimate claim to a state senator in the district composed of Erie, Crawford, and Mercer Counties because the senators for the previous ten years had been elected from the other two.[6] No defense was made for their candidate for the nomination; Erie simply insisted that it was her turn.

The members of the Warren County committee of correspondence had earlier pressed a similar argument in regard to the assembly seat in the district their county shared with Mercer, Erie, Venango, and Crawford. They insisted that the party's assembly candidate must reside in Warren County because no one outside the county could have an accurate knowledge of its needs. Their localism refused to submit to the logic of the idea that a Warren resident was, by the same token, likely to be equally ignorant of the other four counties:

> Those of you acquainted with our [Warren County's] situation, know it to be nearly insular; that we are almost cut off from intercourse with our fellow citizens in other parts of the district, being surrounded on all sides by the state of New York, or by forests scarcely penetrable. Thus situated, our wants are little known, our views and wishes seldom consulted.[7]

The conclusion to this plea for local representation at Harrisburg

---

[5] *Greensburg Gazette,* July 5, and September 6, 1822.

[6] *Erie Gazette,* August 18, 1825.

[7] *Venango Herald* (Franklin) quoted in *Erie Gazette,* August 18, 1821.

revealed an even greater local consciousness. The committee declared that "there is no doubt but that there are members of the legislature who scarcely know that there is such a county in the commonwealth as Warren." A writer from Oil Creek Township in Crawford County agreed with his Warren neighbors. He recognized that no democratic principle was being violated by not passing the offices around, but nevertheless, he asked that such a procedure be followed:

We ask it not as a matter of *right*, but as an act of *courtesy* and *generosity*. The county has been organized more than 20 years. Almost every other township in the county, has been honored, during this period, with the selection of an office of some kind or other, from within its bounds, with the exception of Oil-Creek. What has she done, to be thus treated as a step child? [8]

Such inter-county and inter-township rivalries had contributed greatly to the decentralization of the tottering party machinery and brought politics more and more to the local and personal levels during this decade.

Although the bulk of the activity of a committee of correspondence was centered in the counties to which a given county was leagued in political offices, it was not confined solely to such limits. Committees of correspondence had a responsibility to inform other parts of the state and Union of their actions when an election or problem was of state or national significance. Likewise the committees were to collect relevant material from other areas for presentation to their home counties.[9]

A Greensburg meeting of September 25, 1819, appointed a committee of correspondence to write to members of the Democratic-Republican Party in the different parts of Pennsylvania to ascertain the best possible mode for making the nomination of the next governor of the state. Six days later, before the committee could conceivably have contacted others, it set forth in detail the convention method of nomination. The committee proposed: (1) that a convention of delegates meet somewhere other than the state capital to make the nomination, (2) that delegates be apportioned according to representation in the assembly, and (3) that delegates be paid by the district sending them. The only conclusion that may be reached from this presentation is that the committee, appointed to collect information on the subject and

---

[8] "Oil Creek," *Crawford Messenger,* October 7, 1824.

[9] *Address to the Democratic Republican Citizens of Crawford County* in 1823. Bound with the *Crawford Messenger* for the period 1818-1821 in the Crawford County Historical Society.

present its findings, usurped the right to speak for the other sections. In foisting its will on the public it revealed the tremendous power that committees of correspondence could assume in behalf of their preferred projects or candidates.

Other special committees of correspondence were sometimes created— to promote domestic manufactures, to discuss a state canal project, or to nominate a presidential candidate. For example, the regular county committees of correspondence called public meetings to select and instruct delegates to the Harrisburg Convention in 1824, but the convention, in turn, appointed its own committees of correspondence to promote its sentiments. Since the convention had pledged itself to the support of Andrew Jackson and John C. Calhoun for the presidency and the vice presidency, respectively, these newly-created committees stressed their candidacy. Aside from a state committee of five, including William Wilkins and Robert J. Walker of Allegheny County, to express the general sentiments of the convention, committees of three members each were chosen for every county to advertise and promote the choices of the convention. Men appointed to these committees in the western counties were frequently the same individuals who served on the committees of correspondence that had called the meeting that selected the delegates to the Harrisburg Convention, but this was not always true.[10]

The committee picture was further muddled when segments of the public would not accept the committees of correspondence appointed by the Harrisburg Convention as evidenced by the Greensburg Federal Republicans. They proceeded to appoint another committee, a parallel organization which was also devoted to the promotion of Jackson's candidacy.[11]

COMMITTEES OF VIGILANCE

A public meeting, county-wide in invitation, was the most acceptable means for setting party or faction machinery in motion. This included, not only the committees of correspondence which operated on the county level and outward, but also the committees of vigilance which worked inward. Although both types of committees functioned chiefly in con-

---

[10] *Crawford Messenger,* February 17, and March 30, 1824; *Harrisburg Chronicle,* March 11, 1824.

[11] *Greensburg Gazette,* January 23, and March 19, 1824.

nection with the elections, the committee of correspondence possessed a greater organizational importance. Being the pivotal agent of the political system, it was generally responsible for appointments to the committees of vigilance which were the broad political bases for disseminating ideas among the people of the townships.

After a public meeting or after a committee of correspondence sent forth a call for a delegate meeting to nominate candidates, the committees of vigilance arranged the time and place of the township or ward meetings to select these delegates. The size of these committees generally varied between four and eight members, but extraordinary circumstances at times modified the structure greatly. In 1821 when William Wilkins resigned his assembly seat to accept a judgeship and an immediate replacement was desired, a public meeting, endorsing James C. Gilleland as Wilkins' successor, selected a committee of vigilance for Allegheny County at large. This committee of an unprecedented 70 members was chosen without regard to township or ward lines and with one specific purpose, the promotion of Gilleland for the legislature. Within two weeks after this choice was made public, a special election was conducted and Gilleland was voted the assembly seat.[12]

Then in 1823 when an effort was made to arouse enthusiasm for Andrew Gregg in Pittsburgh, his committee of vigilance for the east ward numbered 69 and that of the west ward totaled 111. The two wards were also assisted by sub-committees of approximately 40 men each, known as the Young Men's committees.[13] Such extraordinary committees were a part of a psychological campaign. It was not intended that all committee members would "beat the drum" for Gregg, but that the names of prominent citizens ascribed to such committee lists would induce the voters to decide in favor of him. At times men's names were used to pad these committees without their knowledge, and on occasion men were placed on committees when they actually favored the opposition candidate. This was a particularly popular practice near an election when no widespread retraction would be possible before the balloting was completed. The activities of this Gregg group suggests such a political maneuver since the 250 committeemen were able to muster only 579 votes for Gregg in Pittsburgh.[14]

---

[12] *Mercury,* January 3, 17, 1821.

[13] *Ibid.,* September 30, 1823.

[14] *Pittsburgh Gazette,* October 24, 1823.

Township meetings called by the committees of vigilance generally followed the pattern of selecting two delegates to represent a given township at a county meeting of all such delegates. This meeting then assumed the task of forming an election slate, and the township committee became inactive until the election campaign when it was responsible for turning out the vote. Quite frequently in this interim the old committees of vigilance were replaced by the new ones for the coming year. Since the new committee of correspondence assumed its duties at this point, it was convenient for the township committees to change at the same time.

As an election approached, the committees of vigilance had the responsibility of distributing the genuine tickets of the party and of preventing "spurious tickets" from being introduced.[15] The second part of this assignment was especially important to the Democratic-Republicans because the Federalists and Independent Republicans often substituted one or two names into a Democratic-Republican ticket with the hope of having several of their candidates ride into office on Democratic-Republican coat-tails. Generally the committees of vigilance performed their task satisfactorily, but a few elections left the public wondering about the political legitimacy of their elected officials.

Occasionally the township meetings called by the committees of vigilance were subjected to criticism because a handful of politicians or several families were always able to have their representatives selected as delegates to the county meetings where the party's candidates were chosen. Frequently the delegate came out a candidate. Since the same cliques kept control in the townships through the years, they were able to bargain and trade off the offices with those of other districts. The more successful were able to play this game on the inter-county and state levels as well, but many agreed with the analysis set forth by a Crawford County citizen:

> At the township meetings we find that our *knowing ones,* by some means or another, almost always get themselves appointed conferees, with the view of carrying a point in their own favour at the general meeting. So that, in general, almost every conferee comes forward with an *axe of his own to grind;* and by *tickling each other's elbows,* in the *axe-grinding way,* it not unfrequently happens that nearly the whole of the candidates are *disinterestedly* selected from their own body, without regard to character or qualification,

---

[15] *Allegheny Democrat,* October 26, 1824; *Crawford Messenger,* June 1, 1816; *Greensburg Gazette,* February 22, 1817.

leaving the public no other share in the business, than that of *"turning the grindstone."* [16]

This general picture was substantiated by the *Washington Examiner* which charged that the family connections of John Reed had established "a court of Inquisition" in Cecil Township of that county. Reed, who served in the state assembly from 1817 to 1822, was campaigning for Findlay's re-election as governor in 1820; and, with his family's help, questioned all those who came to the meeting called by the township's committee of vigilance for the purpose of endorsing a gubernatorial candidate.

The *Examiner* charged that at the township meeting the Reed group refused to receive the vote of any man who attended an earlier Hiester gathering in Washington or who was known to have opposed Findlay in any other manner. The editor felt that this kind of democracy may suit "the *family compact* in Cecil township," but believed that he was obligated to expose it to the public. In the same campaign a man in nearby Canton Township was denied the right to vote for delegates to the county meeting because he opposed the Findlay conferees.[17]

Both actions were based on the theory that all opponents of Findlay did not belong to the true Republican Party, but such charges only encouraged the development of rival committees of vigilance and brought a plea from impartial observers for reform. They suggested that the committees of vigilance see to it that no man who was an avowed candidate be appointed as a delegate to the county meetings and that those appointed give assurances that they would not consent to have their names placed in nomination for any office at the ensuing election. They also urged that the committees of vigilance and the public generally put forth a greater effort to increase the participation in the township or ward meetings. This limited group of reformers was especially desirous of having no repetition of such a fiasco as that experienced in Pittsburgh's east ward in 1818. Only five citizens appeared at the meeting, two who favored Henry Baldwin for Congress and three who endorsed Samuel Douglas. The three, being a majority, appointed two of themselves to represent the whole east ward in the county delegate meeting.[18]

---

[16] "J. G.," *Crawford Messenger,* June 29, 1816.

[17] *Examiner,* September 18, 1820.

[18] *Mercury,* September 25, 1818.

Significant reforms in the committee system, however, failed to gain acceptance. Local problems remained paramount, and local politics continued as the obedient servant of the interested few until after 1823 when state and national projects became popular again. This shift submerged personal politics greatly and instigated a semblance of party organization and discipline.

ELECTION TICKETS

The principal results of the committees of correspondence and the committees of vigilance in the decade 1815 to 1825 are recorded in the successes and failures of the many election tickets proposed during that period. For an evaluation on the basis of these election tickets Western Pennsylvania suggests two distinct patterns, counties where the regular Democratic-Republican slate was literally unopposed and counties where a keen political rivalry sprang up.

The older and more densely settled counties of Allegheny, Washington, and Westmoreland experienced the greatest amount of political badgering and the largest number of conflicting committees.[19] Here the contending forces were sharply divided. The urban business class, known on election slates as the Independent or Federal Republican ticket, was a consistent foe of the more rural and agrarian Democratic-Republican Delegate ticket. Although these were the most frequently used titles for the opposing tickets and parties, they had many substitutes. In Westmoreland County alone the banners of the rivals changed no less than five times in five years. In 1811 the Democratic-Republicans battled the Constitutional Republicans, but in 1812 the Peace, Commerce & Union ticket replaced the latter. The following year both names changed with the Federal or "Don't Give up the Ship" slate attacking the Embargo or "Don't Give up the 'Loaves and Fishes'" ticket. The Farmers and Mechanics ticket did battle with the regular Democratic Republican ballot in 1814, but the next year found the term Federal Republican denominating the opposition to the regular ticket.[20] Several more years passed, however, before the name Independent Republican was a working part of Westmoreland County's political terminology, but the principles for which it stood were well established by 1815.

---

[19] Available evidence suggests that Beaver, Butler, and Fayette Counties also belonged to this group, but such a claim cannot be documented.

[20] *Greensburg Gazette,* September 12, 1811; September 17, 1812; October 9, 1813; October 8, 1814; and September 16, 1815.

In the neighboring county of Allegheny the Delegate ticket repeatedly exhibited more strength at the polls than that of the Independent Republicans. In order to challenge this superior force successfully, the Independents resorted to a shifting array of political maneuvers which defy organization and permit only description. Rather than suffer a stinging defeat in the contests for all offices and demoralize their constituency, the Independent Republican committee of correspondence was content to nominate only partial tickets. If the faction had only three candidates that would run well, its ticket was limited to those three. On occasion, however, such partial tickets were supplemented with the names of Delegate nominees who were regarded as certain front-line runners on election day.

These candidates, involuntarily held in common with the Delegate slate, served the two-fold purpose of affording the Independents the psychological advantage of a partial triumph at the polls and of convincing the general public that the breach between the two factions was not great. Realizing that advantage in political confusion lies with the underdog, these Independent or Federal Republicans exerted their best skills to perplex the voters. In 1817 they proposed first the Independent Republican ticket and followed that with the Independent Delegate ticket which differed very little. Through withdrawals and additions during the final weeks before the election, these two tickets resolved all their candidate differences except the insignificant ones of commissioner and auditor.[21] The first of these tickets was designed to appeal to the voters opposed to the regular Delegate ticket while the second was expected to be confused with the regular Delegate ticket and suggest to the voters that they were voting for the candidates of the other faction.

These confusion tactics were not successful, but several years later the same group again experimented with overlapping tickets to achieve a partial victory. The main core of the Federal Republicans presented the Citizens' ticket which on the Congressional level endorsed common candidates with a special group of Independent Republicans behind Walter Forward and James Allison. The Citizens' ticket also shared candidates for the Pennsylvania legislature with the Delegate ticket. Moses Sullivan of Butler County and James Stevenson of Allegheny were the common choices. The other two assembly posts on the Delegate

---

[21] *Mercury,* September 12, and October 3, 1817.

ticket were allotted to men from Allegheny County while the opposition selected John Gilmore of Butler as one of its nominees.[22]

The endorsement of Gilmore was a new departure in Federal Republican maneuvering, but that of Sullivan had become standard practice by 1822. The Independents of Allegheny County had frequently
made no contest of the choice of assemblyman from Butler County
which shared the same legislative district. To accept nominees for two
of the four positions from the smaller county was an innovation, but
one which spelled partial victory for the Citizens' ticket since Gilmore,
Sullivan, and Stevenson of their ticket were elected.

The Democratic-Republican Party in Washington County, on the
other hand, was not rent by factional strife as early as either Allegheny
or Westmoreland. Not until 1819 did the regular Delegate slate face
serious opposition which, according to Sample of *The Reporter,* came
from a ticket drawn up by the Washington Club. Following the pattern in the other counties, this ticket sponsored two candidates for the
four legislative posts in common with the Delegate ballot, and Sample
charged that the ticket was organized against John Reed and Joseph
Lawrence, the other two men on the Delegate slate. They were both
running for re-election while the Club ticket objected on the basis of
their votes in the preceding session of the legislature where they had
endorsed a measure that compelled all banks to pay specie on demand.
The Club was soundly trounced at the polls and presented no ticket
the following year.[23]

Opposition to the regular Delegate group was, nevertheless, powerful
enough to have the county committee of correspondence submit twice
as many candidates as there were assembly posts. Apparently this type
of ticket also proved a failure to the machinations of the Club because
in 1821 two competing tickets appeared with the Delegate group again
triumphant. On this occasion the Club had difficulty, deliberately or
otherwise, in forming a ticket. Without consulting the men involved,
the Club endorsed James Keys and Joseph Barr, members of the Delegate faction for two of the four assembly seats. This ticket was announced less than two weeks before the election to give the men little
time to declare their position. Keys publicly declined the nomination,
but Barr did not learn that his name was being used until it was too

---

[22] *Mercury,* October 2, 1822.
[23] *Reporter,* September 27, and October 4, 11, 18, 1819.

late to retract it. As a replacement for Keys the Club added Dickerson Roberts, another member of the opposition, on the eve of the election. Like the others, this nomination was without the consent of the nominee, but the effort failed to break the power of the regularly nominated Delegate ticket. Although these three "forced" candidates received a total of 1,875 votes, the leading Club candidate, Parker Campbell, was not able to draw within 500 votes of the lowest ranking Delegate nominee.[24]

Success or failure for a candidate at the polls was conditioned, not only by the strength and vigor of the committees of correspondence that endorsed him, but also by many other factors such as personality and strategic residence which will be discussed in detail in the next chapter. Here the purpose is only to show the limitations of the committees and their tickets.

The Democratic-Republican committee of correspondence in Westmoreland County was successful in electing its candidate, Dr. David Marchand, to Congress in 1816, but the Federal Republicans countered with a clean sweep of the three assembly seats. This represented an about-face on the part of the voters because in 1815 the regular Republican slate had elected all three assemblymen.[25] They returned to this general assembly pattern in 1818 and 1819 with Eli Counter demonstrating his personal popularity by being the lone Federal Republican elected.[26]

In 1820 the "magic" name of Coulter again appeared when Richard Coulter was sent to the lower house in Harrisburg. This election, which again gave two assembly seats to the Delegate ticket, produced another curious shift, making the lines of political organization almost intangible. For Congress the orthodox faction sponsored George Plumer, who endorsed William Findlay for re-election as governor. The opposition nominated Alexander W. Foster for the congressional post, but was inclined toward Joseph Hiester for the governorship. In a close vote Foster defeated Plumer in Westmoreland County, but Hiester and two of the three assembly candidates on the Independent Republican ticket went down in defeat on the same day.[27]

---

[24] *Reporter,* October 8, 15, 1821.

[25] *Greensburg Gazette,* October 14, 1815; October 12, 1816.

[26] *Ibid.,* October 17, 1818.

[27] *Ibid.,* August 25, and October 13, 1820.

As these rival tickets and committees of correspondence developed within the ranks of the Democratic-Republican Party, repeated efforts were made to heal the party wounds. After a bitter campaign had been waged in Allegheny County in 1816 and before the election results of that year were fully known, a call went out for a November meeting to affect an immediate union of all the party's factions on "principles honorable to all" to insure union and success in future elections against the Federalist Party.[28] The group could apparently build no lasting foundation. Although several plans of action were adopted on local levels, they never progressed from that point. The local proposals that gained the widest acceptance were the cooperative or "mongrel" ticket and the double ticket, but the actual names given to such political maneuvers varied from county to county and with opposition or endorsement of a given slate.

The cooperative ticket, which proposed to take part of the candidates from the ticket endorsed by one of the committees of correspondence and the remainder from the other, was generally regarded as a plot by the Federalists and insurgent Republicans to gain a foothold in the government offices. This fear was not without justification since the methods of the "mongrel" ticket reformers were the same as those of the Federal Republicans who endorsed only partial tickets of their own and reenforced them with nominees from the Delegate ticket. In spite of this similarity of method these two groups were striving for entirely different objectives. The sponsors of the cooperative ticket, acting in the name of unity, sought to limit the political animosity that was necessarily engendered by the existence of rival committees of correspondence and competing election tickets. They wished to correct a system that was injurious to the personal character of respected Republican citizens and destructive to party discipline while the Independent Republicans were attempting to break down the whole Delegate system.[29]

Further opposition to this type of union ticket was registered by the citizens of Mifflin Township in Allegheny County. They insisted that the cooperative ticket violated the basic principle of democracy which entitles the people to make a choice on election day. In a public meeting the township organized its own committee of correspondence which

---

[28] *Commonwealth,* October 15, 1816.
[29] *Mercury,* August 15, 22, 1821.

published a newspaper address to their fellow citizens throughout the
county. In denouncing the sponsors of the cooperative type ticket, the
committee declared:

> They have not only thought proper to assume the right of nominating candi-
> dates for our support at the ensuing election, but also to endeavor to deprive
> the people of the privilege of making a choice on the day of election, by
> discontinuing the publication of the two tickets which had been previously
> formed.[30]

The Mifflin group, therefore, wished to retain the concept of rival
Republican candidates, but at the same time was anxious to destroy
competing committees of correspondence. Their meeting was held after
Henry Baldwin and Walter Lowrie had been nominated for Congress
by separate sets of delegates which created their own committees of
correspondence. The Mifflinites believed that the answer to political
harmony was not to be found in the cooperative ticket, but in the double
ticket. Under this proposal all the candidates endorsed by the competing
committees would be listed and the committees would amalgamate.[31]

This plan brought, not only an increased emphasis on personalities,
but also a complete breakdown in party organization. This was especially
true in areas where the number of nominees was not limited to double
the number of offices at stake; the double ticket simply opened the floodgates. In 1821 a committee of correspondence in Washington County
proposed some 20 individuals for the four assembly seats; under such
circumstances political victory was almost totally dependent upon
exogenous, rather than party, factors.[32]

The principle of the double ticket in the densely settled counties was
similar to the political pattern in the counties where the Democratic-
Republican slate faced little opposition. These counties, largely in
Northwestern Pennsylvania, were more area-conscious than problem- or
faction-conscious. In such areas people were more likely to vote for a
candidate on the basis of his home county than any other qualification
or requirement. Only one committee of correspondence generally existed,
and it listed all the congressional and legislative candidates, along with
the counties in which they resided, but without any reference to their
party or faction preferences.[33]

[30] *Pittsburgh Gazette,* September 20, 1816.

[31] *Ibid.,* September 20, 1816; *Commonwealth,* September 24, 1816; *Mercury,*
September 14, 1816.

[32] *Examiner,* October 8, 1821.

[33] *Erie Gazette,* August 12, 1820; August 11, 1821; October 3, 1822.

The editor of the *Erie Gazette* favored Patrick Farrelly of Crawford County over Robert Moore of Beaver County for Congress and
defended his choice by pointing out that Moore had earlier voted for
appropriations to defray the maintenance costs of the "iniquitous" National Road. The editor believed that the road had been "injudiciously
located so as to omit Pittsburgh" and thereby deny Western Pennsylvania its maximum benefit from the commerce that the road undoubtedly
attracted. He insisted that if Moore would appropriate money for the
upkeep of such a road, he would not act for Erie's best local interest
because a man that had no greater concern for his section of the state
than that would be willing to see the naval station at Erie transferred
to another point on the lake in *Ohio*.

> At a time when every portion of the union, struggling with unprecedented
> embarrassments, complains of local wants, and makes claim for separate re-
> lief, we cannot without grossly neglecting ourselves commit the management
> of our affairs to a person whose residence excites in him rival interests; who
> lives on the Ohio, at the extremity of the district.[34]

This area-consciousness also played a major role in the political
maneuvering of the individual candidates in the sparsely settled counties. In 1821 James Weston withdrew from the assembly race in the
legislative district which Erie shared with four other counties. He explained that with other Erie candidates in the field the county's vote
would be so scattered that it was destined to end up without any
representation.[35] By making this magnanimous withdrawal Weston believed that he had not only won the gratitude of his county's constituency, but had also placed himself in a strategic position to gain Erie
County's support the following year. In the campaign of 1822 he reminded the public of his sacrifice for the sake of Erie's representation
and was rewarded with an assembly seat.[36]

The influence of this area-consciousness, along with the scattered
enthusiasm for cooperative and double tickets, limited greatly the
organizational and disciplinary power of the committees of correspond-

---

[34] *Erie Gazette*, October 7, 1820.

[35] James Weston to the Electors of the District composed of Mercer, Erie, Crawford, Venango, and Warren Counties, September 18, 1821, printed in the *Erie
Gazette*, September 22, 1821.

[36] James Weston to the Free and Independent Electors of Erie and **Warren**
Counties, August 13, 1822, printed in the *Erie Gazette*, August 13, 1822;
Pennsylvania, *House Journal* (1822-1823), p. 5.

ence. The fluid line that separated the contending forces in Western Pennsylvania in the decade 1815 to 1825 made the movement of politicians from one camp to the other a frequent practice, and in time the picture of political alignments became so blurred that distinction was impossible. John Wilson of Allegheny County demonstrated this complete breakdown of party discipline and the incapacity of the committee of correspondence to cope with the problem. He was elected to the assembly on the Delegate ticket in 1817 and duplicated the feat on the Independent ticket the following year.[37] While some committees of correspondence strove valiantly to overcome and prevent such paradoxes, others believed that there was political capital to be gained by increasing the confusion.

---

[37] Pennsylvania, *House Journal* (1817-1818), p. 4; (1818-1819), p. 4; *Mercury,* July 17, 1818.

VII

Social and Political Alignments

*Party Spirit—A necessary evil—but may it never interrupt
the course of private friendships.*[1]

JUST as every tide shifts the sands on the seashore, every issue and
nearly every election produced new political alignments in the early
part of the 19th Century. The failure of the committee of correspondence system to develop organization and discipline rendered
meaningless the use of the term "political party," which implies a degree
of permanence. The people of Western Pennsylvania vigorously talked
the language of party, but in reality followed personal preferences and
often in the name of party harmony twisted the muddy political picture
to achieve their own ambitions.

Fortescue Cuming, a widely traveled and intelligent English tourist,
who arrived in Pittsburgh free of local prejudices, commented that
"politicks, throughout the whole of this country, seems to be the most
irritable subject which can be discussed." He observed that the contending forces were not satisfied with vilifying each other on the floor of
the legislature, but delighted in introducing the subject at the bars of
justice and in the pulpits of the churches. Cuming believed that men,
who might otherwise have been on friendly terms with each other, were
avowed enemies because of political differences. He accused even the
women of carrying the spirit of politics into their coteries, so far as to
exclude every female whose husband was of a different political opinion.
To this traveler politics was argued "with more warmth" and was
"productive of more rancour and violence in Pittsburgh than perhaps
any other part of America." [2]

---

[1] Toast proposed at a St. Patrick's Day celebration of the Erin Benevolent
Society of Pittsburgh. *Mercury,* March 25, 1824.

[2] Fortescue Cuming, *Sketches of a Tour to the Western Country through the
States of Ohio and Kentucky,* Vol. IV of *Early Western Travels 1748-1846,*
ed. Reubon G. Thwaites (32 vols.; Cleveland: The Arthur H. Clark Co.,
1904-1907), pp. 72, 85.

Undoubtedly Cuming's description was an exaggeration, but to a visitor whose acquaintance with Western Pennsylvania was limited to five months, it represented an accurate appraisal. People talked as though their political opponents were capable of every crime, but their actions over an extended period, as a parable in *The Gleaner* pointed out, were entirely different:

"Ruined, Ruined," cried my grandfather as he raised his spectacles from his nose to his forehead, and dropped the True American upon his knees: "we are an undone people. . . . A Virginia nabob for President!—A most unnatural war!—Heaven knows it could never prosper!—Take Canada—take a fiddle-stick's end. And then our taxes are doubled—commerce all destroyed—religion and liberty kicked out of doors—I'll tell you, . . . we are a ruined people. Democracy is a bane of freedom—I wouldn't trust a democrat with a field of millstones uncounted." "Poh, poh" said my aunt Hannah, "You are in a passion, father—if a democrat nei'bor wanted any thing you would let him have it." "Have it" cried the old gentleman, "Yes I'd let him have it if it was a halter."

"Grandfather," said my brother Israel, coming in at that moment, "will you lend Mr. Willard your horse to go to [the] mill?" "Why child" said my grand-father, softening his voice, "I was going to town—but he would not ask for him if he didn't want him; yes, he may take him." "I thought," said my aunt Hannah, "you wouldn't trust a democrat, and yet Mr. Willard is the hottest in the neighborhood." "Well, well," said the old gentleman, "he's wrong in his politics—plaguy wrong; but he's a good neighbor, and I believe honest in his error; he's welcome to him."

I couldn't held smiling at my grandfather's political passion, contrasted with his social conduct to his opponents. I turned and went to the Post Office.[3]

This parable moved immediately into a second when the grandson arrived at the post office where he overheard a conversation. One man declared that there was not an honest man in the Federalist Party and assailed the Federalists as a set of rascals, villains, liars, and cheats. In the midst of this tirade he suffered a heart attack which appeared fatal, but his last request was that a Federalist acquaintance settle his estate and act as guardian to his children. The illogical pattern of these two examples was not unique, but commonplace. Political epithets and re-criminations were bandied about everywhere, but generally they were "full of sound and fury-signifying nothing." [4] When there was a genuine sincerity to this language, it was basically the result of personal, rather than political, animosities.

---

[3] *The Gleaner* quoted in the *Pittsburgh Gazette*, May 20, 1815.
[4] *Ibid.*

THE WASHINGTON CLUB

As a result of these political attitudes there were very few continuing alignments in Western Pennsylvania during this decade of good feeling. The political sermons of both the politicians and the general citizenry were always long and spirited, but without text. A notable exception to this pattern of confusion, known as "The Club," developed in the borough of Washington. This organization was created during the political campaign of 1816 and retained its identity for at least ten years.

In the election of that year the Baird brothers, Thomas and George, were candidates for Congress and the state senate, respectively. Both failed to realize their ambitions and placed the responsibility for their defeats on William Sample, the editor of *The Reporter,* because he refused to print their campaign literature which had been prepared by David Acheson. Sample's stubborn refusal was based on the premise that all the candidates should have an equal opportunity in the campaign, and he argued that if his paper published the Bairds' literature, he would be violating this principle.

Superficially at least, Sample's motive seemed both naive and altruistic, but such an attitude was only a part of his total thought process. This apparent unselfishness was, in part, the result of a complex which from time to time has dominated the thinking of editors, lawyers, and other professionals. Realizing that they are entrusted with the defense and protection of particular democratic principles with which their professions are concerned, they have a tendency to exaggerate and even exalt their positions.

Casting himself in the role of protector of freedom of the press and defender of an unbiased political campaign, Sample easily convinced himself that he should not print the literature of the Bairds and their friends who, unfortunately according to him, had been more than occasional officeholders in the early years of the 19th Century.

Although he refused this election material, Sample frequently found editorial space to abuse the character of the Bairds and hasten an irreparable breach with the faction of the party they controlled. Determined upon revenge, the Baird brothers united with Acheson for the special purpose of supplanting *The Reporter* as the local party journal. From that time in 1816 the Washington Club was a reality. The three signed an agreement "binding themselves to bear equal proportions of the expense of purchasing a press, type and editor." [5]

Approximately six months later they moved to fulfill this covenant and established the *Examiner*. Its editor, John Grayson, vigorously denied that his paper was a tool of the Club, but his position was difficult to sustain. Grayson declared that he had been working on a Baltimore newspaper when a friend in Philadelphia advised him that the Republican Party in Washington County was in need of a new editor. Since he had a desire to move westward, Grayson made contact with a "phantom" friend in Washington to whom he outlined his political ideas and editorial policies. Agreement between the two was reached. Grayson later admitted that he asked his unnamed correspondent to assist him in writing the prospectus because he knew nothing of local affairs in Washington.[6] Such a confession linked Grayson unalterably with a local individual or group, even before he published a single issue.

After the details for the prospectus had been agreed upon, Grayson went from Baltimore to Philadelphia to purchase the necessary printing materials, and by coincidence George Baird was there at the time. The parallel was continued when almost simultaneously both appeared in Washington, and within three weeks after Grayson's arrival the first number of the *Examiner* was printed on May 28, 1817, with a subscription list of 400.[7]

For newspapers of that day in areas with such a limited population as Washington, this was an excellent initial circulation and suggests that the groundwork had been laid in advance of the editor's personal appearance. The evidence indicates that he was simply the manager of the *Examiner* for the group designated as the Washington Club which supplied the editorial ideas and the financial backing.

Grayson never admitted that there was any political bond between himself and the Club; in fact, he denied the very existence of the Club. Before he retired from the *Examiner* in 1840, however, he unquestionably attained the independence that he had always professed. The attainment of this goal came only with the gradual disintegration of

---

[5] *Reporter*, September 21, 1818.

[6] *Examiner*, September 7, 1818.

[7] Earle R. Forrest, *History of Washington County, Pennsylvania* (Chicago: J. S. Clarke Publishing Co., 1926) I, 801.

the Club and represented a great departure from the editor's position in 1817.

In those first years of his Washington career Grayson was forced to spend much time and literary effort in refuting, not only the charge that he was the "captive" editor of the Bairds, but also the accusation that he was a Federalist. Both were difficult tasks, the first because it was untrue and the second because of the confusion in party names and principles during this period. His unwavering denials served only to muddle the political picture further, especially since the Club members came from both Federalist and Republican backgrounds.

Undeniably the Baird family, which formed the rallying point of the Club, was originally Democratic-Republican in its political thinking. The family had first come to prominence in Washington County through the military service of Absalom Baird, a noted army surgeon of the Revolutionary War. In 1793 he was appointed brigade inspector of the militia, a post he retained until his death in 1805. Through militia celebrations of Independence Day and military assemblages for other purposes, his popularity grew and gradually assumed a political cast. He represented Washington County in the state assembly in 1798 and was appointed sheriff the following year. Absalom's four sons, John, George, Thomas, and William, elaborated greatly on this inauspicious beginning and began to weave a sturdy political fabric, particularly in the borough of Washington. John was clerk to the county commissioners for five years (1814-1819) while George, who conducted a merchandising store on Main Street, was appointed sheriff in 1811 and was elected in 1816 to fill a vacancy in the state assembly caused by the death of General James Stevenson. William, the youngest of the brothers, followed the legal profession, but likewise enjoyed the lure of politics. He was appointed deputy attorney-general by the governor in 1819 and served for five years.[8]

Thomas H. Baird, the reputed head of the Club, had a more extensive public career than his brothers. After studying law with Joseph Pentecost and gaining admittance to the Washington County bar in 1808, he married Nancy McCullough, the niece of the Acheson brothers, thereby establishing a bond with another important Club family. He

---

[8] Boyd Crumrine (ed.), *History of Washington County, Pennsylvania, with Biographical Sketches of Many of Its Pioneers and Prominent Men* (Philadelphia: L. H. Evarts & Co., 1922), pp. 468-471, 541f.; Pennsylvania, *House Journal* (1815-1816), pp. 322, 340.

served not only as president of the board of directors of the Bank of Washington and as a director of the Washington Steam Mill and Manufacturing Company, along with Thomas Acheson and others, but was also a prominent supporter of internal improvement projects. He solicited subscriptions for the Washington and Williamsport Turnpike Road Company and for the Monongahela Navigation Company. While in partnership with Parker Campbell and Thomas McGiffin, he received a contract, which was sublet, in part, to a number of small contractors, to build the greater part of the National Road from two miles west of Brownsville to the Virginia line.

The contacts afforded by these business enterprises, plus the support that the Club journal had given William Findlay in his successful campaign for the governorship in 1817, brought Thomas Baird a commission the following year as president judge of the Common Pleas Court of Pennsylvania in the newly-created Fourteenth District. The new district, composed of Washington, Greene, Fayette, and Somerset Counties, was modified in 1824 when Somerset was detached. Baird remained as president judge for almost 20 years and commanded the respect of many for his integrity and sincerity. He was noticeably conscious of the dignity due his office, and if others did not show him the proper courtesy, he became impulsive and irascible. When he disbarred lawyers guilty of contempt of court, he was accused of judicial tyranny, but an attempt to have impeachment proceedings brought against him before the Pennsylvania legislature did not succeed.[9]

In the early days of the Club's development the political fortunes of this family seemed most closely linked with the Achesons. There were not only marital and business bonds, but also a direct political kinship since David Acheson, the youngest of four brothers, who had come from Scotland to Western Pennsylvania, assisted George and Thomas Baird in their aforementioned campaigns of 1816.

David Acheson also had a political career in his own right. On three occasions between 1795 and 1804 he had represented Washington County in the Pennsylvania legislature and added further to his political stature by urging that the National Road pass through the borough of Washington. His correspondence with Albert Gallatin on the subject

---

[9] Crumrine, *Washington County,* pp. 244-245, 377, 383, 386, 542, 554; *Commemorative Biographical Record of Washington County, Pennsylvania* . . . (Chicago: J. H. Beers & Co., 1893), p. 153.

was turned over to Thomas Jefferson at a time when the President was not favorably disposed even to a survey of a possible route through the borough. Acheson's arguments prompted Jefferson's reconsideration and won for the young merchant the gratitude and respect of the whole county. Success in persuading people to his point of view was one of Acheson's attributes. He had demonstrated this power in the 1790's when he transported mercantile cargoes from Pittsburgh to New Orleans. He apparently experienced none of the difficulty that marked the efforts of many other merchants to gain the permission of the Spanish authorities to carry their merchandise to the great depot for the Mississippi and Ohio Valleys on the Gulf of Mexico.[10] This power of persuasion made David Acheson a valuable asset to the Club and fortified its position against the Delegate Republicans.

The high command of the Washington Club, which was the county's version of the Independent Republican movement elsewhere, completed its membership when Thomas Morgan joined the group a few years later. Morgan, like the Baird brothers and David Acheson, was the descendant of a well-established and respected Washington family. Being the son of Colonel George Morgan, the famed Revolutionary Indian agent and acquaintance of Aaron Burr, he was called to Richmond to testify in the treason trial of Burr who had been a visitor in his father's home at Morganza on Chartiers Creek near Canonsburg.

While on this mission Morgan met Catherine Duane, the daughter of the Philadelphia publisher Colonel William Duane, and their friendship blossomed into marriage. At the age of 30 Morgan, a neophyte lawyer, was elected to the state assembly in 1814 and then re-elected the following year. He reached for the next rung on the political ladder in 1816 when he was a candidate for the upper house in the district shared by Washington and Greene Counties. George Baird afforded the local opposition while Isaac Weaver was the choice of Greene County. The Washington County Delegate Republicans favored Morgan and with their control of the press successfully stifled Baird's campaign, demonstrating to his supporters the need for such an organization as the Club. Although *The Reporter* urged the election of Morgan, it published an article from a Greene County citizen who deplored the endorsement of Morgan over Weaver. The article dubbed *The Reporter's* own candidate as a former Federalist in the "reign of terror"

---

[10] Crumrine, *Washington County,* pp. 376, 479-480.

under President John Adams and as a western agent for the policies of his father-in-law.[11] Meanwhile, Editor Sample denied the Bairds any editorial space. This action made the breach between the Washington factions of Republicans catastrophic. Weaver's principal support came from his home county, and the split in Washington assured him the senate seat.

In 1817 Morgan parted company with the Delegate Republicans. His endorsement of Joseph Hiester for the governorship caused Sample to charge that Morgan was the mere "journeyman lier" of the Carlisle junto and of William Duane in the Western Country.[12] At that time the Club also favored Findlay to succeed Simon Snyder in the governor's mansion, and Morgan was temporarily left without a place to hang his political hat. Within two years, however, the Club reversed its stand on Findlay who had won the executive post, but nevertheless delayed this shift long enough to have Thomas H. Baird, "the president of the royal family," appointed president judge of a district court by the very governor he was about to condemn.[13]

Just as Findlay rewarded Baird for the assistance that the Club's *Examiner* had given him in the campaign of 1817, he also rewarded *The Reporter* for its support by appointing Sample a prothonotary. The *Examiner's* subsequent denunciation of Findlay in 1819 brought Morgan into the Club which thereafter battled successfully to place Hiester in the executive chair at Harrisburg in 1820.

The complete control of these leaders over the Club was demonstrated in this campaign. A public meeting of "upwards of two hundred" citizens of the county resolved to support Hiester and selected a committee to express more fully the nomination decision. The committee was composed of David Acheson, George Baird, and Thomas Morgan, no more, no less.[14] Probably only the judicial duties of Thomas Baird can account for his absence.

For these Club leaders revenge was sweet. Hiester replaced Sample with Morgan in the Washington County prothonotary's office, but the Club's opposition to Findlay had brought new charges of an alliance with John Binns and the "Philadelphia Hub." [15] The Delegate Re-

---

[11] Crumrine, *Washington County*, p. 867f.; *Reporter,* October 7, 1816.

[12] *Reporter,* July 14, 1817.

[13] *Ibid.,* September 7, 1818.

[14] *Mercury,* October 4, 1820.

[15] *Ibid.,* July 9, 1819.

publicans thus very skillfully identified the Club with both the Binns and the Duane factions in Pennsylvania's eastern metropolis.

Certainly this association was, in part, a manifestation of the urban merchant and manufacturing society in the West. Such pursuits were anathema to the Delegate Republican faction which was composed primarily of self-reliant farmers and tradesmen who held in contempt all those who dealt in such services. These Delegate Republicans believed that the lawyer, the easterner, the merchant, and the manufacturer desired only to exploit them and that the Club was "an artful, cunning set of [such] nabobs apeing at nobility" and prepossessed with the idea that they were born to office. This opposition further denounced the Club leaders as a set of jugglers, neither Whig nor Tory, Federalist nor Democrat, who were supporters of the Delegate position when convenient and enemies when it did not answer the purpose.[16]

> They are in politics, enemies to order and principles; and desperately ambitious—Filled with covetousness and malicious envy; proud inventors of foolish and evil things. Disobedient to republican rules—covenant breakers; implacable and unmerciful.[17]

Aside from presenting the challenge of urban culture to the farming mass of Delegate Republicans, the Club was depicted as a small group of "federal lawyers and disappointed office-seekers" who sought only to achieve personal and family advancement. The "family press," as the *Examiner* was glibly called by its opponents, was definitely established as the result of personality clashes between the editor of *The Reporter* and those who became the Club leaders. In his first issues Editor Grayson attacked the "shallow brain and malignant heart" that ridiculed gentlemen who held no public office and who sought none. Quite clearly this statement had reference to the Bairds' brush with William Sample, but Grayson cloaked its defense of the Bairds and their political family with a resolve to maintain the unity and strength of the Republican Party and with a denial that he was in the employ of the "hated Bairds."[18]

The personal element of the Club quickly came to the foreground, however, when George and Thomas Baird and David Acheson all entered libel suits against Sample. In the first case involving Thomas Baird and the opposition editor, five referees awarded the plaintiff for

---

[16] *Reporter*, March 31, 1817; September 20, 1819.
[17] *Ibid.*, December 16, 1817.
[18] *Ibid.*, August 31, 1818; *Examiner*, June 18, 1817; *Mercury*, June 13, 1817.

damages to his character, $500.00 and thereafter the *Examiner* spoke flippantly of the "convicted libeller" of the rival journal. David Acheson was awarded $50.00 in his case, and the Club paper made political capital of the libel suit on the state, as well as the local, level with slighting references to "Mr. Findlay's prothonotary." The case of George Baird furnished no such propaganda because the evidence was "stolen" and of necessity the suit was dropped.[19]

Both Federalists and "spurious" Republicans constituted the secondary echelon of the Club. Thomas McGiffin and Joseph Pentecost had previously paid allegiance to the former while Parker Campbell, John Wilson, and Alexander Murdoch shared a Republican political ancestry. The first three had all been business associates of Thomas Baird, but in 1818 a rivalry between Baird and McGiffin threatened the unity of the Club. When Baird was awarded the judgeship, his chief competitor was McGiffin. *The Reporter* attempted to foment dissension and strongly endorsed the latter because it favored an "avowed Federalist" to a "hidden aristocrat" like Baird.[20]

This potential rift within the Club organization never developed. A sop was tossed to the Federalist wing when Joseph Pentecost, a "moderate federalist" under whom Thomas Baird had read law, received the Club's wholehearted endorsement for Congress in the fall of the same year. *The Reporter* charged that the Federalist Party, in toto, had become "the kite-tail to the Washington Club" when the Club and Pentecost campaigned vigorously in behalf of increased appropriations to complete the National Road and attempted to pose as the real benefactors of this locally popular internal improvement project.

The opposition pictured Pentecost as a federal lawyer who had repeatedly condemned the Republican administrations of both the United States and Pennsylvania. Their candidate, Thomas Patterson, was a combination humble farmer and manufacturer who earned his bread by the sweat of his brow, who did not treat with contempt a man of ability in tattered garb, and who was opposed to lordly aristocrats who live on the earnings of the laboring class. According to the Delegate Republicans, the election of Patterson, the personification of equal rights and the implacable foe of the pernicious paper money system,

---

[19] *Examiner,* July 12, October 18, and November 29, 1819.
[20] *Reporter,* April 13, 27, and June 8, 1818.

would help adjust the balance in Congress where there were already too many lawyers and merchants and too few farmers and tradesmen.

The Bairds themselves did not openly support Pentecost, nor did the *Examiner*. Such secrecy suggests that perhaps Pentecost was only their pawn. If his well-known sympathy for the National Road would have exhibited enough strength to carry the election, the Club would have taken an important step up the political ladder. On the other hand, failure under such secret conditions would have kept the Club in the good graces of Governor Findlay, and at the same time have retained the loyalty of the Federalist wing.[21]

Sentiment for Patterson, and for the Delegate ticket generally, was too great a hurdle for Pentecost. The Club had to be content with the strengthening of its hold over its Federalist members. In the years that followed, as in 1818, the Club achieved a very limited success at the ballot box; multiform though their political maneuvering was, it succeeded in winning only a few appointment crumbs which fell chiefly to William Baird and Thomas Morgan in 1819 and 1821, respectively.

NON-POLITICAL ALIGNMENTS

In this decade no other county in Western Pennsylvania had a political organization as readily definable as the Washington Club; in fact, the opposition to the Club in Washington County almost defies definition although it won a majority of the political skirmishes. Since only the name of Editor Sample stands out, there is a strong indication that the Delegate Republican organization was largely a mass movement on the part of the farmers of the countryside. Out of force of habit these farmers repeatedly voted for the state and local manifestations of Jeffersonian agrarianism and against the leaders of the growing urban pattern in the borough, particularly the lawyers, merchants, and bankers.

The same type of division was prevalent between the voters of the urban centers and those of the surrounding farm lands in Allegheny, Westmoreland, Crawford, and Erie Counties, but none of these regions could claim such a closely-knit group as the Washington Club. Even Pittsburgh with such prominent political figures as James Ross, William Wilkins, Henry Baldwin, and Walter Forward could not boast of any equivalent alignment. These men, as well as those who enjoyed political

---

[21] *Reporter,* September 7, and October 5, 12, 1818; *Examiner,* October 5, 19, 1818.

good fortune elsewhere in Western Pennsylvania, owed thier success chiefly to overlapping memberships in business, military, civic, and social groups.

The public endorsed candidates because of their personal popularity. Where a man lived, how he gained his livelihood, what organizations he belonged to, and what legislation on a particular subject he, as an individual, was believed to favor, determined his political acceptability. In other words, during this period more people cast their ballots on the principle of a "purer" democracy than under the party system that either preceded or followed the era of good feeling.

No other Western Pennsylvanian so successfully wove a political career out of his non-political activities as William Wilkins. He served the Bank of Pittsburgh, the Monongahela Bridge Company, the Pittsburgh Manufacturing Company, the Greensburg and Pittsburgh Turnpike Company, and the Vigilant Fire Company, and the common council of the city government, all as president. His positions as director of the Permanent Library Company, trustee of the Western University of Pennsylvania, commissioner of the Western Penitentiary, and subscriber to the Ohio Navigation Company bolstered his extensive civic record.

When James Monroe made his swing through New England and the western part of the nation in 1817, he passed through Pittsburgh and was graciously received at the home of William Wilkins. The President was greeted on the edge of town by a delegation of citizens, militia, and city officials. A coach was provided for the honored visitor, but seeing the city officials on foot, he refused to ride and joined them in the procession. The parade proceeded through the streets to the Wilkins' home where Monroe was received "in a manner which reflects great credit on the taste and liberality of that gentleman, to whose politic and public-spirited exertions [the townspeople were] so much indebted on this occasion." [22]

The same year Wilkins was a candidate for the assembly on a ticket that denounced the legislative caucus and endorsed Joseph Hiester for governor. Both went down to defeat, but in 1819 Wilkins was again a candidate for the lower house of the legislature on the anti-caucus ticket. This time the results were different; he was elected and classified as a Federalist when he took his seat.[23]

---

[22] *Pittsburgh Gazette,* September 9, 1817.
[23] Sewell Slick, "The Life of William Wilkins" (Unpublished Master's thesis, History Dept., University of Pittsburgh, 1931), p. 23f.

The following year Wilkins received support for the congressional post which Henry Baldwin had filled for the two preceding terms. In the early summer it appeared that the seat would be contested by these two men, but the Baldwin faction skillfully squelched the possibility of such a political duel. At a public meeting they unanimously sponsored a resolution to the effect that Allegheny County had been ably and satisfactorily represented in both Congress and the general assembly and further declared that any attempt to deprive the district of the talents of the men who had represented them so well would be prejudicial to the district's best interests. Obviously this implied that if both Baldwin and Wilkins were candidates for Congress, the district would be denied the great talents of the defeated one in the legislative councils since Wilkins had previously served in the assembly.

Wilkins was pictured as a man who faced two alternatives: to place the county's interests foremost or to consider his own political ambitions and gamble on dislodging Baldwin from his seat in Washington. He showed deference for the decision of the public meeting which upheld the idea that Baldwin should again be the candidate for Congress while he should campaign for the assembly to promote most effectively the "vital interests of this section of the western country." [24]

This decision placed Wilkins on the same election slate as Baldwin who was an avowed Independent Republican. Both were victorious, but approximately two months after the election Wilkins was appointed president judge of the Common Pleas Court of Pennsylvania for the district composed of Allegheny, Butler, and Beaver Counties by Governor Findlay, a Delegate or Patent Republican. Thus, within a period of 15 months Wilkins had been successfully identified with all three major political factions, Federalists, Independents, and Patent Republicans.

In October 1820 he had run on a political ticket that defeated Findlay, but in December the same governor under dramatic circumstances tendered him the court position. Judge Samuel Roberts had taken sick, and the friends of Wilkins made the preliminary arrangements for his appointment in case the former's illness proved fatal. On the night of December 13 Roberts died, and a special messenger was dispatched to Harrisburg with letters recommending Wilkins' appointment. The courier traveled on horseback, and by changing horses fre-

---

[24] *Mercury,* July 25, 1820.

quently at the stage offices he succeeded in reaching the capital late in the evening of December 18, the last night of Findlay's term. The governor was aroused between 11:00 p.m. and midnight to validate the commission; any delay in the ride would probably have resulted in another judge.[25]

This appointment carried Wilkins to the brink of his career in national politics which was destined to rival his success in state and local offices. In 1824 he was elevated to a federal judgeship in the Western District of Pennsylvania by President Monroe, but four years later he returned as an active campaigner. Running for Congress on the Jackson ticket, Wilkins was easily elected, but resigned the post before ever taking his seat. Shortly thereafter the Pennsylvania legislature honored him with an appointment to the United States Senate where he shared the responsibility of serving the Keystone State with his brother-in-law, George Mifflin Dallas. He was later called by President Jackson to represent his government in Russia and by President Tyler to administer the War Department.

Quite obviously Wilkins had been asked to assume each of these responsibilities because of competent service in previous assignments, but to determine his initial springboard into politics is not an easy task. The difficulty is common, however, to the foundations of all political careers that were laid in the era of good feeling. With the fluid party line of this decade, political success was of necessity conditioned largely by multiform non-political activities. The problem of determining, where in this non-political background of Wilkins and his political contemporaries the emphasis should be placed, defies an accurate solution. Since the comparative strengths of the various non-political activities cannot be calculated because of inconclusive records and different circumstances in each community, they can only be individually described.

Citizens with both a profession and a yearn for political office quickly learned that the former was a valuable asset, not possessed by men of other occupations, in the attainment of public office. The only notable exception to such success stemmed from the farmers' antipathy for lawyers. In spite of this one political handicap, however, lawyers enjoyed a marked advantage over all others, even their fellow professionals, in the contests for offices.

Necessity generally demanded that lawyers practice in several counties

---

[25] Klein, *Pennsylvania Politics,* p. 68.

to gain a livelihood; some were away from their homes and offices half the time, traveling with the court officials from one county seat to another on horseback. The lawyer's mobile office which made him always ready for business, was a sack slung across the saddle and containing legal papers and a few books.[26]

The nature of this law practice established a definite correlation between the profession on the one hand and both county and inter-county office-holding on the other. William Wilkins and Henry Baldwin of Pittsburgh traveled as far as Crawford County to practice while Patrick Farrelly of Meadville, another successful lawyer-politician, likewise spent much time on the road. He was present at almost every session of the court in Erie County, and his practice at the Erie bar was estimated to be larger than that of all the lawyers residing in the town.[27]

This contact in Erie undoubtedly strengthened Farrelly's political position for the congressional contests of 1822 and 1824. On these two occasions he opposed Samuel Williamson of Mercer County, who had no such Erie activities, in a multi-county district of which Erie was part. As was the prevailing custom in Northwestern Pennsylvania, both men were listed on the ticket simply as Republicans, and the people of Erie were required to vote on their personal knowledge of the candidates. In 1822 Farrelly received 992 votes in Erie County to 136 for Williamson, and two years later the result was even more lopsided, 1,030 to 68.[28] Although it is impossible to ascertain how many of these votes were directly or indirectly traceable to Farrelly's law practice, they nevertheless represent the most definable explanation of his victories.

Public meetings concerned with the nomination and endorsement of candidates for political office were, whenever feasible, held at the county seats during the last week that the court was in session there. Such an arrangement found the lawyers of the local and surrounding counties as the only group present with any common denominator except, of course, the townspeople who frequently did not constitute a political bloc. These circumstances gave the local lawyers the necessary advantage to dominate the meetings and nominations with perhaps an

---

[26] Samuel P. Bates, *History of Erie County, Pennsylvania,* . . . (Chicago: Warner, Beers & Co., 1884), p. 324.

[27] Bates, *History of Erie County,* pp. 346, 349.

[28] *Ibid.*

assist from the people of the town. The inevitable result was a breach between the lawyers and townspeople, on the one hand, and the rural population, which rapidly developed a feeling of inferiority, on the other.[29]

The presence of lawyers from the nearby counties tended further to promote "deals" concerning the choice of a candidate who was to represent the several counties concerned. Candidates for county office in Erie, for example, were willing to support Farrelly of Crawford County for Congress in their multi-county district in exchange for his endorsement of their candidacy for local office. Farrelly's support carried a personal meaning to the great number of Erie citizens who constituted his clientage and, therefore, aided the local political aspirants.

These political features of the legal profession caused it to become the instrument of many intelligent and ambitious young men who desired an entree to politics. Of all the pursuits that an aspiring man might undertake anywhere in the West to raise himself quickly and easily above the level of his neighbors and within the aristocracy of his western community, that of a lawyer was the most promising.

Others, without the spirit of personal and public betterment, followed the same profession. Since it offered attractive rewards and was, at the same time, easily attainable by reading with a practicing attorney or judge, many insincere and materialistic practitioners made their appearance. They were especially numerous in an area like Western Pennsylvania where land titles were constantly in dispute. The courts were clogged with much litigation, not only because land laws and legal codes were new and imperfect, but also because individual citizens believed they were being maneuvered out of land that was rightfully theirs by such groups as the Croghan heirs and the Holland Land Company.[30]

The nature of these land battles and the material mind of many an unscrupulous lawyer joined forces to produce a widespread prejudice against the legal profession in rural districts. Add to these ingredients two others, the principle that people tend to fear what they do not understand and the near-absence of academic training in rural Western Pennsylvania, and the legal and judicial systems became all the more mysterious to the farm population. In a society where energies were spent largely in back-breaking toil, a display of learning such as a

---

[29] "A Citizen of Crawford county," *Crawford Messenger,* August 31, 1816.

[30] Miller, *Genesis of Western Culture,* p. 57f.

mastery of the law, was regarded as a conspicuous waste. According to the rural attitude, learning and leisure were synonymous, and both were, in turn, contemptuous to the energetic farmer. This made it difficult for well-educated men such as Albert Gallatin and Hugh Henry Brackenridge to get along well in the Western Pennsylvania of these years.[31]

Rural editors were subsequently aroused to oppose lawyers for political office, and the Washington *Reporter* felt compelled to remark that:

> Last winters debating in congress will satisfy any man, lawyers excepted, that there are too many lawyers already in congress—there are 122. Too much money has been spent in speechifying. Lawyers are a troublesome set at best.[32]

"A Farmer" enlarged upon this theme in a *Westmoreland Republican* editorial. He insisted that there were too few farmers and mechanics in government offices and urged the people of the countryside to endorse the Democratic ticket of four farmers and a mechanic rather than the Federalist choices of two lawyers and three storekeepers. In calling the roll of the Democratic standard-bearers individually, "A Farmer" pointed out that Dr. David Marchand, the nominee for Congress, had been a farmer until three years before and implied that the constituency should vote for him on that basis.

The Washington *Reporter* had indulged in a converse bit of logic in 1816 when it urged its readers to vote against Thomas Baird because of his legal background. Such suggestions were widely accepted and became the cornerstones of the agrarian political philosophy.

> The farmers and mechanics compose the largest part of our population, and should be permitted to have a little of the sport too. They should, indeed, have an interest in our legislative councils through their representatives. It might prevent law from selling at too high a rate, and keep store goods from becoming too cheap.—The idea of getting new clothes for next thing to nothing, might operate powerfully on our senses, divert us from our primitive simplicity, and compel us that we, who once were only Clodhoppers, would soon become nabobs, and arrive at the very pinnacle of perfection.[33]

"A Farmer" further charged that the Federalist ticket was designed to impede the development of domestic manufactures and force the rural population to continue as it was, "nothing but farmers." This comment

---

[31] Dangerfield, *Era of Good Feelings,* p. 114.

[32] *Reporter*, September 18, 1820.

[33] *Westmoreland Republican*, October 10, 1818.

THOMAS ATKINSON
Crawford Messenger (Meadville)

JOHN M. SNOWDEN
Mercury (Pittsburgh)

Courtesy of Observer Publishing
Company

Courtesy of great-granddaughter,
Mrs. Alexander Murdoch

WILLIAM SAMPLE
Reporter (Washington)

JOHN GRAYSON
Washington Examiner

suggests, not only the farmers' inferiority complex, but also his desire to share in the spreading urban economy.

"A Farmer" verified this trend in farm philosophy in a later article which admitted that two of the Democratic nominees, whom he had labeled as farmers, were now storekeepers. He stumbled over this apparent contradiction with the assertions that they had been farmers and that their interests were almost exclusively connected with agriculture. Even with restatement it was readily discernible that "A Farmer" was attempting to hold onto an argument that was becoming less valid with every passing year. The farm population was undeniably being modified by the growing influence of town culture.

In Washington County a similar opposition to lawyers prevailed. There the rival newspapers tried to depict each other as the instrument of the "federal junto of lawyers." The *Examiner* declared that local lawyers had recently come to regard the *Reporter* as "their paper" and that they accordingly endeavored "to put down every *democrat* who may have independence enough to oppose their wicked schemes, thinking thereby to change the politics of Washington county!!!" This accusation resulted from the *Reporter's* support of Thomas McGiffin for a judgeship after it had earlier denounced this avowed Federalist as an "illiterate attorney."

In its counterendorsement of Thomas H. Baird, the *Examiner* announced that success for McGiffin and his Federalist junto would incite a re-appearance of the "reign of terror." The *Examiner,* which ironically pledged its allegiance to the lawyer-studded Washington Club, superficially at least, campaigned to defeat Federalist judges who would sit in the courthouse and contemptuously insult respectable citizens "as had been their custom." Editor Grayson scathingly recalled the case of Nicholas Little, a farmer of Strabane Township, who on an earlier occasion had been admonished by McGiffin to leave the courthouse with the allegation: "Little, you nor none of your sort are wanted here."

Using the theme that there were too many attorneys in Congress, the *Reporter* concurred in these anti-lawyer sentiments. Paralleling Grayson's charge that the *Reporter* repudiated every Democrat with any independence of mind, came Editor Sample's insistence that the county's "Old School" organization was dominated by lawyers from the borough who were conniving to disrupt the Democratic-Republican Party. He predicted, however, that the loyal army of farmers from the countryside would thwart their machinations. This feat was to be accomplished in spite of the direction that the local legal junto unstintingly received from Pittsburgh's "federal lawyers" headed by that "fox in politics," Walter Forward.[34]

Such charges and countercharges reveal the widespread antipathy of farmers and their spokesmen for the lawyer class. At the same time that they castigated lawyers generally, the rural population and their supporting journals exhibited both faith and trust in individual lawyers whom they frequently knew personally. This condition, plus the lawyer's indispensable role in western society and the desire of the rural citizenry to be well represented in the state and national councils, eclipsed any disfavor the lawyer incited and made his profession the most accessible path to the highway of politics.

Aside from the lawyers, the doctors represented the most active civic and politically-minded professionals in Western Pennsylvania. Interestingly enough, most of the doctors who exercised any degree of political power had served in either the American Revolution or the War of 1812.

Henry Adams' belief that an imposing presence contributes greatly to political success was especially manifest in this era of local political emphasis. This imposing influence doubly served the doctors, lawyers, and other professionals who held ranking militia offices. Particularly in Allegheny, Erie, Fayette, and Westmoreland Counties were doctors with military careers active as political campaigners, presiding officers at political meetings, and as members of committees of correspondence and vigilance.

Felix Brunot, the foster brother of the Marquis de Lafayette, who came to America with him, and George Stevenson became two of Pittsburgh's most public-spirited physicians. Both had served in the colonial army at Brandywine before migrating to Western Pennsylvania to pursue their medical careers. Stevenson's decision to reside there had been reached by indirection. Upon President Washington's call for militia units in 1794 to suppress the Whiskey Insurrection, he organized the Carlisle Infantry to march on Pittsburgh, but became so attracted to the area that instead of capturing Pittsburgh the city took him captive.

---

[34] *Examiner,* May 4, 1818; *Reporter,* October 7, 1816; August 11, 1817; October 12, 1818.

He entered into the affairs of the town and acquitted himself as a good citizen. In 1801 he was elected chief burgess and was a member of the first select council when Pittsburgh was incorporated as a city in 1816. Stevenson further demonstrated his service to the community by serving as the first president of the board of trustees for the Western University of Pennsylvania and by acting with James Ross, Walter Lowrie, and David Evans as commissioners in charge of the construction of the Western Penitentiary of Pennsylvania.[35]

Brunot, on the other hand, showed a reluctance for public office, but his name was repeatedly affixed to committee lists and reports of public meetings. Although the nature of his political power was more indirect, its impact on Allegheny County affairs was neither slight nor unique. Brunot's leadership was similar to that of John C. Wallace, the first resident physician of Erie County active in the local militia. Doctors Benjamin Prother, James Estep, and James Beatty enjoyed correspondingly prominent roles in political committee assignments in the county of Westmoreland.

Joining Stevenson and Brunot among Pittsburgh's "medico-politicos" was Joel Lewis, the first president of the Pittsburgh Medical Society which was founded at the close of the War of 1812. At the tender age of 31, Lewis was also elected brigadier-general of the 15th Division of the Pennsylvania militia in 1821. He quickly capitalized on this combination of the medical society and the militia command to launch a whirl-wind political career. After an active year in grass-root politics, Lewis gained the nomination for Congress on the Delegate Republican ticket in 1822. In spite of his defeat by Walter Forward in the election, the nomination itself attests to his ability to amass political support, based on his army and professional relationships, quickly. Death intervened in 1824 to cut short a budding political career.[36]

Politics in Westmoreland and Fayette Counties also witnessed the influence of local physicians. Dr. David Marchand, who had been appointed by Governor Snyder to the rank of major general of the militia with the command of the 13th Division of the state's troops in the War of 1812, was the Westmoreland leader. After the war he was elected to two successive terms in Congress; and thereafter gave a guiding hand

---

[35] Theodore Diller, *Pioneer Medicine in Western Pennsylvania* (New York: Paul B. Hoeber, Inc., 1927), pp. 44, 51, 60; *Mercury*, July 6, 1816.

[36] Diller, *Pioneer Medicine*, pp. 51, 102; *Mercury*, June 13, 1821; July 31, 1822.

to local politics by serving as prothonotary in his home county and by directing public-spirited meetings and committees.[37]

Across the county line in Fayette Dr. Daniel Sturgeon, without the benefit of a military past or present, entered politics forthrightly in 1818. He served four consecutive terms in the Pennsylvania Assembly before surrendering the post to concentrate on his medical career. His absence from politics was only temporary, however. When the ideas of the Jackson party caught his imagination, he actively rejoined the political fight and was a candidate for the state senate in 1826. The subsequent election results bear testimony of Sturgeon's personal appeal; the voters showed little political consistency in sending Sturgeon to the state senate and Andrew Stewart, a Clay Whig, to Congress.[38]

Except for Sturgeon, all the leading "medico-politicos" of Western Pennsylvania in these years had military experience. Since the same is true of numerous other classes of citizens who enjoyed political success, these military contacts cannot be minimized.

Military assemblages represented the most extensive gatherings of a cross-section of the population in the western end of the state at this time. Especially in Allegheny, Butler, Erie, and Westmoreland Counties were these military organizations vigorously supported. Pittsburgh alone had five militia companies, plus a chapter of the Society of the Cincinnati. In 1820 all of these Pittsburgh militia groups were united under one authority and known collectively as the Pittsburgh Volunteers. The oldest component of the organization, the Independent Blues, had served in the Northwest under General William Henry Harrison during the War of 1812.[39]

These numerous rifle, artillery, and infantry companies assembled frequently to satisfy a variety of needs: to train, to hunt destructive animals, to greet visitors, to conduct funerals, and to celebrate occasions of importance. Training Day, which was most closely allied to the basic functions of a militia group, was primarily devoted to close-order drill rather than to the use of equipment. Nevertheless, a rudimentary training in the use of firearms, while on a mass maneuver, was conducted in the northwestern counties at least. There militia units were deployed to hunt and destroy bears, wolves, deer and other wild animals

---

[37] Boucher, *Westmoreland County,* III, 357.

[38] Roadman, "Daniel Sturgeon," pp. 25, 27.

[39] John E. Parke, *Recollections of Seventy Years and Historical Gleanings of Allegheny, Pennsylvania* (Boston: Rand, Avery & Co., 1886), pp. 33-35.

that menaced the farmers' livestock and field crops. In 1820 Butler County conducted a "grand hunt" which involved four divisions, each commanded by a resident militia leader who was actively or potentially a political personality. Meetings with such large groups of citizens engaged in such a worthy community enterprise were a great political asset to militia leaders, especially in an era of limited communication facilities and meager party discipline. Generally they made the most of it, as the great number of militiamen in politics would attest.[40]

In contrast to these informal musters, the militia assembled on many formal and ceremonial occasions. When President Monroe visited the area in 1817 and LaFayette in 1825, the militia units had their most significant opportunities to pay their respects to distinguished visitors. In the course of these formations the militiamen were afforded opportunities to discuss and exchange ideas among themselves, and it is not unreasonable to assume that the subject of politics was explored because, where two or three Americans of any era have been gathered together, politics has invariably crept into the conversation. A similar setting for political discourse was provided when militia units assembled to participate in the funeral services of a departed member who was customarily buried with military honors.

These more serious and somber militia gatherings were counterbalanced by celebrations and dedications. Festive occasions ranged from the dedication of such public improvements as the Allegheny Bridge in 1819, to which the Pittsburgh Blues had been invited to take part, to the annual celebration of Independence Day. At the former celebration all the city and county dignitaries were given opportunities to propose toasts, and the Blues appropriately responded to each with a volley of gunfire.[41]

Aside from the performance of this type of public service, militia units held celebrations of their own, sometimes privately, but frequently in the company of guests, to commemorate a part of our national heritage. For example, units such as the Washington Guards of Birmingham and the Washington Artillery of Erie, which had been named for the famed Revolutionary War general, celebrated his birthday with a dinner and a series of speeches.

---

[40] Brown, *History of Butler County,* I, 71.

[41] John H. Niebaum, "The Pittsburgh Blues," *The Western Pennsylvania Historical Magazine,* IV (1921), 266.

In 1824 other politically-minded militiamen of Western Pennsylvania began to pay homage to the great hero of the second war against Britain, Andrew Jackson. On January 8 of that year the Pittsburgh Volunteers, composed of the City Blues, the City Guards, the Washington Guards, the Pittsburgh Greens, and the newly-formed Jackson Independent Blues, met ostensibly to celebrate the New Orleans victory, but actually to promote Jackson's candidacy for the presidency.

The combination of this newly-created company of militiamen bearing the name of a political candidate and the general celebration of the Pittsburgh Volunteers on both January 8 and July 4 of that year marked the culmination of direct "politicking" within Western Pennsylvania's militia during this decade of good feeling. After firing a salute to Old Hickory in honor of his New Orleans victory, they gathered at the First Presbyterian Church where an address was delivered by Algernon S. T. Mountain, an enterprising young lawyer with political ambitions. Following this service the Jackson Independent Blues, accompanied by invited guests, adjourned to a local hotel and continued the celebration with a dinner and entertainment. After the dinner numerous toasts were proposed, some of which were directed to Jackson's military past, but most of which were drunk to his anticipated political future in the White House. The most loquacious proposer was Edward Patchell, a self-appointed Jackson leader in Pittsburgh, who toasted the general on no less than four occasions.[42]

Generally speaking, Patchell's toasts stated the theme of the day— that Andrew Jackson, the first front-ranking military nominee since Washington, was vitally needed by the nation to defend the monument of the father of our country. At the dinner table Washington's portrait was hung at the head and Jackson's at the foot to establish even a pictorial identity between the two; a vote for Jackson was implied to mean a vote for the principles and leadership of George Washington. The Tennessean was toasted as "the hero of New Orleans" and "Second only to Washington 'in war, in peace, and in the affections of his countrymen.' "

Needless to say, the Jackson political star grew brighter in Western Pennsylvania with this militia support. Dominated in most areas by the militia, Independence Day celebrations had assumed a decided politi-

---

[42] Niebaum, "Pittsburgh Blues," *West. Penna. Hist. Mag.,* IV, 266-267; *Pittsburgh Gazette,* January 16, 1824; *Mercury,* January 13, 1824.

cal tinge in Western Pennsylvania by 1818 or 1819, giving the occasion
a firm political foundation by the time Jackson's candidacy first made
itself manifest. Actually, as early as 1814 Butler County had given
political significance to this holiday by conducting an official party
meeting in the afternoon. Delegates from the townships of the county
assembled at the courthouse on this date to select their candidates for
the next general election.[43]

Generally the militia units, where there were more than one in an
immediate area, would assemble on the morning of the nation's birthday
and go through a brief close-order drill and inspection with their families
and the general public looking on. Thereafter the units went their
several ways to picnic groves or meadows to eat a basket lunch. Each
had its own program, but they all adhered to a basic pattern which
included the reading of the Declaration of Independence, followed by
speeches and toasts which became increasingly political with each passing
year of the decade.

Reading the Declaration of Independence and delivering an oration
on this national holiday carried an unexplained prestige. The limited
available evidence reveals that Dr. Joel Lewis's first semi-political action
was the reading of the Declaration of Independence at a celebration in
1817, but from that beginning he went forward to be a candidate for
Congress five years later. Algernon S. T. Mountain and Robert J.
Walker, who became enthusiastic Jackson supporters, first gained public
attention with holiday orations.

Since the commanders of militia companies could select these speakers
and thereby control to a limited degree the political ideas expressed in
these celebrations, their positions also carried an extraordinary political
power. Until he was elected brigadier general of the militia in 1824,
Edward Patchell, by his own admission, had no remote claim to fame,
aside from his many Jackson toasts, offered on every possible occasion,
unless the distinction of manufacturing the first waterproof hat west of
the mountains is so considered.

These conditions suggest that the people's preference for Jackson was
the determining factor in their selection of Patchell who, with a great
flourish and display of egotism, explained the circumstances of his election in a letter to Jackson. In his grandiose style Patchell described for
Old Hickory how there had been eight nominations for the post of

[43] Myers, "Committees of Correspondence," p. 61.

brigadier general before the 1,000 citizens of Allegheny County who assembled at the courthouse. A voice-vote for several of the candidates was taken

> when they ware severally hissed by nine tenths of the multitude; Untill my name was reached on the list, when shouts of Old Hickory resounded from all parts of the hourse, nine cheers for Old Hickory, was the word, "when the crowd burst in upon me where I was seated at the counsel table" and bore me out on their shoulders into the public square; I assure you General I felt more proud of your nick name "than I now feel of the Generalship, notwithstanding I have been elected by a much larger majority than any other of my predecessors for any office whatever in this County since the beginning. And I must confess had not it been for your sake I never would have yielded to become a candidate at this stage of life.[44]

Patchell, with an unfathomed belief in his ability to do great things, further advised Jackson that when he had first been asked by the Jacksonites in Pittsburgh to run for the office, he declined. To the exaltation of Old Hickory's enemies, the pro-Jackson militiamen were forced to sponsor a man who was not well-known through the brigade. In telling Jackson that the man was not popular enough to "warrant or justify the risque to your honour," Patchell dramatized his decision upon further appeals to make the supreme sacrifice and campaign for the position.[45]

Then in closing his letter a new zenith of emotion and egotism was reached. He told Jackson that he desired no thanks for his support.

> I must repeat it, I have done no more than my duty, and I even forbid you "return me thanks: And should we fail this Election, I will pray my God" to spare life untill I see Andrew Jackson President of the U States. and then let me close my eyes in peace, adue [46]

Although this letter to Jackson was designed to demonstrate the author's importance, it also reveals the political significance attached to militia organizations. Patchell's position as brigadier general had appointive powers which he could and did use as a political instrument. He brought John McFarland from Harrisburg to edit a pro-Jackson paper in Pittsburgh and appointed him a brigade major so that he might extend his influence and strengthen his *Allegheny Democrat*. Since militia elections were frequently regarded as "trial balloons," indicating

---

[44] Patchell to Jackson, August 7, 1824. Bassett, *Correspondence of Jackson,* III, 262.

[45] *Ibid.*

[46] *Ibid.* III, 264.

the local strength of candidates for major state and national offices, newspaper support assisted the Jacksonites of the militia in maintaining and promoting their candidate, without and within their organization.

SECONDARY NON-POLITICAL ALIGNMENTS

Other non-political activities that conditioned a citizen's fitness for a career in politics had their centers in the social and business institutions of the local community. In an era of relatively little government responsibility for individual security, benevolent and charitable demands upon private generosity were enormous. Any man that could demonstrate leadership in meeting these demands became recognized as a public-spirited and righteous inspiration to his contemporaries, a designation which never impeded a political career.

The oldest and most extensive social institution in promoting political success was the local church and its affiliates. In Western Pennsylvania no congregation was more closely allied with the development of political leadership for its community than the First Presbyterian Church of Pittsburgh where James O'Hara, the city's foremost industrialist, was president of the board of trustees. Associated with him on the board were other prominent business leaders such as Isaac Craig and John Wilkins. The church rolls also displayed the names of James Ross, Ebenezer Denny, John Scull, and John M. Snowden whose talents added immeasurably to the prestige of the congregation. In this era people purchased particular pews in a church because of a concern for the families in the pews around them, and the fact that these business and political leaders attended the First Presbyterian Church encouraged others who were business and political aspirants to do likewise.

Among the religious organizations allied to the Pittsburgh churches were the Pittsburgh Bible Society in which Walter Forward served first as a manager and later as president, the Young Men's Western Auxiliary Bible Society in which Harmar Denny filled the office of president, and the Sabbath School Society which at this time was not directed by a political leader.[47] No other community of Western Penn-

---

[47] *Pittsburgh Directory* (1815), p. 120; *Pittsburgh Directory* (1819), p. 123; William W. McKinney, *Early Pittsburgh Presbyterianism: Tracing the Development of the Presbyterian Church, United States of America, in Pittsburgh, Pennsylvania, from 1758-1839* (Pittsburgh: Gibson Press, 1938), p. 135.

sylvania could boast of such an elaborate development of religious organizations in these years, but no matter how limited the religious life of his town, a politician's relationship to it had an important bearing on his career. In fact, the inhabitants of the smaller communities possessed a complete personal knowledge of their candidates' religious habits and practices which guided their judgments.

The religious-minded were also civic-minded; some sought to advance education while others endeavored to save the city from the ravages of fire. As early as 1815 the Permanent Library Company was founded in Pittsburgh, and among the directors were the names of Walter Forward, Henry Baldwin, and William Wilkins who shared the community's political leadership in the decade that ensued.[48] The three further demonstrated their support of education by serving with the first board of trustees for the Western University of Pennsylvania, and in this endeavor they were joined by Dr. George Stevenson, John Darragh, and John Gilmore who also went forward to political success.[49]

Such civic-minded citizens were also inspired to organize and maintain fire protection companies. The Eagle Fire Company, which pioneered this development in Pittsburgh in 1810, was assisted by three others throughout Allegheny County before the end of a decade. These companies were administered by a board which included a president, vice president, secretary-treasurer, engineer, four directors and lesser officials, all chosen at annual elections. To win these elections was indicative of popularity and prestige; needless to say, leadership in the fire companies was often equivalent to local political leadership. William Wilkins discharged the duties of president in the Vigilant Fire Company while Alexander Brackenridge and Harmar Denny served as president and vice president, respectively, of the Eagle Fire Company in 1819 before their political careers blossomed. Ebenezer Denny directed the course of the Allegheny Fire Company while Robert Patterson, John Darragh, and William Lecky held lesser posts with the various companies and thereby increased their political availability.[50]

In the realm of social organizations none was so important to the politician as the Masonic Order. Lodge No. 45 of the Ancient York

---

[48] *Pittsburgh Directory* (1815), p. 124f.
[49] *Ibid.* (1819), p. 115.
[50] *Ibid.* (1815), pp. 125-127; (1819), p. 124f.

Masons, established in 1785, represented the oldest and most influential fraternal organization in Pittsburgh, and on its rolls appeared the names of the community's leading citizens. This lodge, together with its later affiliates in Western Pennsylvania, produced a staggering array of political leaders headed by United States Senators James Ross, Walter Lowrie, and William Marks, and Congressmen Henry Baldwin, Walter Forward, Adamson Tannehill, John Gilmore, James S. Stevenson, Robert Moore, James Allison, and Robert Orr. Masonic members of the state legislature at various times included Forward, Lowrie, Ross Wilkins, James S. Craft, Samuel Pettigrew, Samuel Douglas, William Irish, Alexander Brackenridge, George Cochran, and Samuel Powers. Of the judges in Western Pennsylvania Hugh Henry Brackenridge, Jonathan Walker, Charles Shaler, and James Riddle embraced this same fraternal order.[51]

Some of these Masons joined with others who aspired to political fortunes. They further spread the seeds of their civic-mindedness by daubing themselves with grease and appearing in amateur theatrical productions. The instrument of this activity was the Thespian Society, organized in Pittsburgh for the purpose of holding benefit performances to raise funds for the relief of the poor and afflicted. Prominent among the players were William Wilkins, Alexander Brackenridge, Charles Shaler, James S. Craft, and Morgan Neville.[52]

Still another type of social organization with political overtones took form in Pittsburgh, the political headquarters of Western Pennsylvania. Established in 1815 on the basis of common national ancestry, the Erin Benovelent Society of Pittsburgh, like so many other institutions of the day, was designed to promote charity and philanthropy, but nevertheless could not avoid sporadic political tendencies. The society's constitution called for an annual meeting and election of the customary officers on March 17, and it also established a three-man visiting committee for each of the city's two wards. These committees afforded an excellent potential for political contacts, but incomplete records render impossible any detailed study of their manipulation toward this end.

In 1817, however, without reference to the Erin Benevolent Society by name, a meeting, strongly reflecting the society's influence, was held

---

[51] "Citizens of Allegheny, Beaver, Armstrong, and Butler Counties." Undated handbill pertaining to the campaign of 1829. Denny-O'Hara Papers, Box 50.

[52] Parke, *Recollections,* p. 104.

to select an election ticket which claimed at least to favor "principles and not men." This premise was contradicted by the group in a second resolve which urged nominations without regard for party feeling and prejudice. The site of the meeting was the home of Dennis Flagherty where Phelin McGuigan presided with Arthur O'Farrin as secretary. Resulting from this meeting was an election slate of inconsequential nominees, along with a committee of correspondence composed of McGuigan, O'Farrin, Roger O'Rourke, Patrick O'Blarney, and Neal MacFail, to advance their candidacy.[53] If the Erin Benevolent Society did not openly sponsor this meeting, it can reasonably be concluded that it did incite a nucleus of leaders.

Although the society demonstrated no party preference of its own, its endorsement was solicited by candidates who ran on the more popular tickets. In 1821 an unidentified group of non-Irish-Americans recognized the political wisdom in celebrating St. Patrick's Day. During their festivities they selected a committee, with the aspiring Dr. Joel Lewis as chairman, to call upon the Erin Benevolent Society in the midst of its celebration and offer a toast of best wishes. Dr. Lewis proposed:

> The Erin Benevolent Society of Pittsburgh. We respect them as friends of the same human family; we admire and revere the principles of charity and benevolence on which their institution is founded. Although, by their constitution, many of us cannot be admitted among them, yet we hail them as coworkers in the great cause of philanthropy.[54]

By 1823 invitation to the society's March 17 celebration was extended by the members to the distinguished citizens of the community. The political guests, including Baldwin, Forward, William Wilkins, Algernon S. T. Mountain, Harmar Denny and Dr. George Stevenson, responded on the occasion with optimistic toasts which were civic rather than political in theme. Baldwin with his toast to "General Jackson" sounded the only political note, but this trend should not be taken to imply that the society was losing its political overtones. In the gubernatorial campaign of that year the political connotation of the society was revealed by a member who lashed out against the opponents of Andrew Gregg who denounced him as the son of an Irishman. In a letter to the *Mercury* he declared: "You will agree with me in opinion, that the son of an *Irishman* is as well calculated to make a good governor,

---

[53] *Mercury*, April 2, 1817; *Pittsburgh Gazette*, August 22, 1817.
[54] *Mercury*, March 28, 1821.

as the son of a *German*." [55] Although this denoted no official protest by the society, the writer nevertheless thought that by signing his name "Erin" he would rally the society behind Gregg's candidacy.

Paralleling this influence of social and fraternal organizations on a budding career was one's business and occupational pursuits. This was especially true if the aspiring politician was interested in pursuits which the public regarded as essential and edifying to the community. In these years the promotion of both domestic manufactures and agriculture represented the most urgent needs of Western Pennsylvania, and those concerned with their advancement enjoyed a political advantage.

A society to encourage domestic manufactures was initiated as early as 1807 in Meadville, but it proved ineffectual. A second start was made ten years later at Pittsburgh where a more or less permanent organization, with officers and fixed annual dues, resulted from a public meeting. The first officers included James Ross as president with Benjamin Bakewell, Alexander McClurg, James S. Stevenson, Robert Patterson, and Anthony Beelen among the twelve managers. Eventually the organization was chartered as the Pittsburgh Manufacturing Association which established a warehouse, from which articles manufactured by members of the association could be sold.

Since actual selling was difficult in these years because of a scarcity of money, the association was also prepared to barter manufactured articles for country produce and raw materials. It was willing to accept iron, wool, cotton, sugar, salt, whiskey, butter, rags, flaxseed oil, and many other basic requirements of an industrial town in exchange for such agrarian needs as axes, sugar, assorted brushes, copper stills, window glass, hatchets, hoes, nails, ploughs, shot, and saddles. Under the direction of George Cochran, it first agent, the Association did not limit itself to the exclusive handling of Pittsburgh products, but kept its warehouse stocked with flour from distant mills, broadcloths from the Steubenville Woolen Factory, and supplies of every description that could be obtained.[56]

Outside of Pittsburgh there was little thought, if any, given to the promotion of the factory system with the result that the other communities of Western Pennsylvania possessed a different concept of

---

[55] *Mercury,* March 25, and October 7, 1823.
[56] *Pittsburgh Gazette,* March 18, 1817; October 29, 1819; *Commonwealth,* March 25, 1817; Wilson, *History of Pittsburg,* p. 160.

domestic manufactures. Although the Washington *Reporter,* for example, blamed imported goods for the depression times, it did nothing to promote the protective tariff or support the work of Henry Baldwin in Congress. No one would gather from the files of either Washington paper in these years that there was a tariff controversy raging. They took a more literal meaning of the term and encouraged only manufacturing done in the home.[57]

The presence of these conflicting concepts of domestic manufactures tended to complicate the problem; but since the whole economy was upset by 1820, it was obvious that even complete cooperation and understanding by all those concerned with domestic manufactures of every sort could not reach a solution alone. A public meeting of the citizens of Pittsburgh and vicinity sponsored the formation of another association for the advancement of the whole domestic economy, agrarian as well as industrial.

With Charles Shaler presiding and Alexander McClurg as secretary, the group decided that since innumerable petitions to the state and national governments had failed to produce any program to curb their general economic distress, they would seek to chart their own destiny. "The Society for the Promotion of Agriculture and Domestic Manufactures for the County of Allegheny" was organized and application for a charter honored by the Pennsylvania legislature. Leadership in the new society devolved upon the prominent or aspiring politicians. William Wilkins was elected president with Henry Baldwin assuming the role of vice president. The Denny father-and-son combination of Ebenezer and Harmar served as treasurer and secretary, respectively, and other businessmen of the community dominated the board of directors.[58]

Chief among the duties of the officers was the conduct of correspondence with similar societies, which were springing up elsewhere throughout the nation, for the purpose of collecting and disseminating information that might be useful in accomplishing the society's objective. Locally the organization attempted to encourage agricultural and industrial progress by granting monetary rewards to individuals who contributed substantially to the human knowledge of these pursuits. The introduction of new grains, grasses, or roots, an increase in the

---

[57] *Reporter,* December 6, 1819.
[58] *Mercury,* February 18, 1820; November 21, 1821.

yield of grain per acre, the invention of new and useful implements of husbandry, and improvements in breeding horses, cattle, sheep, and hogs constituted the society's major classes of interest and recognition.

In 1822 this enterprising group in Allegheny County began sponsoring an exhibition and fair. Farmers and domestic manufacturers were invited to display their staples which were homogeneously grouped and judged in a spirited competition. Thirty-two prizes totalling $197.00 were awarded at the first fair, but both the number of prizes and their value were increased by approximately 50 per cent the following year. In 1824 a new category, known as agricultural implements, was added. The spectators were also treated to a bit of action when ploughing contests, featuring both horses and oxen, were introduced.

The fairs and exhibitions grew into gala occasions. The managers of the Allegheny and Monongahela Bridges demonstrated their interest in the advancement of the county's economy by declaring their bridges free of toll to all those exhibiting, buying, or selling at the fairs. People were given every inducement to participate, and among the results of these enterprises which stirred a large part of the countryside was the spread of the popularity of the officers and judges. The fairs always featured an address by the society's president to acquaint the public with the purpose of the organization. This appearance placed the president before the citizenry as a sincere civic-minded leader while the other officers and the judges of the various competitions shared the same public reaction for their roles in this endeavor to promote the area's economy.[59]

Although the society was established to promote both agriculture and industry, its leadership was supplied almost wholly by businessmen. As a group, they served their communities in many other capacities as well, with the result that they were properly conditioned to lend politics a directing hand. Whether it meant serving on boards of bank directors or on public committees to draft memorials to the state and federal legislatures recommending legislation to satisfy local needs, these businessmen, especially in the Pittsburgh area, were the aggressive community leaders. George Anshutz, William B. Foster, John Arthers, Alexander McClurg, Thomas and Benjamin Bakewell, Henry Beltzhoover, John McNickle, and most of the other business leaders were not active political campaigners, but they always played an active role

---

[59] *Mercury,* May 29, and October 23, 1822; July 1, 1823; February 17, 1824.

on committees of correspondence and vigilance and in the direction of public meetings concerned with the selection of political candidates. Since nine of the 13 directors of the Westmoreland Bank of Pennsylvania in 1821 also enjoyed this type of relationship with the political life of that county, it must not be attributed to Pittsburgh alone simply because the evidence is too limited to trace it elsewhere.[60]

The influence of this non-political activity on politicians and elections cannot be accurately ascertained, but the repetitious appearance of names is proof of popularity and prestige which in the absence of party discipline were tantamount to political power. While William Wilkins, Henry Baldwin, Ebenezer Denny, and David Marchand are indicative of the political leadership of this era, there is no evidence that any one of them developed a great political machine. In fact, they obviously did not possess such an organization; but nevertheless they did achieve and maintain political power. An extensive network of non-political activities offers the only logical explanation. The same is true of the succeeding wave of politicians who reached manhood and first gained public attention of any description in this era. Harmar Denny, Algernon S. T. Mountain, James Stevenson, Edward Patchell, and Joel Lewis, all entered politics after an active and comprehensive non-political, then semi-political, life which in these years of Western Pennsylvania's development afforded the only entree to political attainment.

---

[60] *Greensburg Gazette,* November 23, 1821.

PART THREE

The Major Campaigns

VIII

Helmsmen of the Good Ship Pennsylvania

Rotation in office—may honest men turn out rogues.[1]

FROM 1808 to 1817 the administration of Pennsylvania was under the command of Governor Simon Snyder who in 1817 was concluding the last of the three successive terms permitted under the Constitution of 1790. He had come to power with a plea for "rotation in office," but then conveniently forgot about this plank in his platform.

In the western counties Abner Lacock "was always an octave above the whole choir" in presenting the Snyder "line," but by 1817 the evolution of Western Pennsylvania society and the appearance of a new wave of aspiring politicians insisted that rotation was overdue. Ironically they began to assault the Snyder faction with its own arguments. "Power too long possessed has corrupted the possessors" was their charge, and their prescription to safeguard liberty and human rights called for freer elections at the stated intervals. Such reform was deemed necessary because the "Snyder demagogues" had utilized the caucus to thwart the democratic process and prevent an expression of the public will.[2]

When a Harrisburg caucus of "mongrel breed, half office holders and half hungry expectants" nominated William Findlay, who had served the preceding nine years as state treasurer under Snyder, many assumed that the old machine would continue intact if Findlay were elected. Most office holders whose tenure rested solely on the discretion of the governor believed that they would be retained by Findlay.

---

[1] Toast proposed at an Independence Day celebration in the borough of Erie. *Erie Gazette,* July 8, 1820.

[2] "Tracy," *Crawford Messenger,* July 4, 1817; "Independence," *Crawford Messenger,* September 5, 1817.

This evaluation of the gubernatorial election alarmed John M. Snowden of the *Mercury* who recognized the threat to the democratic system posed by the caucus. He led the fight in Pittsburgh against Findlay and in behalf of General Joseph Hiester who was the choice of a Carlisle meeting. The editor denounced the caucus as corruption of the worst kind because it gradually destroyed a sense of responsibility in the rulers and fostered in the few office holders a spirit of domination which would ultimately destroy the fabric of civil liberty. Thus the caucus was viewed as a contrivance of the "eager office seekers to cheat the people out of their rights of self-government" by combinations among themselves.[3]

Victory for Findlay was interpreted to mean that the freedom and purity of elections had disappeared and that office holders, instead of being the followers, had become the leaders of the public will. Instead of serving the people, they would not only serve themselves, but require the people to serve them as well. In order to free the state of this vicious exploitation, Snowden endeavored to demonstrate that Hiester had been nominated by a convention, not by incumbents to office or those wishing to preserve the influence of the governor. The Carlisle meeting was described as more liberal, more republican, and more virtuous in spirit than the Harrisburg caucus because the delegates were animated only by the idea that the people should select any candidate they desired.[4] This was the same defense adopted by the Independents on the county level the year before when they rejected the caucus nomination for Congress and endorsed Henry Baldwin.

The Findlayites countered with the charge that the only sources of opposition to their candidate west of the mountains sprang from a few discontented office hunters in Washington and Allegheny Counties where they had established newspapers to disseminate their doctrines of abuse. In general, this analysis was correct although among the densely-populated counties Westmoreland proved to be more troublesome to the Patentees than Washington.

In these large counties both factions exercised their talents extensively to label the other as Federalist or proto-Federalist. Hiester, who had served 14 years in Congress, was berated for having openly sup-

---

[3] "Tracy," *Crawford Messenger,* July 4, 1817; *Mercury,* June 27, and July 18, 1817.

[4] *Mercury,* June 13, and July 11, 1817.

ported Federalist principles and candidates since 1804, especially was he arraigned for having failed to endorse a single Republican candidate for governor since that time—meaning, of course, Snyder on four occasions.

Hiesterites were indicted as "an amalgamation of the fragments of faction" uniting the doctrines of Old Schoolism, Federalism, Quidism, and Toryism to destroy the Republican Party in Pennsylvania. Collectively they were called Independents, but the Findlayites pointed out that in numbers they were truly the "dependents." Henry Baldwin, who had overcome the unfortunate connotations of all these titles the year before in winning the right to represent his district in Congress, was elected to the Allegheny County committee of correspondence to promote Hiester's candidacy. With his letter writing and speaking campaign in the summer of 1817 Baldwin assumed the leadership of the Western Pennsylvania politicians who campaigned to elevate a fellow Independent to the highest office in the state.[5]

Not only did the Hiesterites answer the accusations against them, but also set forth similar countercharges against the Patentees. Findlayites were quoted as telling Federalists that their candidate was a Republican in name, but that only a shade of difference existed between the two groups. Independents slyly reported that Federalists of Findlay's home county of Franklin, who had the best opportunity to know his character, preferred him even to men of their own party. Fearing that such publicity would be ruinous, the Findlayites, according to the *Patriot* of Williamsport in Washington County, launched a more violent campaign than Western Pennsylvania had witnessed since the "whiskey days of '93." Truth and honesty were shelved when the possibility of defeat loomed before the Patentees who recognized that many people might think and act for themselves, independent of the caucus. With this mounting suspicion the character of the Findlay press sank "to a level with the tenants of a fish market"; in fact, Findlay papers even slandered each other.[6]

In the borough of Washington, for example, there were two journals that endorsed Findlay, and each wanted to prove that it was the true

---

[5] *American Telegraph,* May 7, 1817; *Commonwealth,* August 30, 1817; *Reporter,* October 6, 1817; Taylor, "Henry Baldwin," p. 46.

[6] Pamphlet: *The Crisis* reprinted in *Reporter,* February 24, 1817; *The Patriot* (then Williamsport, but now Monongahela) quoted in *Aurora,* May 13, 1817.

friend of the state treasurer. After Findlay was elected governor, *The Examiner* charged that *The Reporter* would have been equally well satisfied if the Federalist candidate, meaning Hiester, had been victorious because Editor Sample was under the secret influence of the Federalist Party.[7]

Aside from party orthodoxy and the method of nomination, the only other important issue in this election to arouse the people of Western Pennsylvania was Findlay's financial morality during his career as state treasurer. The *Western Register,* a Federalist press in Washington under the influence of Thomas Morgan, who supported his father-in-law's endorsement of Hiester,[8] denounced Findlay as "the greatest villain that ever offered himself as a candidate for the office of governor." The basis for this vituperation, which Hiester spokesmen throughout the state quoted, was a reputed monetary exchange at Harrisburg in 1815 which reflected a misappropriation of state funds by the treasurer.[9]

According to the *Register* General Thomas Acheson, a Washington merchant on his way to purchase goods in Philadelphia, had stopped at the treasury where Findlay willingly exchanged $5,000 to $10,000 of western and middle county paper for Philadelphia notes or paper accepted at par in the eastern metropolis.[10] Attending a session of the legislature in Harrisburg at the time, Morgan met his fellow-townsman who casually told him that Findlay had saved him a six to ten per cent discount by exchanging the funds. The Acheson-Findlay bargain was corroborated by Robert Darragh of Beaver County who made a similar request of the treasurer. He refused most undiplomatically. Not only did he claim that he had given all the Philadelphia notes he could spare to Acheson, but at the same time paid Darragh money that the state owed him in "country paper." The situation was all the more galling

---

[7] *Examiner,* September 28, 1818.

[8] Thomas Morgan was married to Catherine Duane, the daughter of William Duane, the Philadelphia publisher who opposed Findlay.

[9] *Western Register* quoted in *Examiner,* August 6, 1817.

[10] Reports differed on the amounts of money involved in the exchange. Morgan originally held that it was $10,000, but later confided that it could have been less. Robert Darragh said simply that Acheson gave Findlay between $5,000 and $10,000 in "country paper" which he accepted in an even exchange for Philadelphia notes.

because Darragh, like Acheson, was on his way to Philadelphia where eastern paper would have afforded him a similar advantage.[11]

James Mitchell of Burgettstown, Washington County, was also irked at the exchange. He was purchasing goods in Philadelphia for Hugh Hagerty, a Washington competitor of Acheson, when he met the general who boasted that he had made good purchases because he had all par money. When Mitchell remarked that he had been unable to get that kind of paper in Washington, Acheson confided that he had been equally unsuccessful, but had been enterprising enough to make the exchange at Harrisburg.[12]

Both the *Examiner* and *The Reporter* in Washington denied these "Federalist" charges against Findlay. In the face of the evidence the latter eventually admitted that the exchange did take place, but attempted to disguise its significance by pointing out that it came at a time when there was no difference in value between eastern and western paper. David Acheson, the brother of Thomas who had died between the date of the alleged exchange and its exposure in 1817, swore that since he was in partnership with his brother, no such transaction could have transpired without his knowledge. Since he was unaware of the exchange, he concluded that the whole account was Hiester propaganda.

Within the next three years, however, he altered his views considerably. Along with Morgan and Editor Grayson of the *Examiner,* he joined forces with the Bairds to form the high command of the Washington Club which anathematized both Findlay and *The Reporter.* In a pamphlet circulated on the eve of the 1820 election, in which Findlay sought re-election, Acheson presented his revised opinion of the exchange. In order to expose Findlay and advance the Club, he admitted that the transaction could have taken place and probably did.[13]

John I. Scull of the *Pittsburgh Gazette,* who had originally declared himself a neutral in this gubernatorial contest of 1817 between two Republicans, used this opportunity to alter his position. Believing that the best interests of Western Pennsylvania were not being served by treasury manipulations which granted special privilege to rich, influential merchants, Scull announced his opposition to Findlay.[14] The treasury

[11] *Western Register* quoted in *Aurora,* May 5, 1817; "Somnambulist," *Examiner,* July 30, 1817; *Mercury,* August 15, 1817.
[12] *Mercury,* August 15, 1817.
[13] *Examiner,* July 9, 1817; *Genius of Liberty,* October 9, 1820.
[14] *Pittsburgh Gazette,* August 29, 1817.

exposure, however, had no effect on the *Mercury's* campaign. Snowden held to the theory that the corruption of public opinion was worse than the bribery suggested by the exchange and continued his campaign against Findlay on the basis of his caucus nomination.

On the positive side the Hiester managers sent Valentine Brobst through the western counties ostensibly to purchase land, but actually to conduct a subtle electioneering tour. He spoke with farmers, mechanics, and others concerning Findlay's unethical practices and Hiester's virtue and patriotism. The latter's Revolutionary career especially was recalled. Brobst told how Hiester, after raising a company of 80 men in 1775 to fight for the cause of independence, joined Washington's forces only to be captured in the battle of Long Island. He spent nearly a year on a British prisonship, but upon release he demonstrated his willingness to make an additional sacrifice for the American cause by rejoining Washington in 1777.[15]

The Findlay opposition painted an entirely different picture of Hiester's Revolutionary career and portrayed him as a coward who ran from battle at Brandywine. This aroused the righteous indignation of Thomas Atkinson of the *Crawford Messenger* who called upon the people of the state, who cherished a fond recollection of the sacrifices and sufferings of the departed heroes of the Revolution, to be mindful of the merits and claims of the living heroes as well. A vote for Findlay, he declared, was a treasonous sanction of the falsehoods spread against this hero of independence, and in a second editorial of the same number of the *Messenger* the people were urged to endorse Hiester because he was the *"last old revolutionary character . . . likely to be a candidate for governor."* This was to be the last chance for Pennsylvania voters to demonstrate their gratitude to the heroes of the independence movement.[16]

All of these arguments were of no avail. Findlay carried the election by almost a two to one majority in the western counties. Only Allegheny and Crawford Counties gave Hiester scant majorities of 37 and 6 votes, respectively. The bulk of Findlay's strength was concentrated in the four southwestern counties of Greene, Fayette, Washington, and Westmoreland which registered a greater vote for the Patentee candi-

---

[15] *Reporter,* September 22, 1817; William H. Egle, *Pennsylvania: Civil, Political, and Military,* . . . (Harrisburg: DeWitt C. Goodrich, 1877), p. 243.

[16] *Crawford Messenger,* September 5, 1817.

date than the entire region of Western Pennsylvania cast for his opponent. Except for 78 votes the victor's state margin of 7,005 was
compiled in the 13 western counties that gave him a plurality.[17]

This strength in the West may probably be attributed to the fact
that Findlay was a candidate of the regular Republican Party [18] and to
the conservatism of the farmers who continued to dominate the population of Western Pennsylvania. As a writer in the *Crawford Messenger*
reported:

> By the election of Mr. Findlay we shall have a moral certainty that there
> will be no change in the politics of the state. Pennsylvania will be respected
> for the stability of her character and institutions—we shall fear no dangerous
> innovations—the citizens and the laws will be preserved unviolated—and
> grateful for the abundant mercies we enjoy. . . .[19]

COMPETITORS RE-MATCHED

In many respects the gubernatorial contest of 1820 was a carbon
copy of the one in 1817. The same candidates, the same issues, and the
same electioneering methods reappeared, but a few additions and altera-
tions reversed the decision and sent Hiester to Harrisburg as governor.

Scarcely had Findlay pulled his chair up to the governor's desk in
1817 than his opponents in the legislature took steps to embarrass and
undermine his administration. Desiring to learn more about the campaign charges: (1) that Findlay had made monetary exchanges to
injure individual creditors and purchase the political support of others
and (2) that he acquired short-term loans from private banks to cover
deficiencies in the treasury, the legislature passed a resolution to investigate the governor's conduct during his term as state treasurer.
William Marks and Andrew Stewart of the western counties were appointed to the committee which made the investigation and exonerated
Findlay. On March 18, 1818, Stewart read the committee's report to
the assembly and concluded that the governor's demeanor as treasurer
had been faithful, meritorious, and beneficial to the state and that he
was entitled to the thanks and gratitude of his fellow citizens.[20]

Aware that this report would pass its second reading with the same

---

[17] For complete election statistics of the western counties see Appendix C.
[18] Klein, *Pennsylvania Politics,* p. 95 f.
[19] "A Farmer," *Crawford Messenger,* August 22, 1817.
[20] Pennsylvania, *House Journal* (1817-1818), pp. 16, 666-675.

finality it enjoyed on the first, the opposition attempted to halt this formal acquittal by restating the charges and by proposing a resolution to require the next session of the legislature to study the governor's record further. The Findlayites defeated this maneuver and adopted the committee's report.

Undaunted by this defeat, the opposition, which was becoming known as the Anti-Corruptionists in contrast to Findlay and his Corruptionists, insisted that the governor had impeded the investigation. They worked with this spark of corruption until the 1819-1820 session of the assembly when they again fanned it into a glowing flame. The suspicion of corruption surrounding appointments to office and the charge of subsidizing public officials into silence produced a new committee to examine Findlay's conduct as governor. William Wilkins and James Todd of Allegheny and Fayette Counties, respectively, were appointed to this committee which analyzed eight separate charges, plus the one condemning the governor for hindering the earlier investigation. In spite of the efforts of Josiah Randall, a Philadelphia henchman of John Binns, who presented the original petition for the inquiry to the house, and who was chairman of the investigating committee, the group declared that the petition was founded only on rumor and absolved the governor of any misconduct.[21]

This unrelenting attack on Findlay was largely eastern-sponsored, but its reverberations were felt throughout the state. Although vindicated by both investigations, the governor was hurt politically by the incidents themselves because they kept hinting at the possibilities of corruption. When impeachment appeared unlikely, the Anti-Corruptionists assaulted the men responsible for clearing the governor's record.

William Wilkins was the center of this diverted attack. Binns not only labeled him a Federalist, but also attempted to demonstrate that he was the spokesman for the administration in the assembly. As further proof that Findlay was backed by the Federalists, Binns linked Wilkins' success in winning the assembly seat in 1819 with support from such Federalist journals as the *Pittsburgh Gazette*. According to Binns, since Wilkins was "allied to one of the most influential republican families in the state," the *Gazette* hoped to obtain advantages for Pittsburgh and vicinity through the influence of Wilkins who was the brother-in-law of George M. Dallas who was the brother-in-law of Richard Bache

---

[21] Pennsylvania, *House Journal* (1819-1820), pp. 10, 586-612.

who was the brother-in-law of Thomas Sergeant.[22] Wilkins and his connection, dubbed the Family Party, were accused of harboring Federalist ideas and of perpetuating a corrupt governor in office.

After Wilkins had directed the house committee to the conclusion that the governor was guilty of no misconduct, the rumor spread that he was in line for an appointment to a judgeship by the governor. To this the *Washington Examiner* bluntly commented: "the labourer is worthy of his hire," and the apparent alliance between Findlay and this Family Party with Federalist tendencies caused Editor Grayson to charge that the governor had betrayed the Republican Party that elected him. Binns echoed these sentiments, and both editors expressed their suspicion of Findlay's political loyalties. They based their contention on the fact that within two years of his election he threw himself into the arms of leading Federalists to "avoid being consumed by a blaze of public indignation which his own acts of corruption had enkindled about him." [23]

If Wilkins personally tended any further in the direction of Federalism than the average Independent Republican, he successfully hid his convictions from the public in the autumn elections of 1820. He was supported for re-election to the assembly by the same people that endorsed Baldwin's return to Congress. Although Wilkins campaigned on his personal record and tied his candidacy in no way to the gubernatorial race, the facts do not preclude a secret alliance with Findlay.

The election results of 1817 had demonstrated that Findlay did not run comparatively well in Allegheny County where Wilkins was required to win his major support, and nothing happened in the succeeding three years to make the prospects of 1820 any more optimistic. Because of this situation the most effective assistance to Findlay that Wilkins could render was obviously in the legislature, and by ignoring the governor's candidacy for re-election Wilkins charted the best course to gain that strategic assembly seat.

After his victory and Findlay's defeat, Wilkins further clouded the issue by campaigning for the speakership as a Hiesterite. On the surface at least, this seemed to nullify the charge of a secret pact between Wilkins and Findlay, but actually the former was motivated by opportunism. Both his personal career and the Family Party stood to gain if he

---

[22] *Democratic Press,* February 18, 1820.
[23] *Ibid.,* April 5, 1820; *Examiner,* March 13, 1820.

were chosen speaker, but beaten by John Gilmore of Butler County, a true Independent, Wilkins was forced to accept the failure of his political maneuver. The governor, however, did not regard him as either a fair-weather friend or an enemy of long standing. Completely satisfied with Wilkins' conduct on the investigating committee, in the election campaign, and in the speakership contest, Findlay paid his obligation in full in the last official act of his administration in December 1820. Wilkins was appointed president judge of the Fifth Judicial District of Pennsylvania, and the Family Party, which held the balance of power in the legislature, in turn, showed its gratitude in 1821 by successfully sponsoring Findlay for the vacant seat in the United States Senate.[24]

The charge of corruption which had dogged the governor throughout his term proved to be a hurdle he could not jump. If he had been required to answer only this complaint, he might have won re-election, but he was also faced with the most challenging type of problem set before an incumbent administrator. Findlay's three years as governor were years of depression, and like so many other incumbent candidates and parties after him, he was unable to overcome the reaction against the party and administrator in power which demands that they assume the responsibility for economic collapse.

The Hiester block in Western Pennsylvania linked depression conditions with what was termed the unprecedented manner in which Findlay doled out the patronage. This charge formed the theme for their campaign propaganda in 1820. The governor experienced a significant loss of public confidence in Beaver, Fayette, Mercer, Washington, and Westmoreland Counties when large numbers of voters became dissatisfied with his appointments and policies which, they were led to believe, contributed to the depression. The *Western Argus* of Beaver was most vociferous in registering objections to the governor for his failure to reduce salaries in the face of the troubled times and for his numerous appointments of justices of the peace in that county without regard for the public good.[25]

The effectiveness of these editorials revealed that the county's political sceptre had passed from the hand of ex-Senator Abner Lacock to the

---

[24] *Democratic Press,* November 28, and December 8, 14, 1820.

[25] *Mercury,* March 17, 1820; *Western Argus* (Beaver) quoted in *Aurora,* September 28, 1820.

politically-minded Logan Brothers of the *Western Argus*. The completeness of their victory was disclosed by the election results in 1820 when Hiester recorded a 242 majority over Lacock-sponsored Findlay who had gained a 272 margin over the same opponent three years before.

The Logans and other Hiesterites in the western counties attacked Findlay with basic Jeffersonian philosophy by denouncing the "high cost of government"; his administration was condemned for costing more than Federalism ever did. While the price of the farmer's flour dropped to $2.00 per barrel, oats to 15 cents a bushel, and butter to 10 cents a pound in the depression, the cost of "Mr. Findlay's democracy keeps up still."

> Was not the government which they [the soldiers of the Revolution] fought for, and established, a good and cheap one? Theirs was the real, true democracy: at least I think so. I prefer it much to this new-fangled democracy, which seems to be made for nothing but noise and extravagance. . . . I want a cheap government—such as we had twelve years ago. . . . [26]

Although this bit of frontier farm philosophy was designed to injure the political acceptability of Findlay, the election results demonstrated that it had little, if any, effect on the farm vote of Western Pennsylvania. In the rural counties of Armstrong, Greene, Indiana, and Jefferson, Findlay actually increased his margin of victory over Hiester from what it had been in 1817. The relationship between the two remained static in Allegheny, Crawford, Erie, Venango, and Warren Counties where the difference between the two did not vary more than ten votes from the 1817 margins.[27]

Except for Greene and Allegheny Counties, the anti-Findlay trend in Western Pennsylvania was registered in the other five largest counties which were developing more-urban populations. Although Findlay carried all the western counties in 1820 except Allegheny and Beaver, his margin of victory was so reduced over his comparative rating with Hiester in 1817 that he obviously lost the campaign for re-election in the region that had made him victorious three years before.

The decrease of Findlay's strength in Washington, Westmoreland, and Beaver Counties alone more than offset Hiester's margin of victory throughout the state. The governor's greatest decline was in Washington County where the Club had risen in opposition. Both the *Examiner*

---

[26] "A Democrat," *Mercury*, October 4, 1820.
[27] See Appendix C.

and the *Reporter* had endorsed Findlay in 1817—indicating that at that time there was no disagreement over politics at the state level, but a wide gulf between the two journals opened in the following three years.

Because of issues that were local in character, the Club's *Examiner* threw its support behind Hiester in 1820. Superficially the Club talked of corruption and the governor's failure to meet the depression, but in reality Findlay's appointment of William Sample, rather than George Baird, as prothonotary had stirred the Club's jealousy. The removal of Alexander Murdoch and Isaac Kerr of the Club's lower echelon from office after the 1817 election supplied additional fuel for the destructive fire kindled by the *Examiner*.[28]

Although the Findlayites countered with the epithet "dissappointed office-seekers" and predicted that the Club was preparing to join "in wedlock with *New England Federalism*," the *Examiner's* campaign moved forward.[29] In fact, the Independents made marked progress in all the densely-settled western counties where they received a favorable press. In 1817 the public had viewed the Independents with suspicion and identified all opposition to the regular Delegate ticket as Federalists, but by 1820 that misconception was dispelled.

The public only gradually became aware of the split in the Republican ranks and recognized that Federalists, in order to vote at all, had to endorse one or the other of the new Republican alignments. Mindful that Federalist support did not necessarily make an alignment Federalist-dominated, as many had feared in 1817, they were not so willing to accept the Findlayite charges of Federalism. The *Pittsburgh Gazette,* the *Mercury,* the *Western Argus,* and the *Greensburg Gazette* joined forces with the *Examiner* to promote this idea which proved decisive in the second Findlay-Hiester contest.

PREVIEW OF THE PRESIDENTIAL RACE

After Hiester took office, support fell away on all sides. Binns withdrew his endorsement and returned to the Patentee fold, Duane passed from the scene, and the depression lingered to cause added embarrassment. More than ever the Independent alignment appeared to be only a cloak for Federalism. Politicians generally were disgruntled with the administration, and Hiester evinced no desire for a second term.[30]

[28] *Reporter,* September 4, 11, 1820.
[29] *Ibid.*
[30] Klein, *Pennsylvania Politics,* p. 145.

Dissatisfaction in the western counties promoted the idea that the next governor would of necessity have to be a westerner. The *Mercury* went so far as to suggest that a western convention, denounced in the East as a caucus of the worst sort, be held to make certain that this goal was reached, and the names of William Wilkins and Walter Lowrie were frequently associated with such a nomination. Moses Sullivan, the Butler County delegate, was directed to cast his ballot for Lowrie at the Harrisburg Convention of 1823 while the Allegheny County representatives were urged to push the Wilkins' nomination with the utmost assiduity. Believing that Wilkins could unite the diverse factions of the western part of the state at least, Snowden heartily concurred in his endorsement.[31]

The Harrisburg conclave of the regular Republican Party, however, ignored these desires and nominated John Andrew Shulze while a Lewistown Convention of Independents selected Andrew Gregg as his opponent. Disapproving a nomination at the capital, Snowden was quick to declare Gregg a good choice. During the spring session of the United States district court in Pittsburgh in 1823, a public meeting of the citizens from the different western counties, in which Snowden played a prominent role, met to denounce the Harrisburg meeting as a caucus, and to map campaign strategy for Gregg.[32]

Snowden followed the same anti-caucus theme in attacking Shulze that had characterized his assaults on Findlay in 1817 and 1820. In this argument he was joined by the *Pittsburgh Gazette* and the "Gregarious" enthusiasts of Fayette County. Together they charged that an endorsement of this legislative interference in elections was an attempt to rob the people of their democratic right to nominate candidates for office and to throttle the advocates of liberty.

When these Gregg supporters in Fayette County questioned the authenticity of information concerning their candidate published in Thomas Patton's *Genius of Liberty,* they were forced to resort to handbills to explain their cause. Being a partisan editor, Patton adhered to the Delegate doctrine and said nothing favorable about Gregg although his was the only press in the Uniontown area. He condemned the charge that the members of the legislature had usurped the right of electing the governor as an artful insinuation because they had only recom-

---

[31] *Aurora,* November 2, 1822; *Pittsburgh Gazette,* February 14, 21, 1823; *Mercury,* February 18, 1823.
[32] *Mercury,* June 10, 1823.

mended Shulze, a member of their own body. "Surely," declared a writer in the *Examiner,* "it will not be contended that they are incompetent judges of his qualifications, particularly when it is recollected he has been associated with them so long in the legislature." [33]

While the Patton press passed off the Harrisburg nomination as a mere recommendation, the pamphleteers asked the public:

> Why then did they appoint committees all over the state with *giant* instructions from the *caucus* how to deal with you to the best advantage? . . . The county committees meet and appoint sub-committees in each township to *drill the people, march them to the polls, and place in their hands the ticket they must vote.*[34]

The Lewistown meeting was defended as a genuine convention because it only recommended Gregg; no committees, no sub-committees, and no "whippers in" were appointed. When not affirming this position, the Greggites were engaged in replying to the charge that their candidate was a Federalist. He was accused on the basis of the "Peace Letter" which he had supposedly written to the "peace party committee" at the outbreak of the War of 1812. In deploring the fact that the "golden harvest of wealth and happiness" enjoyed by all classes of citizens had been swept away and replaced with war, debt, and taxation, the letter in question identified Gregg with the Pennsylvania wing of the "Hartford stampers."

Although Gregg declared that he had never authored such a letter, his managers could not deny that he received Federalist support. Like many previous Independent leaders, they pointed out that this was no innovation; the Fayette pamphleteers used the example of Andrew Stewart who had received Federalist aid in his congressional campaign although no one suspected him of being a member of that party. Since Federalists had to vote for one of two Republicans or forfeit their vote, they were praised for their wise choice in endorsing Gregg.[35]

In order to offset the Federalist label pinned on Gregg, Shulze was depicted as an advocate of foreign commerce who, if elected, would cripple and retard the development of internal improvements and domestic manufacturing. He was further indicted as an aristocrat who

---

[33] Pamphlet: "Benjamin Franklin," *To the Electors of Fayette County.* Dated October 7, 1823, and bound with the *Genius of Liberty* in the Uniontown Public Library. "A Democratic Republican," *Examiner,* March 29, 1823.

[34] Pamphlet: *To the Electors of Fayette County.*

[35] *Ibid.; Examiner,* August 30, 1823.

posed as a Republican while advocating the anti-Republican doctrine
of the legislative caucus.

The Independents also discovered William H. Crawford, a caucusite
boomed for the presidency in the 1824 election, lurking in the background of the Shulze campaign. Since Shulze and Crawford were endorsed by the same people, Gregg's Republican record was compared
with that of the latter who was not popular in Western Pennsylvania.
The Independent was found to be a more uniform Republican than
Crawford because in 1798 he was in Congress to oppose John Adams'
reign of terror while Crawford united with the Federalists to perpetuate
it. Again in 1807 when Gregg was in the United States Senate, he
assisted the Jeffersonians in passing the Embargo Act while Crawford
cast his ballot with the opposition.[36]

In a further effort to embarrass Shulze's candidacy, other politicians
unacceptable to large blocs of voters in the western counties, were linked
to his campaign. Among them were John C. Calhoun, the most prominent rival to Crawford for the caucus nomination for the presidency,
and Abner Lacock who had accused Gregg of writing the "Peace
Letter." The public was also encouraged to vote against Shulze because
he was a "bitter and malignant persecutor" of Andrew Jackson who
already was the most popular choice in Western Pennsylvania for the
presidency in 1824. Lacock, like another Patentee, Albert Gallatin,
was in particular disrepute in Allegheny County because of his vote for
the Cumberland Road. These men were joined by Walter and Matthew
Lowrie, Ephraim Pentland, William Marks, and James Stevenson in
their endorsement of the caucus nominations, namely, Shulze for the
governorship and Crawford unofficially for the presidency. All were
condemned by the Independents for taking part in this scheme to cheat
the people out of either of their favorite candidates for the presidency—
Jackson or Henry Clay.[37]

The Independents also argued conversely that a vote for Gregg
meant support for Jackson for the presidency the following year. This
appeared to be a master stroke politically since numerous groups in
Western Pennsylvania had already endorsed Jackson. The Westmore-

---

[36] *Mercury,* September 16, and October 13, 1823.

[37] *Genius of Liberty,* August 5, 1823, quoted in *Pittsburgh Gazette,* August 15,
1823; "Notalacock," *Pittsburgh Gazette,* September 12, 1823; Pamphlet: *To
the Electors of Fayette County.*

land County meeting that had selected delegates to the Lewistown Convention also recommended that Jackson be supported for the presidency. In the course of the 1823 campaign a public meeting in Pittsburgh appointed James Ross and Henry Baldwin to head a committee to promote Jackson's nomination. The Independent leaders pictured defeat for Shulze as a defeat for the congressional caucus and encouragement for Jackson, but the balloting of Western Pennsylvania in 1823 and 1824 revealed that the public did not hold a similar view. Instead the people judged the elections individually, preventing the Independents from gaining the strength they expected from their unofficial attachment to Jackson.[38]

After Shulze's triumph Snowden urged him to disarm his opposition throughout the state by announcing his support of Jackson for the presidency. The editor feared that success for Shulze after his Harrisburg nomination would be construed as an approval by the people of Pennsylvania of the caucus method for selecting a presidential nominee.[39] Actually Crawford's stock in the state's political market did rise sharply after Shulze's victory because many of the rank and file leaders identified Shulze with Crawford and recognized the powerful patronage position afforded the governor under the existing state constitution. State appointments after the election left the governor with an extensive grass-root control which he could turn in favor of the presidential aspirant of his choice, if he so desired.

These election results in 1823 revealed that the western counties endorsed the nominee of the regular Republican Party with more vigor than exhibited at any time since Simon Snyder had held the reins of state politics tightly in his hands. Only Warren of the 15 western counties did not register a majority vote for Shulze, and while the state at large cast 58 per cent of its total vote for the victor, Western Pennsylvania turned in 69 per cent. Although Pittsburgh remained in the Independent column by a narrow margin, Allegheny County voted three to two for Shulze.

The distribution of the results in Allegheny and Washington Counties revealed conclusively that personal loyalties were gradually being replaced by faction regularity. In Allegheny both the Regular and the

---

[38] *Mercury,* February 25, 1823; *Pittsburgh Gazette,* September 5, 1823.
[39] *Mercury,* November 4, 1823.

Independent slates followed with a consistency not experienced since the War of 1812.[40]

The Independent movement, sponsored by the Club in Washington County, all but gave up the ghost in this election; Club strength had ebbed to the point that no Independent ticket for the legislative posts was set forth. The Club's *Examiner* did assist, however, in the campaign against Shulze, but based its arguments wholly on local considerations. A victory for Shulze was taken to mean that Sample would be reappointed prothonotary and his former clerk Joseph Henderson would assume the offices of register, recorder, and clerk of the courts. Since inevitable victory also loomed before Sample's brother-in-law, Samuel Workman, in his quest of the sheriff's office, the *Examiner* jealously talked of this political prize for which Sample's "family" was contending.[41] Recognizing the inability of the Club to upset the local Patentee ticket, the *Examiner* placed its hopes for Club resurgence on a Gregg victory and the subsequent local appointments, neither of which materialized.

Throughout the county Shulze's vote was 4,188 to 1,414 for Gregg, but the four unopposed regular Republican candidates for the state assembly did little better. They registered 4,281 4,272, 4,271 and 4,209 votes, respectively, indicating that probably most of Gregg's supporters possessed enough party conviction to abstain from voting for these legislative nominees.[42]

---

[40] According to the *Pittsburgh Gazette*, October 24, 1823, the regular Republican ticket in Allegheny County, composed of Shulze for governor, Samuel Power for state senator, and James S. Stevenson, James Patterson, John Brown, and Moses Sullivan for assemblymen, was supported in its entirety with marked consistency. The voting pattern in eight of the county's 17 townships follows:

Townships	Shulze	Power	Stevenson	Patterson	Brown	Sullivan
Moon	71	73	73	73	71	73
Findlay	137	147	141	141	141	141
Ohio	153	158	163	163	159	163
Pine	95	99	100	106	101	100
Ross	151	150	158	145	152	149
Plum	160	164	168	160	156	162
St. Clair	166	163	187	170	170	177
Robinson	111	117	120	122	117	120

[41] *Examiner*, October 6, 1823.

[42] *Ibid.*, October 18, 1823.

Of course, this failure to provide a complete ticket of their own spelled doom for the Club, a stronghold of Republican insurgence in the western counties over the last six years. With these evidences of total victory in Washington and Allegheny Counties in 1823 the Republican organization throughout Western Pennsylvania exhibited a stronger tendency toward unity than at any time in the preceding decade.

IX

The Unpopular Election

Lord Packingham[1] *and King Caucus. Andrew Jackson
defended the country against the arms of the one, the
country will defend him against the arts of the other.*[2]

THE gubernatorial election of 1823 was in no way indicative of
simultaneous developments on the national scene. Shulze's victory revealed a trend toward both Republican harmony and
caucus nominations, especially in the state's western counties, but neither
of these concepts reflected contemporaneous politics at the national level.

The confusion that reigned there was, in part, the outgrowth of
Monroe's re-election in 1820. Although the party line in state and local
politics had been fluid since 1815, the national shell of the Republican
Party had remained relatively firm. Politicians had come to regard the
presidency, especially a second administration, as the grand finale to a
highly successful political career. Monroe was no exception and wanted
only to relax and enjoy his last years on the political stage. In assuming
this attitude he gradually lost control of many of the party's strongest
men who regarded themselves as presidential aspirants and began
jockeying for position. They recognized that the President had become
a mere setting sun in the world of politics.

By April 1822 Hezekiah Niles had estimated that there were at
least 16 candidates actively engaged to win the necessary support to
succeed Monroe in the White House. All of these leading candidates
professed the same political ideas, at least to such an extent that any
one of them could have been heartily supported by the whole Republican Party, a supposed prerequisite since this was the only alignment
throughout the nation with more than a local existence.[3]

---

[1] General Edward Pakenham who commanded the British forces in the battle at
New Orleans.

[2] Toast proposed by Neville B. Craig at the Jackson Blues' celebration of the
ninth anniversary of the New Orleans victory. *Mercury*, January 13, 1824.

[3] Edward Stanwood, *History of the Presidency* (new ed.; Boston: Houghton,
Mifflin Co., 1928), I, 126 f.

Western Pennsylvania, however, extended its solid front into the realm of national politics with a near unanimity on a presidential choice for 1824. As early as the autumn of 1821 the region's better analysts recognized that the legislative and executive powers of the state had done everything possible to promote internal improvements and tariff protection, but had failed. They perceived that they must turn the eyes of the general citizenry toward the central government to gain the desired assistance.[4] This they did in one accord. The western counties voted overwhelmingly for Jackson in 1824 but, in so doing, they exhibited at least an indifference toward the methods of nominating candidates, if not a complete reversal of the pro-caucus tendency in the previous year.

A CROWDED BANDWAGON

After Shulze's caucus nomination and sweeping victory in the autumn of 1823, the caucusites were encouraged to expect substantial support from Pennsylvania for any candidate they might nominate. Their congressional caucus assembled on February 14, 1824, with only three Pennsylvanians numbered among the 66 members present; two of these, Walter Forward and Walter Lowrie, represented the western counties. Since this meeting was obviously attended by only a minority of the 261 members of Congress, it was an inspiring signal to sundry non-caucus candidates to enter the presidential race against the choices made at the nation's capital. William H. Crawford of Georgia and Albert Gallatin of Pennsylvania were tapped for the presidency and vice presidency, respectively, by the legislators, and it was hoped that the latter's selection would swing the Keystone State into the Crawford column on election day. An ultimate Jackson-Calhoun coalition, plus the political impotence of Gallatin evidenced at a later Harrisburg convention, upset the plans of the Crawford group which grew more and more desperate as the campaign progressed.[5]

At the time of the caucus nominations the presidential enthusiasm of the people in Western Pennsylvania centered around Andrew Jackson. Old Hickory, as the general was familiarly known, had first gained

---

[4] "A Republican," *Mercury*, September 19, 1821.

[5] *Mercury*, February 24, 1824; *Pittsburgh Gazette*, February 27, 1824; Everett S. Brown, "The Presidential Election of 1824-1825," *Political Science Quarterly*, XL (1925), 395 f.

the popular acclaim of the state's western counties during the War of 1812 when western newspapers needed copy desperately. The general and his staff supplied military reports in abundance. Most of them got into print and now began to pay valuable political dividends. Along with his nationally well-known exploits, they literally made the name of Jackson a household byword in Western Pennsylvania.

As early as September 17, 1822, the *Crawford Messenger* suggested Jackson's name for the presidency two years hence. The friends of the general in Westmoreland County held a public meeting in Greensburg on December 28 of the same year to add their approval to the Meadville recommendation.[6] Not until August 6, 1823, however, did the people of Allegheny County endorse Jackson in a public meeting although Henry Baldwin had entertained such an idea many months before. In January he had written to Jackson to determine whether or not he would consent to run for the presidency. The general informed him that he thought it consistent with republican principles not to solicit any public office, but at the same time declared that he would not decline any public demand upon his services.[7]

Following the lead of the other counties, Allegheny made this demand when an estimated 600 or 700 citizens almost unanimously selected Jackson as their presidential preference. In the words of the *Pittsburgh Gazette* the August meeting

> was composed of every class of people, and of every political denomination, and after a full and orderly discussion, in which every candidate, whose name has been before the public, was fairly nominated and respectfully treated, the Hero of New Orleans was taken up, with a burst of enthusiasm, and with a degree of unanimity never before witnessed in this place.[8]

A committee of correspondence, including Baldwin, James Ross, James Riddle, John M. Snowden, Edward Patchell, Morgan Neville, and Ross Wilkins, was selected to contact the friends of Jackson throughout Pennsylvania.[9] After a lapse of three months a second Jackson meeting in Pittsburgh was called for November 29, 1823, ostensibly to decide whether or not the general should be the official candidate of the Re-

---

[6] *Crawford Messenger,* September 17, 1822; *Westmoreland Republican,* January, 3, 1823.

[7] Jackson to Baldwin, January 24, 1823. Bassett, *Correspondence of Jackson,* III, 184.

[8] *Pittsburgh Gazette,* August 8, 1823.

[9] *Mercury,* August 12, 1823.

publican Party of Allegheny County. From the beginning the meeting
was prejudiced in the affirmative. The sponsors simply hoped to whip
up more enthusiasm and to plan a Jackson celebration for January 8,
the anniversary of his renowned New Orleans victory.

On this occasion Robert J. Walker, the twenty-two-year-old lawyer-
son of Judge Jonathan Walker, delivered a spirited address in favor of
Jackson and in opposition to the caucus system. The group responded by
instructing the legislators of their district to abstain from nominating
an electoral slate for Pennsylvania in order both to circumvent the
selection of a candidate other than Jackson and to prevent the defiling
of Jackson's political purity through identification with a legislative
caucus. For similar reasons their congressmen were advised not to take
part in any caucus at Washington designed to nominate a presidential
candidate. Along with Walker, Patchell of the original Jackson committee of correspondence appointed in August was the most active in
support of these resolutions.[10]

The absence of Baldwin, Ross, Riddle, and Neville of the same committee was conspicuous and apparently indicative of a rift in the Jackson leadership of Allegheny County. A new committee of correspondence, composed of young Walker, William Stewart, Robert Steele, and
14 other political unknowns, was appointed, and from the tone of the
address that they subsequently published, this group of new young men
was attempting to control the Jackson nomination to the exclusion of
all other political groups.

In praising Jackson as "the unyielding champion of Democracy" who
was *"not the reluctant convert driven in from prostrate Federalism,
monopolizing the rewards of Democracy,"* the committee showed its
resentment of the entrenched political leaders, particularly Baldwin and
Ross whose ideas were strongly tinged with Federalist philosophy.
The address also attacked the caucusites by pointing out that the campaign issue was simply to determine whether the Congress or the people
should select the party's candidate. Through this endorsement of a
caucus-free nominee and stern denunciation of Jackson's Federalist and
Independent adherents, the committee wished to place itself in command of the Jackson movement of Allegheny County. These Jackson
sponsors further demonstrated the sagacity of their choice by identifying
him with Thomas Jefferson, the father of the party, who had once

---

[10] *Pittsburgh Gazette,* December 5, 1823.

toasted Old Hickory with "honor and gratitude to the man who has filled the measure of his country's honour!" [11]

A public meeting in nearby Beaver resolved to approve the measures adopted by the Democratic-Republicans of Allegheny County to promote the nomination of Jackson. The "Federal Republican friends of General Jackson" in Westmoreland County took similar action. In the latter county a committee of seven was appointed to address the local citizenry on the subject of the election in the *Greensburg Gazette*. The committee pointed out that the caucus had been responsible for the elections of Jefferson, Madison, and Monroe, and now favored the Crawford-Gallatin ticket. By inference the group charged that caucus Democrats were behind Crawford while Federal or Independent Republicans deserved credit for sponsoring Jackson. Although the Baldwin faction subscribed to this interpretation, it was obviously counter to the Patchell-Walker adherents of Allegheny County and the Marchand Democrats of Westmoreland County.[12]

With similar dissension among the Jackson forces threatening elsewhere in Western Pennsylvania, the various counties of the state selected delegates to the Harrisburg Convention of March 4, 1824, to nominate a presidential candidate. At the time some of the pro-Jackson counties made their choices, they believed that they were selecting delegates to a convention at Huntingdon because they feared that the Calhoun men would dominate the Harrisburg meeting. Determined to nominate and elect Jackson, they had no desire to weaken his support by risking a showing against Calhoun at Harrisburg, but the withdrawal of a significant bloc of Calhoun's strength encouraged the two groups to sit down together. Samuel D. Ingham, George M. Dallas, and their Family Party decided at the last moment to withhold their support from Calhoun's campaign for the presidential nomination in favor of a Jackson-Calhoun ticket. This shift was sufficient to bring enough members of both groups to one convention at Harrisburg that the Huntingdon meeting was never held.[13]

Before this coalition occurred Abner Lacock, who was unable to control the selection of a delegate in his home county of Beaver, jour-

---

[11] *Pittsburgh Gazette,* December 19, 1823; *Mercury,* December 23, 1823.

[12] *Western Argus* quoted in *The Commonwealth* (Harrisburg), February 3, 1824; *Greensburg Gazette,* January 23, and February 27, 1824.

[13] Klein, *Pennsylvania Politics,* p. 161 f.

neyed to Pittsburgh through 18 inches of snow to stir up support for Crawford at the Harrisburg Convention. His hope was to win convention approval for the nominee already selected by the congressional caucus, but his scheme was rejected when the people of Allegheny County selected four Jacksonites to represent them at the convention. Available records show that at least 11 Western Pennsylvania counties were in attendance, and all of their 23 delegates voted for Jackson; in fact, only Jonathan Roberts of the 125 delegates voted against him.[14]

The convention did not enjoy as much unanimity as this one vote suggests. When Robert J. Walker of Pittsburgh proposed that Jackson be linked with a vice presidential nominee as the Family Party desired, some delegates opposed, arguing that a running mate might endanger Jackson's election. The principal objection of these opponents was based on local considerations. Headed by John H. Wise of Westmoreland County, these politicians sensed Jackson's personal popularity and recognized that it would assist local tickets throughout the state, but at the same time they did not want to be committed to a vice presidential nominee who held tenets contradictory to their own and to those of their local candidates. Walker insisted that a vice presidential choice would "fortify and support the General throughout the Union" because no other body would be convened thereafter that could nominate a better man. He declared that a bold stand by Pennsylvania on a vice presidential nominee would assure the defeat of the caucus rival, Albert Gallatin.[15]

The convention decided to follow Walker's recommendation, and the nod went to Calhoun who registered 87 votes to ten each for Clay and Gallatin. This meager demonstration of Gallatin's strength in his home state was an early indication of the difficulties that the Crawford-Gallatin ticket was to face in the campaign.[16]

Many delegates were unhappy as they departed for their homes, not only because of the choice of Calhoun, but also because of other circumstances surrounding the convention. Some of the original sponsors of Jackson were disgruntled because they had been passed over in the selection of committees and because too many persons who had formerly been supporters of Calhoun were placed on the Jackson ticket. There was

---

[14] Klein, *Pennsylvania Politics*, p. 164 f.; *Pittsburgh Gazette*, February 20, 1824.

[15] *Commonwealth* (Harrisburg), March 9, 1824; *Mercury*, March 23, 1824.

[16] *Pittsburgh Gazette*, March 12, 1824.

particular criticism of the recommendation by the Allegheny County delegates when they proposed Charles Kenny of Mifflin Township for the position of presidential elector instead of Edward Patchell. The latter was defended in the Harrisburg *Commonwealth* as an early and most active supporter of the general while Kenny merely belonged to the "new levies." [17]

This solicitude for Patchell, shown by Editor John McFarland who insisted that the Pittsburgher had been unjustly denied the political courtesy of serving as a presidential elector, won his admiration. Patchell believed that the local papers supporting Jackson, the *Mercury* and particularly the *Gazette,* where still tinged with Federalism and did not represent the true friends of the general as satisfactorily as this Harrisburg editor who had championed him personally. Probably this impression caused Patchell to invite McFarland to Pittsburgh a few months later to edit the *Allegheny Democrat,* an emotional Jackson press founded in June 1824.

After the Harrisburg Convention a general fear that not all the advocates of the Jackson cause were sincere, but were motivated instead by opportunism, spread throughout the state. J. T. Sullivan of Philadelphia charged that Federalists had thrust themselves into the ranks of the Jacksonians merely for local and personal advantages. John Boyd of Erie, Henry Baldwin, and William Wilkins in the western counties were most frequently rumored as disloyal to the Jackson cause. The Harrisburg *Commonwealth* editorially reprimanded Boyd, who had been appointed one of Pennsylvania's presidential electors by the convention, for his refusal to serve on a Jackson committee during the campaign.[18]

This fear that there were traitors in the Jackson camp spread to Baldwin and his cohorts. Although not a delegate to the convention, Baldwin was present in Harrisburg, inciting much agitation and speculation. As a result of the indirect report he received on the Harrisburg conclave, John Q. Adams deduced that Baldwin was "a Crawfordite under a Jackson mask." [19] Adams, like so many of Jackson's own supporters, believed that the general was simply being used as an instrument to advance the candidacy of Crawford, and Baldwin's clandestine actions appeared to be proof of this anticipated pattern.

[17] *Mercury,* March 23, 1824; *Commonwealth* (Harrisburg), March 23, 1824.
[18] *Commonwealth* (Harrisburg), March 23, 1824.
[19] Adams, *Memoirs,* VI, 254.

Although this evaluation of Baldwin was unjust, it is difficult to define his role in the campaign. Calhoun had always been prominently connected with the Henry Clay concept of the American System. The same was true of Baldwin, and as early as 1821 Congressman Thomas J. Rogers, a manufacturer, and Samuel D. Ingham began organizing Pennsylvania politicians for Calhoun.[20]

Although Pennsylvania farmers, particularly the Scotch-Irish of the western counties, showed little interest in him, Baldwin who later in his career declared that the tariff had been his one interest in politics and that the "original Jacksonmen" were "tariff men of the old faith," at least flirted with the possibility of joining the Calhoun school in spite of his constituents' apathy. Undoubtedly the voters' wishes acted somewhat as a deterrent as did the unfolding of events in the 1824 campaign, especially when the major Calhoun support came from the Family Party which hated Baldwin because of his Independent Republican connections.[21]

Baldwin, in the meantime, had demonstrated himself to be a friend to the national military hero from Tennessee. He could justly claim that he had supported Old Hickory from the time the Lacock committee condemned him for the Florida Incident. The senatorial charges produced an outburst of public sympathy, and from that point the general's political star began to rise with the Baldwin label clearly visible. In 1829 Baldwin boasted that he had been a friend of Jackson

from the time he was ARRAIGNED BEFORE CONGRESS as a CRIMINAL. . . . He was my *first* and *last* choice for the Presidency, with me it was a voluntary, deliberate preference. I did not wait for public opinion to *kick me into his support,* but gave an impulse to the feeling which first brought him before the people.[22]

This Baldwin could prove by his letter to Jackson on January 2, 1823, in which he asked if Jackson would consent to be a presidential candidate; in fact, he was the only man with a political reputation in Pennsylvania who even timorously took Jackson's candidacy seriously

---

[20] John Spencer Bassett, *The Life of Andrew Jackson* (New York: Macmillan Co., 1928), p. 331.

[21] Baldwin to Stephen Simpson, October 7, 1829. Henry Baldwin, *Hypocrisy Unmasked* (Philadelphia: S. Probasco, 1832), p. 5 f.; Klein, *Pennsylvania Politics,* p. 157.

[22] Baldwin to Simpson, October 7, 1829. Baldwin, *Hypocrisy Unmasked,* p. 8 f.

and had courage enough to go on record for Jackson at that early date. Although Jackson's reply was in the affirmative, he pointed out that he "had gone into retirement with a desire rather to be a spectator, than actor in the passing scenes of life." [23] Perhaps the implied attitude led Baldwin to believe that he would not make a fight for the nomination, and certainly the Pittsburgh Independent was anxious to support a winner.

If this Jackson response influenced Baldwin's at all, it was not in the immediate future; months passed before any anti-Jackson trend was discernible. In August 1823 he played a major role in Pittsburgh's first Jackson meeting. He stated the purpose of the meeting to those who assembled, accepted an appointment to a Jackson committee of correspondence, and, according to Patchell, was commissioned to write an address to the Democratic-Republicans of the nation on the advisability of nominating Jackson for the presidency. The same source declared that the very next day Baldwin was persuaded by Judge James Riddle, associate judge of the Pittsburgh court of common pleas and likewise a member of the Jackson committee of correspondence, that the caucus would nominate and elect Crawford.[24]

From that date Baldwin appeared to take no active part in the local campaign either for or against Jackson. Patchell, described by John Spencer Bassett as "an ignorant preacher of the neighborhood," assumed control and seemed to develop an obsession that Jackson must be elected President. He became so closely identified with the Jackson cause that he too was nicknamed Old Hickory and in his copious writing to Jackson, whom he had never met, explained his efforts in the general's behalf in Pittsburgh and vicinity. He reported that, if Baldwin had done as he promised, he (Patchell) would not have faced half the difficulty "in turning the people on the straight course." Patchell modestly admitted that with the help of a few assistants he had reduced the Jackson opposition in Pittsburgh from 10,000 to something less than 50, but in reality the Pittsburgh population, men, women, and children, did not surpass the 10,000 figure.[25]

---

[23] Jackson to Baldwin, January 24, 1823. Bassett, *Correspondence of Jackson*, III, 184.

[24] Patchell to Jackson, August 7, 1824. Bassett, *Correspondence of Jackson*, III, 263.

[25] *Ibid.*

If Baldwin did turn his back on the Jackson campaign locally, as charged, he apparently had no desire to give that impression abroad. James Tallmadge of New York wrote to Baldwin in 1832, implying that he possessed a letter, several pamphlets, and handbills in behalf of Jackson which Baldwin had sent him in 1824. He sympathized with Baldwin whom he regarded as an "original and true friend" of the general and attempted to console him by pointing out that the "new levies" were always trying to separate Jackson from those who stood by him in 1818 and 1824 as Baldwin had done.[26]

Aside from taking Jackson's statement that he desired to be a "spectator" literally, Baldwin and his cohorts were undoubtedly disturbed by the composition of the committee of correspondence selected in August 1823 to advance the name of Jackson. Many very young men and others who were political novices gained prominent positions on the committee. At any rate John M. Snowden, an ardent Jacksonite who had been a close ally of Baldwin in previous political battles, spoke out against this leadership. He opposed their frequent public meetings which he regarded as extremely injudicious and "calculated more to make the nominations a burlesque than to render any essential aid."

> We consider them, as having been got up by a few intemperate young men, who appear to be anxious to force themselves into the front rank; and to take the lead in a business which more properly belongs to the age and experience of society.[27]

The Washington *Reporter* confirmed this analysis of the Jackson leaders after the Harrisburg Convention; except for a few members of the assembly, the "chief actors" were aspiring young men who had recently embraced the Republican ranks.[28] This situation inevitably widened the rift between the Jackson factions of Western Pennsylvania as Frederick J. Cope, editor of the *Greensburg Gazette*, attested. While attending a Jackson celebration in Pittsburgh on Independence Day in company with some 200 other guests including former Governor William Findlay, Walter Forward, William Wilkins, and Edward Patchell, Cope discovered that Patchell was rather ungraciously received by the group. When his high rank in the militia and outspoken support of a

---

[26] James Tallmadge to Baldwin, June 27, 1832. Henry Baldwin, Correspondence in the possession of James R. Shryock, Meadville.

[27] *Mercury,* January 13, 1824.

[28] "Native," *Reporter,* August 2, 1824.

common candidate are considered, the only possible conclusion to be drawn is that the Jackson forces were openly divided.[29]

Included in the Patchell faction were numerous young attorneys headed by Robert J. Walker and Algernon S. T. Mountain, who were both too young to have voted in a presidential election prior to 1824. Likewise James S. Craft and, for a part of the campaign at least, Ross Wilkins, nephew of the judge, lent their youthful legal talents to the alignment. Walker and Wilkins, however, were identified with an Allegheny County nominating convention in June 1824. This group ignored the presidential race, since the Republicans had made their choice at Harrisburg, and proceeded to nominate what proved to be the local anti-Jackson ticket. Since Wilkins served as secretary during the meeting, his true allegiance was left in doubt. Both he and Walker were honored with appointments to the county committee of correspondence for the ensuing year, along with such prominent caucusites as Charles Shaler and Ephraim Pentland. Although the conclave selected William Beatty of Butler and John Brown of Allegheny as assembly candidates in common with the Jackson slate, James C. Gilleland and Robert Moore, two avowed opponents of Old Hickory, were also among their endorsements.[30]

In the face of his otherwise staunch support of Jackson and a complete Jackson ticket, Walker's apparent split-political personality should not be considered seriously. He was probably an unwilling victim of the meeting. As was the custom in these years, groups frequently selected men to their committees who were known to hold diverse political sentiments with the hope of making political capital from the resulting confusion. The failure of Wilkins to identify himself with the Jackson campaign after this meeting, plus his role as secretary, makes it impossible to assume that he stood by his original Jackson declarations.

Aside from the young hopeful attorneys the faction's leadership was supplied by Patchell himself and the bankrupt editor John McFarland, whom he had brought from the East in the heat of the campaign. Both were older men, but like the lawyers, without political experience.

Although the Baldwinites were disturbed at the composition of this Patchell organization, it may have been incidental to their decision to withdraw from the high ground taken in behalf of the general. If the

---

[29] *Greensburg Gazette,* July 9, 1824.
[30] *Allegheny Democrat,* June 22, and August 3, 1824.

action of the whole Baldwin group were gauged by the conduct of Walter Forward, opportunism would represent their strongest motivation. Although Forward had attended the congressional caucus and voted for Crawford, he belonged to the Baldwin supporters of Jackson. To add to the confusion among the Jacksonites, the *Allegheny Democrat* pointed out that Forward now called himself a Jackson candidate for Congress while his pamphlets and handbills were being printed by caucus leaders. His most active friends were also supporters of James C. Gilleland, an assembly candidate with a consistent caucus record. Perhaps the Baldwinites were prepared to climb on whatever bandwagon seemed most likely to succeed.[31]

The same motivation caused James Ross and the remnants of Western Pennsylvania Federalism, some of whom now labored under the Independent banner, to advocate Jackson's election. Since the general had written to President-elect Monroe in 1816 requesting the appointment of a Federalist as secretary of war, all those who looked to Ross for leadership regarded Jackson as the most friendly to their ideas on government. Furthermore, they believed that since their party had been absent from national administrations for so long, the election of Jackson with their endorsement would enhance their prestige, in spite of the fact that he was not exclusively their nominee.[32]

Certainly this proved to be an important factor in the unanimous endorsement given Jackson by Western Pennsylvania delegates at the Harrisburg Convention and by the western counties themselves on election day. Other Federalist and Independent encouragement for the uniform support of Jackson came from the editors of the *Pittsburgh Gazette* and *Mercury* who based their arguments on "sound" democratic principle. Morgan Neville was most emphatic in denying the caucus charge that Federalist support for Jackson was temporary and insincere and would ultimately switch to Adams. Although Federalists still respected Adams, Neville pointed out that the primary issue in Pennsylvania was simply "caucus or no caucus," and on this issue the Federalists stood squarely behind Old Hickory and against Crawford.[33]

---

[31] *Allegheny Democrat,* October 5, 1824; Robert M. Ewing, "Hon. Walter Forward," *The Western Pennsylvania Historical Magazine,* VIII (1925), 83.
[32] Schoyer, "James Ross," p. 100.
[33] *Pittsburgh Gazette,* November 5, 1824.

A POORLY CONTESTED RACE

Although Crawford had been nominated by a congressional caucus, his followers in Pennsylvania felt the need of a delegate convention to confirm the nomination and win the support of those whose political scruples refused to permit them to accept the caucus system. Under the guise that Pennsylvania caucusites could either confirm Crawford or select another candidate of their own choosing, they planned a Harrisburg convention of their own.

This decision held little meaning for the people of Western Pennsylvania, but in Allegheny County, at least, a call for a public meeting to select delegates to the convention was advertised by men on horseback who spread handbills throughout the county. Response from only 19 citizens was an indication of Crawford's weakness. Obviously there were many caucusites who failed to put in an appearance because they recognized that any anti-Jackson exhibition would weaken their local caucus tickets for which they had hopes in spite of Jackson's personal strength.[34]

The Jacksonites were relatively undisturbed by the proposed conference. Even McFarland, Jackson's emotional oracle of Western Pennsylvania, believed that it was of little importance whether the caucus at Harrisburg decided to continue its intrigue in the campaign under Crawford or switch to an Adams label. According to the editor Old Hickory was as secure in the Keystone state as life itself; "if he lives he will receive 28 votes from Pennsylvania." [35]

The campaign of the caucusites was built on a theme of party harmony. "Stick to the ticket as it now stands" (with Crawford and Gallatin) and "don't divide the party" were their most impassioned cries. Of course, Jacksonites insisted that Pennsylvania caucusites had divided the party themselves by joining southern Federalists in supporting Crawford. In rebuttal the Pennsylvania caucus group held that nominations should be made with due regard for every part of the nation or else local jealousies would increase until they destroyed the Union. Both candidates on the Jackson ticket were from the South, with Jackson even having been born in Calhoun's home state. According to local caucusite reasoning, there was surely someone in a non-slave-holding state that was qualified to hold one of these two offices;

---

[34] Patchell to Jackson, August 7, 1824. Bassett, *Correspondence of Jackson,* III, 265.

[35] *Allegheny Democrat,* August 17, 1824.

the Virginia dynasty itself had not been guilty of such an error in its presentation of Crawford and Gallatin to the public.[36]

Throughout the campaign the caucusites minimized the caucus as an issue. Crawford was simply endorsed as the party's best hope to close the breaches in the Republican ranks. At the same time the Crawford-ites said very little against Jackson, but attacked those who endorsed him instead.

This produced an ineffective campaign since the real contest in Western Pennsylvania was between Crawford and Jackson; the candidacy of both Adams and Clay remained incidental throughout. Adams did not enter the Pennsylvania presidential picture until July 1824 and then conducted no campaign at all in the western counties. Even the *Pittsburgh Gazette* with its tendency toward Federalism did not get around to acknowledging his candidacy, or that of Clay, until October 15, 1824:

> The reader will perceive that the friends of Mr. Adams are about forming an electoral ticket for him in this state. We have hitherto neglected to mention that preparatory measures have also been adopted for the formation of a Clay ticket in Pennsylvania.—Let them proceed, it is fair and proper enough that they should make the trial of their strength; and we have little doubt that either of these candidates may out-poll Mr. Crawford.[37]

Such casual treatment of these tickets was also adopted by the populace of the western counties, and it proved all the more ironical when the same two captured the presidency and the portfolio of the state department a few months later. Adams at no time actively sought Pennsylvania's support, but merely sanctioned the use of his name by state enthusiasts. On the other hand, Clay expected support as a result of his tariff and internal improvement programs, but it was not forth-coming.

All four of the presidential candidates permitted their local managers to picture them as tariff and internal improvement sponsors, but none had compiled a better record than Clay. At the outset of the campaign in Western Pennsylvania the tariff had loomed as the dominant factor in the election and it gave the Clay-men a reasonable hope for victory. This issue was relegated to a secondary role, however, by the abrupt emergence of the Jackson personality, and curiously enough, the trend

---

[36] *Allegheny Democrat,* August 3, 1824; P. P. F. De Grand, "Side-Lights upon the Presidential Campaign of 1824-25," *The Magazine of American History,* VIII (1882), 629.

[37] *Pittsburgh Gazette,* October 15, 1824.

developed without Jackson making any dogmatic pronouncements on either the tariff or internal improvements over which his Western Pennsylvania following could cheer.[38]

More so than the promoters of any other presidential candidate, the Jacksonites encouraged support for a whole ticket. At a meeting in August of the election year, the Allegheny County group resolved to oppose any individual for Congress and the state legislature who was opposed to the election of the general. Other groups held that the presidential race was completely divorced from congressional, state, and local elections. In echoing the sentiments of the Jackson leaders, McFarland argued that their ticket should be supported because all true followers of Old Hickory endorsed the democratic principle that the people should nominate and elect the President. Anything else was denounced as "elective despotism" and contrary to the firm conviction "of the framers of our constitution that the President should be selected *by the people throughout the union* and not *by a combination of politicians at the capitol.*"[39]

Simultaneously with the approach of the election, there was a quickening of the spirit of nationalism and of pride in representative government. Boastful talk of aiding republicanism everywhere that it enkindled the smallest flame became rather commonplace. Pride in the new Latin American republics and optimism for the success of the Greek movement for independence flowed from many an editor's pen and from the lips of such outstanding American statesmen as Clay, Monroe, and Gallatin, bringing back memories of our own national achievements. They were further revived by newspaper articles which began appearing in early 1824 to the effect that an invitation had been tendered and accepted by the Marquis de LaFayette to visit the United States as the nation's guest.

In anticipation of the event thoughts were turned to our military accomplishments, and Jackson's New Orleans victory shone like a beacon on a darkened hillside. More living people had shared in this engagement or could recall it from their personal experience than any other great national feat. All such extraneous development assisted in

[38] Klein, *Pennsylvania Politics,* pp. 172, 174; Eiselen, *Pennsylvania Protectionism,* p. 65 f.

[39] *Allegheny Democrat,* June 22, August 17, and September 28, 1824; Herman Hailperin, "Pro-Jackson Sentiment in Pennsylvania 1820-1828" (Unpublished Master's thesis, History Dept., University of Pittsburgh, 1925), p. 8.

the advancement of Jackson's candidacy since he, more so than any of his political opponents, was a national idol. A Pittsburgh militia unit under young Captain Harmar Denny demonstrates this point well. At a meeting on December 17, 1823, the company unanimously resolved that because of Jackson's gallant military services it would thereafter be known as the "Jackson Independent Blues." A dinner was planned for the anniversary of his New Orleans victory to celebrate their newly adopted name and, incidentally, to lend a psychological lift to his campaign for nomination and election.[40]

As the only surviving hero of the Revolution, Jackson was frequently mentioned in the same breath as George Washington during the presidential campaign. Because he had "attacked the perfidious Spaniard in his fort" and "fought the haughty Briton in the open field," Old Hickory was hailed as "second only to the father of our country" in the admiration and confidence of his fellow countrymen.[41]

Since military glory has a particular appeal to youth, this identification of Jackson with the nation's heritage was of paramount significance in Western Pennsylvania where "mere boys" were most aggressive to elect him. In the words of the *Allegheny Democrat*, Old Hickory's opponents referred to these supporters as "misguided youths, who are led away by the specious trappings of a 'tinselled' coat and military fame, to follow the fortunes of Gen. Jackson." [42]

With few exceptions even the general's political adversaries had nothing but praise for his military exploits, but one of them was afforded by a Crawford meeting in Uniontown where the sons of Albert Gallatin took an active part in the proceedings. Jackson was denounced as a Federalist, murderer, and violator of the Constitution. Adams-men also made his military career a target of sporadic attack with charges of cruelty, blood-thirsty murder, and conduct unbecoming a Christian because of his action in Florida. The Jackson presses countered with anecdotes showing his tenderness and humility. In domestic affairs he

---

[40] *Pittsburgh Gazette,* December 26, 1823. The Jackson Independent Blues became the twin company of the Pittsburgh Independent Blues, but a slightly different interpretation of their origin is presented by Niebaum, "Pittsburgh Blues," *West. Penna. Hist. Mag.,* IV, 266-267.

[41] *Mercury,* February 10, 1824.

[42] *Allegheny Democrat,* June 29, 1824.

was described as "meek as a lamb," but on the field of battle as "bold as a lion." [43]

In spite of such testimonials there were those who praised Jackson as a military leader, but believed that it would be endangering the civil and political liberties of the nation to place him at the head of the government. In cautioning that a political leader should have more than military merit and success on the battlefield to recommend him, a writer in the Washington *Reporter* observed that "one man is a warrior, and another is a statesman." This proved to be his indirect way of criticizing Jackson for taking a vague stand on internal improvements and for voting "variously" on tariff measures.[44]

The general suffered very little because of these attacks on his military career which certainly proved more of an advantage than a hinderance. Being the hero of New Orleans, he was able, according to former Senator Jonathan Roberts, to captivate "crowds of a deluded people," but Jackson's opponents in Western Pennsylvania sought to snap the public from this blind worship by challenging his party orthodoxy. The man responsible for this caucusite scheme was United States Senator Walter Lowrie of Butler County who had successfully replaced Abner Lacock as the caucus leader in the western counties. His plan was based on the thesis that a genuine party man considers it a matter of conscience never to vote a ticket composed of Federalists, in whole or in part, or even supported by Federalists. Although Jackson, Adams, and Clay tickets were all at least endorsed by some ex-Federalists, the caucusites feared only Jackson, and Lowrie convinced himself that he had found a point on which Old Hickory was vulnerable.[45]

Since Jackson had now come forward as a presidential candidate, the senator contended that the public should be informed of his sentiments on party politics. Lowrie believed that the general's views were incontrovertibly stated in one of his letters to Monroe who had read it to Senator Findlay and himself in 1821 without realizing the implication.

They had approached the President to protest the reappointment of William B. Irish as marshal of the Western District of Pennsylvania

---

[43] Gallatin to Badollet, July 29, 1824. Henry Adams, *The Life of Albert Gallatin* (New York: J. B. Lippincott & Co., 1879), p. 599; *Genius of Liberty* quoted in *Allegheny Democrat,* July 6, 1824.

[44] "Native," *Reporter,* August 2, 1824.

[45] *Pittsburgh Gazette,* November 19, 1824; Hailperin, "Pro-Jackson Sentiment," p. 9; Roberts Memoirs, II, 142.

on the grounds that he was a Federalist. In defending the reappointment, Monroe quoted from the Jackson letter in question which he
had received more than four years before in December 1816 when he
was President-elect. In it the general had suggested that Monroe invite
two Republicans and two Federalists into his cabinet because there
were worthy and competent members of the Federalist Party who had
severed their relationship with that party during the War of 1812. They
then "gallantly served their country in the field" and furnished the
proofs of "patriotism and attachment to free government that entitle
them to the highest confidence." [46]

In a later epistle to Monroe the general set forth a similar argument.
He denounced the leaders of the Hartford conclave as monarchists and
traitors to the nation, but insisted that there were "men who are called
Federalist that are honest, virtuous, and really attached to our Government." [47]

In the face of this evidence, plus Monroe's reply to the earlier letter
which was lost to posterity, Lowrie's charge cannot be denied. Writing
on December 14, 1816, Monroe pointed out to Old Hickory that he
agreed with him in principle to the effect that the chief magistrate of
the country ought not to be the head of a party, but of the nation itself.
He proposed to bring this state of affairs to pass by basing his administration strongly on the Republican Party for the present, but at the
same time "indulging toward the other, a spirit of moderation, and
evincing a desire to discriminate between its members and to bring the
whole into the republican fold, as quick as possible." Likewise Monroe
was anxious not to disgust the members of his own party "by too hasty
an act of liberality to the other party, thereby breaking the generous
spirit of the republican party, and keeping alive that of the Federalist."[48]

Although Monroe thus refused Jackson's suggestion for party amalgamation in 1816, he was willing to make use of Old Hickory's argument in 1821 to defend his action in sending the name of Irish to the
Senate for confirmation. Even though the Senate agreed that Irish had

---

[46] This apparently is Monroe's paraphrase of a statement in Jackson's letter
making such a request. Monroe to Jackson, December 14, 1816. Bassett, *Correspondence of Jackson*, II, 266.

[47] Jackson to Monroe, January 6, 1817. Bassett, *Correspondence of Jackson*, II,
272 f.

[48] Monroe to Jackson, December 14, 1816. Bassett, *Correspondence of Jackson*,
II, 266, 268.

previously given perfect satisfaction in the discharge of his duties, it failed in a secret session to confirm his reappointment. When discussion began, Martin Van Buren, a Crawfordite from New York, asked if there was anyone present that could answer whether Irish had voted for Hiester or Findlay in Pennsylvania's gubernatorial election of 1820. Aware that Findlay, now a senator himself, was in the chamber, Van Buren received the reply he desired. Findlay declared that Irish had voted for his opponent. Upon hearing this testimony, the New Yorker urged Senate Republicans to unite with him in refusing office to all but party members of the "genuine stamp." Irish was rejected.[49]

With the implication that Jackson would support an administration composed partly of Federalists in the future, Lowrie presented additional evidence of the general's proposal to Monroe. He introduced vouchers from Jonathan Roberts, Jesse B. Thomas, and Benjamin Ruggles to further substantiate his charges. Roberts, who had cast the only ballot for Crawford in the Harrisburg Convention, admitted in a letter to the Butler senator that the President had quoted to him from the Jackson letter in queston. Thomas, an Illinois senator appointed by Crawford to inspect the western land offices, and Senator Ruggles of Ohio, the chairman of the 1824 congressional caucus, declared that both Findlay and Lowrie had talked in their presence about having the letter read to them by Monroe. Findlay did not unequivocally deny that the President had read the letter to him, but "in his true character had no memory of it." [50]

Since Findlay, who was now endorsing Jackson in the presidential race, would not corroborate the charges of his Pennsylvania colleague in the Senate, all the testimony concerning the general's "soft" policy toward Federalists was presented by Crawford managers. Such a realization was all that was necessary to destroy Lowrie's whole argument. All loyal Jacksonites were convinced that the whole incident was contemptuously designed to thwart the desire of the people to nominate and elect a President of their own choice.

---

[49] *National Gazette* (Washington, D. C.), quoted in *Democratic Press,* March 13, 1822; *Mercury,* April 3, 1822; "Pennsylvania," *Reporter,* May 17, 1824.

[50] Jonathan Roberts to Walter Lowrie, April 25, 1824, printed in the *Pittsburgh Gazette,* May 14, 1824; Lowrie to Roberts, May 23, 1824, Jonathan Roberts Papers; Roberts Memoirs, II, 140; *Pittsburgh Gazette,* April 30, and May 7, 14, 1824; *Reporter,* May 17, 1824.

Lowrie's exposure was intended to break the solid front of Jackson's political army, but the general cleverly kept his forces intact by saying nothing about the situation that would alienate either Republican or Federalist followers. The *Butler Sentinel*, edited by Lowrie's brother-in-law John Sullivan, hoped to initiate an editorial trend away from Jackson after the disclosure of the incident. Desiring to be the conductor of a consistently Republican journal and now aware of Jackson's lack of regard for Republican principles and institutions, Sullivan regarded it his duty to turn toward another candidate. In further identifying the general with Federalist tactics, he charged that the doctrine, that party distinctions are only bubbles, was the party line of the Jackson type as far back as 1798.[51]

Lowrie and Sullivan together were unable to attract enough followers to this leadership to affect the Jackson strength appreciably. The *Western Press* at Mercer, the Washington *Reporter,* and the *Statesman* in Pittsburgh voiced similar sentiments, but their assistance was not enough to make either the caucus or the caucus candidate popular in Western Pennsylvania. In fact, with every passing week the caucus outlook grew dimmer and dimmer throughout the nation until it was recognized that Crawford's only salavation rested on the hope that Clay could be persuaded to accept the position of a vice presidential candidate on a Crawford ticket. Such a South-West coalition offered strong possibilities for success against the Jackson-Calhoun alignment.

In September before the election Van Buren approached Gallatin with a formal recommendation that he withdraw to make a place for Clay.[52] Gallatin was relieved at being permitted to escape what appeared to be inevitable defeat even in this manner, but declared that he would leave the decision to withdraw to the central committee of correspondence for Virginia. He felt particularly bound to that state since the caucus nominations had been confirmed by the Republican members of the Virginia legislature. Clay, however, refused to be molded to the Crawford pattern, and the presidential contestants went "down to the wire in a dead heat." [53]

---

[51] *Butler Sentinel* quoted in *Democratic Press,* July 31, 1824; *Allegheny Democrat,* August 31, 1824.

[52] Adams, *Life of Gallatin,* p. 602.

[53] Gallatin to Lowrie, October 2, 1824, printed in Adams, *Life of Gallatin,* p. 604.

HENRY BALDWIN

WILLIAM WILKINS

THOMAS H. BAIRD

ABNER LACOCK

VICTORY WITHOUT OFFICE

As was customary in this era, the state elections preceded the selection of presidential electors by a month. Generally these earlier results represented a good barometer of the popular will to be expressed in the presidential race, but the October returns of Western Pennsylvania in 1824 gave no indication that Jackson would sweep all 15 western counties by more than a three to one margin. In most western counties there were only as many nominees for office as vacancies in the legislature and Congress. Occasionally additional names appeared on the ballot; except for a few instances, however, they were too few and too disunited to constitute a rival ticket or to influence the outcome.

Even where rival tickets existed, it was difficult to discern a trend in this election, especially in the race for the two congressional seats shared by Allegheny, Armstrong, Beaver, and Butler Counties. The victors in Allegheny were James Allison, a Jacksonite, and a caucus nominee, James S. Stevenson, while Forward of the Jackson camp and Stevenson dominated the voting in Armstrong County. Beaver likewise divided its allegiance between these two factions, but in so doing endorsed two local men, Allison and Robert Moore. Dissatisfied with all these choices, Butler supported two other candidates who did not run well in any of the other three counties. When these diverse results were brought together, Allison and Stevenson, a follower of Old Hickory and a Crawfordite, respectively, had won the right to represent the district in Congress.[54] The fact that Walter Forward who was prominently connected with the Baldwin branch of the Jackson clan ran third in his home county of Allegheny would suggest a weakness in the general's ticket, but it was certainly not prevalent in the November voting.

The assembly race in Allegheny and Butler Counties, where competing tickets were marshaled against each other, followed a more consistent pattern, but not one that would indicate the outcome of the presidential battle. John Brown was a candidate on both Crawford and Jackson tickets to assure his election, but the other three seats were hotly contested. Robert J. Walker, Samuel Cochran, and William Beatty, the Jackson standard-bearers, were successful in Allegheny County, but all of them suffered defeat by greater margins in Butler County. This permitted the caucus nominees, James Patterson, James C. Gilleland, and Moses Sullivan to represent the district in Harrisburg.[55]

[54] *Pittsburgh Gazette,* October 22, 1824.
[55] *Ibid.*

This trial run indicated that Jackson would win by a slight majority in Allegheny, but would be defeated in Butler if the public adhered to the party line with the same consistency in November. When his presidential electors carried Butler by a two to one margin and Allegheny by three to one, Jackson demonstrated that his personal appeal rather than party alignment was responsible for his victory. In no western county was the combined vote for Jackson's opposition equal to his own, but in spite of this overwhelming success the western counties exhibited very little more strength in behalf of Old Hickory than did the state as a whole. Within Western Pennsylvania the general's greatest margins of victory were, with the exception of Westmoreland, in the rural counties, namely Armstrong, Greene, Indiana, Jefferson, Venango, and Warren.[56]

If Jackson could be said to have had political weaknesses in Western Pennsylvania, they were in Washington and Butler Counties, but even in both he enjoyed a two to one majority. With the exception of Washington in every county where he experienced any significant opposition, it came from one candidate. In this one county, however, all four contenders received 120 or more votes of the 1482 total. The remnants of Federalism in the borough accounted for the Adams strength while *The Reporter* delivered several pungent editorials in behalf of Crawford without extending him an open endorsement. Clay, however, afforded the major opposition; his strength was based on the encouragement he had given the National Road which passed across the county. The only other county in which Clay compiled a respectable vote was Fayette, the other of Western Pennsylvania's counties to gain substantially from the road.

In Butler County Jackson's opposition came wholly from the caucusites. John Sullivan operated the *Sentinel,* his major attack-weapon, with assistance from his brother, Moses, who was a successful assembly candidate in 1824, and his brother-in-law, Senator Lowrie, who had been an avowed Crawfordite from the days of the congressional caucus. They were ably seconded by Barnet Gilleland, the brother of a victorious caucus nominee for the assembly from Allegheny County. The Butler family faction, meanwhile, extended a similar liaison to their Allegheny neighbors through Walter Lowrie's brother Matthew, a Pittsburgh merchant, who actively supported the entire Crawford

---

[56] See Appendix D for details.

ticket. In Butler the family faction was successful only to the extent of keeping Jackson's margin of victory smaller than it was in all other western counties except Washington.[57]

Aside from Jackson's victory in every western county the most notable aspect of the election was the "light" vote. In comparison with the October state election, the gubernatorial election of 1823, and the election of local officers in 1825, there were few ballots cast. In Armstrong County only 28 per cent of the voters in the October election turned out the following month to declare their preferences for presidential electors. At first glance after viewing the presidential results these facts would seem to indicate that the public regarded a Jackson victory as inevitable and, therefore, recognized no urgency to vote for electors.

Such a conclusion has no basis in fact. The limited available records on the local elections in October, as indicated above, gave no evidence of a decisive Jackson victory. Furthermore, if such an apathy did condition the voter, it certainly would have curtailed the October vote in Washington County where there were only as many candidates as there were assigned seats in the assembly and Congress. In reality there were 50 per cent more voters on hand in the earlier election although the contest over presidential electors in the county was an open battle.

Slightly more than one-fourth of the voters who cast ballots in the gubernatorial race of 1823 voted for presidential electors the following year. Similar results were achieved in later years. In 1825 three times as many people voiced their opinions on a proposed state constitutional convention as voted for or against Jackson in 1824. The 1828 vote for electors in the western counties was almost four times as great as that of the previous presidential race, and the facts do not suggest that those who had believed Jackson wronged in 1824 turned out to make certain that he did not meet the same fate again. Actually his margin of victory in Western Pennsylvania was less in 1828 than in 1824.

By the process of elimination there are only a few plausible explanations for the limited vote in this election, and collectively they add up to confusion. The appearance of four candidates professing, through their local managers, similar views on the principal issues before the voters was in itself disconcerting, but division within the Jackson camp afforded further complications. The failure of this large bloc to pull

[57] *Allegheny Democrat,* October 5, 1824.

together, plus the caucusite practice of campaigning for state and local tickets of their own while frequently supporting Jackson for the presidency, so befuddled many voters that the issues and personalities became meaningless to them. Others believed that they had performed their duty by exercising their franchise in October, but at the same time they had not re-discovered the national government as a valuable instrument through which their wants and desires, attainable through government, could be fulfilled.

Such a trend toward a greater reliance on the central government was developing, but it was not pronounced in 1824. Without this realization many Western Pennsylvania citizens made no effort to share in the selection of presidential electors. An election studded with prominent national personalities and the explosive caucus issue was, therefore, permitted to pass by without exciting as much interest as the choice of an assemblyman.

X

The Aftermath of Battle

*Pennsylvania—A bright star in the political firmament—
though clouds may occasionally obscure its brilliancy they
soon pass over, without obscuring its brightness.*[1]

JACKSON'S large popular vote in the national balloting and his
electoral plurality at first caused his adherents to assume that the
choice of a President by the House of Representatives would be
routine. When the House eventually disregarded their presumption
and selected Adams, the verdict was received with mixed emotions in
Western Pennsylvania. The more reserved Jacksonites, headed by the
Baldwin faction, believed that they had salvaged at least a little from
the campaign by assisting in the defeat of Crawford. The *Pittsburgh
Gazette* accurately summarized their attitude by pointing out that "if
this result be not exactly what a majority of the people wished, it is
yet a triumph of the people over the unconstitutional caucus system,
and had been arrived at in accordance with the constitution as it
stands." [2]

Although there is a dearth of data on the reverberations of the election, that available indicates that this was the general spirit of the
region's reaction. The one notable exception was the Patchell clan.
Dominated by young office-seeking hopefuls, this group became almost
insane with rage. In their first move, which came before the lower
house of Congress declared its choice of Adams, Editor McFarland
warned the aristocrats of that body that they would not be safe if they
elected any candidate other than Jackson because the indignant feelings
of the people would not be confined to effigy burnings. Later he openly
suggested that any intrigue to defeat Old Hickory in the House should
be resisted "at the point of the bayonet." [3]

[1] Toast proposed at an Independence Day celebration in Pittsburgh. *Mercury,*
July 11, 1821.
[2] *Pittsburgh Gazette,* February 18, 1825.
[3] *Allegheny Democrat,* November 9, and December 28, 1824.

When he heard the decision of the House, McFarland charged that Adams was being smuggled into the presidency under "an aristocratic clause in the federal constitution." He predicted that "the *black cockade* days of John the *first*" were about to be revived under "John second." Aware that the new President had been a minority choice by both the people and the members of Congress, the editor became increasingly invective. Under the circumstances he declared that he expected the king of England and "all usurpers against the liberties of the people" to write congratulatory notes to their "dear and trustworthy *cozen,* John the *second,* for his finesse in suppressing the voice of the majority." [4]

BARGAIN AND SALE

The hatred of the Patchell alignment that had been directed against Crawford in the campaign was now diverted to Adams and Clay, particularly the latter. Even before his appointment as secretary of state, Clay was denounced as a traitor for accomplishing in miniature what Benedict Arnold and Aaron Burr had been preparing to execute on a larger scale. He was characterized with Arnold and Burr as:

The American A. B. C.

Those three, brothers be.[5]

Thus the *Allegheny Democrat* strove in its own iniquitous way to encourage disobedience to the government summoned to power by the presidential choice made in the House. In February 1825 McFarland, Patchell, and five of their henchmen were indicted before the Mayor's Court in Pittsburgh for inciting a riot. According to McFarland's own report, they had been taken into custody for holding out inducements to other citizens to roast an effigy of the "Kentucky Gambler" over a burning tar barrel. William Wilkins and Richard Biddle were counsel for the Commonwealth while A. S. T. Mountain served among the defense attorneys for the enraged Jacksonites. After much debate the trial jury could not agree on a verdict, and when one juror became ill, it was obvious that no decision could be reached. The jury was dismissed, and the defendants discharged with a *nolle prosequi* entry in the court record. Some 60 witnesses brought into court to testify for the defendants were denied their pay on the technicality that the court had

---

[4] *Allegheny Democrat,* April 26, and August 30, 1825; August 22, 1826.
[5] *Ibid.,* February 8, and May 3, 1825.

not proceeded to a logical conclusion. Totally disgusted with the procedure, McFarland quipped: "Lord what a Court." [6]

More than a month later another effigy of Clay was found in Pittsburgh suspended from a signpost with a pack of cards in its fist to connote the dealer. Several hundred citizens were on hand to view the spectacle, but the only one indicted for rioting was a poor negro who had cut down the stuffed figure and was "quietly and peaceably conveying the representative of our worthy Secretary of State to the river in a wheelbarrow with the charitable intention of sending him home to Kentuck." The official statistics compiled by McFarland's journal revealed that this marked the 153rd time that Clay had been burned in effigy by the American public which had also accorded him seven formal burials. [7]

Running through McFarland's harangues were ideas which were later reflected in Jackson's strategy, as well as in his campaign theme for 1828. As the editor indicated, the caucus was destined to be replaced as the implacable foe to majority rule by the threat of secretarial succession. Especially after Clay told the people of his congressional district that he saw in the election of Adams the establishment of no dangerous example, did the Jacksonites believe that the "secretary dynasty" would have to be crushed at once.

In declaring that he viewed the election of 1824 only as a conformity to the safe precedents established by Jefferson, Madison, and Monroe who had filled the same office from which Adams had been called to the White House, Clay concluded that it was proper for Adams to accede to the presidency. Jackson leaders quickly translated this to mean that Clay considered it proper for a President to nominate his secretary of state as a successor. Under existing circumstances they recognized that Adams was more deeply obligated to his secretary of state than any of his predecessors had ever been. [8]

This interpretation in itself went a long way in stirring up a stop-Clay movement among the Jacksonites and accounts for much of the vigor with which the corrupt bargain charge was pressed. Further reenforcements were added to the Jackson organization when the Tennessee legislature in 1825 nominated the general for the presidency three

---

[6] *Allegheny Democrat,* March 8, 1825; *Pittsburgh Gazette,* February 25, 1825.

[7] *Allegheny Democrat,* April 5, 1825.

[8] *Examiner,* April 30, 1825.

years hence. This was sufficient signal for him to resign his seat in the United States Senate the same year and lend a personal touch to the charges of bargain and sale, secretarial succession, and domination of government by the eastern aristocracy. Thus the Jackson leaders began building on the theme that they had been swindled out of the presidency in 1824, and in this endeavor the *Allegheny Democrat* proved to be an important sounding board for all such propaganda.

Together these forces were ushering in a new era of political excitement which had its genesis in the circumstances surrounding the House selection in 1825. Jacksonians became arrayed against the Adams-Clay coalition, and the purely personal considerations of the presidential election in 1824 were gradually being pushed aside.[9]

The Old Hickory sponsors had already exhibited strength in numbers, but were painfully aware that this power would have to be organized for an electoral superiority as well, before they could successfully seat a President. They set about their task by playing and replaying the old refrain of election fraud. As the new President struggled to ward off this attack, he discovered moderate strength in the patronage at his disposal, but the emergence of disguised Federalists from the Republican ranks to support him openly gave the alignment its most reasonable hope for success in the next four years.

From the outset the corrupt bargain indictment was the most challenging obstacle standing between the Adams-Clay faction and a successful administration. In order to steal the initiative from their opponents, these conservatives tried to convince the public that fate had been kind in preventing the election of a military leader like Jackson. Basing their contention on the testimony of an unidentified army officer who had fought under Jackson in his "southern army,"[10] they charged that the general made certain confessions which marked him as a military dictator. The alleged meeting of Jackson and his former officer had taken place at the hotel of James Briceland in Washington, Pennsylvania, on the evening of November 29, 1824. Old Hickory was en route to the next session of the United States Senate when he stopped at Briceland's hotel to spend the night and, by chance, met the army

---

[9] Lynch, *Party Warfare,* pp. 275, 277.

[10] The account does not elaborate further on which "southern army" is meant, but obviously the choice is between Jackson's command during the War of 1812 and the army he led into Florida in 1817-1818.

officer who had stopped from his westward journey to seek lodging at the same establishment.

According to this countercharge to the corrupt bargain, Jackson chatted intimately with his military comrade of yesteryear in a private compartment and confided that he had "little faith in the stability of Republics" because "they fall an easy prey to the ambitions of rivals for power." He even offered an example from his own career by observing that the insolence of the governor of Georgia had once tempted him to march a hostile army into the state "in pursuit of personal revenge," and admittedly his very presence in the presidential race of 1824 had been prompted by the same motive. He declared that he had been encouraged by a political leader in New York to take immediate action to unite the West behind him before another aspirant of that section, obviously Henry Clay, would use his popularity and intrigue to secure the nomination and presidency for himself. Since this aspirant was an implacable personal enemy, Jackson directed his adherents in the Tennessee legislature to nominate him.[11]

Apparently designed to depreciate the value of a military President and to weaken Jackson's strength in the South and West, this account was first reported in Nashville and promptly accepted by Philadelphia's *Democratic Press*. From this beginning it quickly became a controversial reprint throughout the nation in spite of Jackson's denial that he had ever held such a conversation and Briceland's assertion that he had no roomers other than the Jackson party on the night of the alleged confessions.

Just as quickly the issue passed into oblivion. Only a few months were required to prove that this effort to divert the Jackson enthusiasts from their self-appointed task was ineffectual; actually an overwhelming majority of Old Hickory's followers in Western Pennsylvania became more determined than ever to place him in the presidency.

PROSPERITY ROUNDS THE CORNER

While Western Pennsylvania was absorbed in crucial political battles from 1823 to 1825, prosperity returned. Pittsburgh, once the outpost of a scattered population, now became the center of this growing wealth and the fortress of expanding industry in the western counties. After a general retardation of all the nation's manufacturing interests in the

---

[11] *Allegheny Democrat*, April 15, 1825; *Reporter*, April 18, 1825.

previous years because of the inroads of British manufactures to our domestic market, the city surged forward with fresh energy to become the unrivaled center of manufacturing skill and ingenuity west of the mountains. As the hub of this reviving commerce and industry, Pittsburgh increased in population from 8,000 in 1822 to approximately 11,000 three years later.[12]

A definite trend toward an expansion of the city's manufacturing capacities was noted in the same years. In 1822 James McCracken and Adams, Allen & Company both opened factories for the manufacture of cotton textiles; employment for many was anticipated, and a genuine prosperity was forecast. By 1825 the iron industry reported similar progress. Bar and sheet iron, nails, and wire, and to a lesser extent metals for axes, scythes, sickles, shovels, and other pieces of hardware poured from the city's seven steam rolling mills. Eight air foundries, six steam engine factories, and a cupola furnace added to the diversity of iron production and placed stoves, plough castings, hollow ware, shafts and wheels for steam machinery, and steam engines themselves on the market. Since three of Western Pennsylvania's nine paper mills were powered by steam and since the boatyards in and around Pittsburgh built 21 steamboats in the three-year period ending in 1825, the domestically produced steam engine appeared to have a most revolutionizing effect on the region's economy.[13]

Obviously Pittsburgh was not an isle of progress in a region languishing in depression; the areas around the city also shared in this industrial prosperity. Five blast furnaces along the Allegheny and its tributaries in Butler, Armstrong, Venango, and Crawford Counties supplied roughly finished metals to Pittsburgh mills. During one week in the early spring of 1825 the flat boats and arks of the river brought to the city 500 tons of bar iron and 500 tons of pig metals, as well as other non-industrial products including 7,000 barrels of salt. Iron furnaces in Beaver, Fayette, and Westmoreland Counties also contributed to the region's developing prosperity and rising industrial greatness as did the glass factories that dotted Western Pennsylvania. Although the glass industry had been started in the western counties as early as 1798 by

[12] *Statesman* quoted in the *Democratic Press,* January 7, 1825; Gray, "Industries and Transportation," p. 4.

[13] *Mercury,* April 10, and June 26, 1822; Leander Bishop, *A History of American Manufactures from 1608 to 1860* (Philadelphia: Edward Young & Co., 1864), II, 301.

James O'Hara, its success remained in doubt for years, especially when this captain of industry was brought to the verge of ruin in the depression that swept the region in 1818. By 1825, however, the number of glass producers had multiplied to nine with the major concentration in Allegheny and Fayette Counties.[14]

In spite of the fact that many other manufacturing areas in the nation suffered financial distress in 1825, the industrial prospects of Western Pennsylvania were bright. Pittsburgh was awakened to her potential market in Ohio, Indiana, Illinois, and the Michigan Territory with the realization that those areas could not obtain such articles as manufactured in the Emporium of the West at such reasonable prices from any other production area.[15]

Furthermore, Western Pennsylvania glass was competing successfully with imported glass in eastern cities, and Pittsburgh steam engines were being sold as far east as the Phoenix Iron Works near Philadelphia. With glass, steam engines, cotton textiles, iron, and nails leading the exports, Pittsburgh was finally able to boast a surplus of exports over imports by the end of 1825.[16]

Hand in hand with this industrial prosperity came the promotion of commerce through natural waterways and internal improvement projects. The completion of the Erie Canal alerted the extreme northwestern counties to the possibilities of a bright economic future while the inhabitants of Western Pennsylvania's other counties were able to share either directly or indirectly in Pittsburgh's prosperity because the rivers of the region radiated from this hub like the spokes of a wheel through the Monongahela, Allegheny, and Ohio River valleys.[17]

In 1825 the *American* became the first steamboat to ascend the Monongahela with full freight and passengers as far as Brownsville. Since the soil of this valley was unexcelled anywhere on western waters, the people of the area recognized that a ready market for their agricultural produce, as well as for the iron of their furnaces, existed in Pittsburgh and beyond.[18]

---

[14] *Poulson's Advertiser,* March 29, 1825; Bishop, *American Manufactures,* II, 301.

[15] Bishop, *American Manufactures,* II, 302.

[16] *Ibid.,* II, 301; Samuel Jones, *Pittsburgh in the Year Eighteen Hundred and Twenty-six,* ... (Pittsburgh: Johnston & Stockton, 1826), p. 86f.

[17] Reiser, *Pittsburgh's Commercial Development,* p. 29.

[18] "Monongahelian," *Pittsburgh Gazette,* April 8, 1825.

Thus with the advent of steam navigation to Brownsville, the surrounding countryside could look east and west along the National Road and north via the Monongahela for easily accessible markets. The people of the Allegheny Valley could likewise look in several directions for views of potential outlets for their products. To the southwest they were inspired, not only by the needs of industrial Pittsburgh, but also by the broader realization that the waters of French Creek were now united with the Gulf of Mexico at New Orleans in an upstream, as well as a downstream, traffic. By way of Lake Erie, the Erie Canal, and the rivers of New York to the northeast these inhabitants were also joined to the Atlantic Ocean. The vision of a waterway connecting Lake Erie, the Allegheny, and the Susquehanna across Pennsylvania further encouraged settlement and improvement of the fertile agricultural lands of the northwestern counties.[19]

The cooperation of state and national authorities in the removal of obstructions at the entrance to Erie harbor seemed destined to make Erie superior to any other lake port and to stimulate a flow of surplus produce via that point to New York in quest of a foreign market. Hope for the future rested, not only in this exportation route, but also in the knowledge that these farm communities could be supplied with their eastern needs at 50 per cent less than current transportation costs. In a confident tone the editor of the *Crawford Messenger* reported that "these results are as sure and as certain as the principles of gravity." He advised the farmers:

Clear more land—improve your fences—cleanse your old fields; and by every possible care and attention endeavour to improve your system of agriculture, for rest assured the time is not remote when you will cease to complain for the want of a market for the product of your labour.[20]

Naturally there was a high correlation between this actual and anticipated prosperity on the one hand and the amount of capital available for industrial development and internal improvements on the other. All Western Pennsylvania was optimistic about the establishment of a satisfactory transmontane channel for commerce in these years. The attitude had grown partly out of the founding of "The Pennsylvania Society for the Promotion of Internal Improvements in the Commonwealth" at Philadelphia in the fall of 1824 and partly out of the experiences of the depression.

---

[19] "Mutius Scaevola," *Pittsburgh Gazette,* May 28, 1824.
[20] *Crawford Messenger,* January 6, 1824.

There is a contagion in despair. Men who believe that they are destined to sink together are apt to discover in each other amiable characteristics which, under more fortunate circumstances, might have been completely overlooked.[21] This became increasingly true of the various groups of farmers, mechanics, merchants, and manufacturers in Western Pennsylvania, as well as throughout the state as a whole. As prosperity returned, the eastern and western parts of the state were more amenable to the task of solving their mutual problems, and within Western Pennsylvania the various economic groups and areas were also willing to modify many of their demands in the interest of positive political action. The farmer, the merchant, and the manufacturer each learned that success for the other two was the best guarantee of his own continued prosperity. Cooperation on the portage canal system which was under consideration at the time was ample proof that they were aware of their interdependence.

Early in February 1825 the citizens of Western Pennsylvania sent a memorial to the state legislature declaring that there was a better means than turnpike roads for carrying commerce across the mountains between the extremities of the state. These memorialists pointed out that the answer lay in a canal system and suggested that the best line of communication between the Ohio River and the eastern slopes of the Appalachian Mountains was via the Allegheny, Kiskiminetas, Conemaugh, Juniata, and Susquehanna Rivers. Although the legislature did not accept the suggested route, it did respond favorably in April by authorizing the governor to appoint five commissioners to survey for a canal system connecting eastern and western waters. The project gathered momentum, culminating in a Canal Convention at Harrisburg the following August to decide the fate of transmontane transportation. Practically all of the counties in the state responded by sending delegates who represented a cross section of economic endeavor. When they voted to carry the proposed Pennsylvania System into reality, the convention took on the appearance of a united, state-wide opinion.[22]

East-West relations, between Philadelphia and Pittsburgh, improved

[21] Richard I. Shelling, "Philadelphia and the Agitation in 1825 for the Pennsylvania Canal," *The Pennsylvania Magazine of History and Biography,* LXII (1938), 175; Dangerfield, *Era of Good Feelings,* p. 4.

[22] *Pittsburgh Gazette,* February 4, 1825; Hartz, *Economic Policy,* p. 132f.

considerably in the next decade while the Pennsylvania System was being built, but beneath the surface local jealousies and tensions remained. Rural areas across the state battled to have the waterway pass along their streams while turnpike owners, innkeepers, and wagoners fought to prevent their investments from being jeopardized by the re-routing of commerce over the canal system. Since these groups cut across regional lines, they were far less damaging to positive action than the rift between eastern and western Pennsylvania in the 1815-1825 decade.[23]

PARTY SPIRIT REBORN

On the political scene at the close of this decade new party alignments were becoming fairly distinct.[24] People who work and plan together, as the various occupational groups in Western Pennsylvania were doing after the return of prosperity, are likely to vote for the same candidates. In December 1824 Albert Gallatin admitted that a new era was dawning and that the Republican Party of the preceding years had now lost its effectiveness at the national level just as it had done in the internal politics of many states in previous years. While evaluating his defeat, the vice presidential nominee confided to his son that personal politics had now reached the national government, the last vestige of party power. In the presidential election personalities had proved stronger than party and principle because of the Constitution's "monarchical" concept of voting for a popular candidate rather than for a program.[25]

Although this emphasis on personalities in 1824 succeeded in throttling the outworn caucus system at the national level, the organization of the opposition's various elements, necessary to achieve victory, was still lacking. Only a coalition of two of the personalities seated a President, and the antagonism resulting from this solution gave a pronounced impetus to the revival of party organization.

Once the hollow national shell of party politics collapsed in the election of 1824 and lay in a jumbled heap with the personal and local politics which had dominated many states for years, new alignments

---

[23] Hartz, *Economic Policy,* p. 134; Reiser, *Pittsburgh's Commercial Development,* p. 151.

[24] Hockett, *Western Influences on Political Parties,* p. 127.

[25] Adams, *Life of Gallatin,* p. 606.

could take form more easily. The age of political confusion was passing; personal prejudices were no longer confounded with political principles, and selfish feeling was no longer mistaken for civil philanthropy. The discriminating shades of opinion and action, which had politically separated men from each other in the years of healthy party conflict, but had become so blended in the era of good feeling that the most acute observation could not distinguish them, were beginning to reappear.

The trend away from personal and local allegiance toward faction responsibility was prevalent in both the rural and urban counties of Western Pennsylvania. In Crawford County in 1824 one man declined to be a candidate for the assembly and another for county commissioner because they did not wish to divide the Jackson organization on local issues.

The elections of Butler County in the same year found the people voting against William Beatty, a *local* candidate for the assembly in the district composed of Butler and Allegheny Counties, by almost a two to one margin because he supported Old Hickory against the locally powerful Lowrie-Sullivan caucus forces. In his campaign for the same office in the same district, James C. Gilleland, a caucusite from Allegheny County, experienced similar treatment in his home county because of the strong Jackson organization there. He ran last in a race of six candidates for the three assembly seats of the district to show, not only increased party discipline, but also greater attention to national politics.

At the same time that these alignments were forming at the county level, Western Pennsylvania voiced a determination to weaken the prestige of the governor whose appointive powers had made him the dominant influence in Pennsylvania's political life at the state, national, and even local levels. Through his appointments of justices of the peace and judges of state courts, as well as recorders, sheriffs, and other local officials, he was always able to inject his ideas and preferences into local politics and sway the elections of legislators who, in turn, appointed the United States Senators.

In the era of good feeling the senators who represented Pennsylvania had belonged to the alignment of the governor during whose administration they had been appointed. The one exception was William Findlay. Although he was chosen over an administration nominee, his appointment does not detract from the gubernatorial control over senatorial assignment. Since he was elected only a year after his own term as governor had expired, it might appropriately be argued that the machine he, as governor, had been responsible for establishing was still powerful enough to effect the appointment.

With the growing use of executive patronage for personal advantage, the public was aroused more and more to support reform. From 1820 to 1825 there was an increasing number of petitions calling for the passage of an act to provide for a convention to revise the state constitution, especially in regard to the extensive patronage of the governor.[26] Western Pennsylvania remained relatively quiet on the subject until 1823 when Beaver and Crawford County journals joined the *Mercury* in seeking reform. The *Western Argus* suggested that the governor's power be curtailed by establishing definite terms with fixed expiration dates for justices of the peace and many other local officials under his control. By recommending that the advice and consent of a majority of the state senate be required before such appointments became valid, the *Argus* added another proposal for further pruning the governor's personal patronage. The *Crawford Messenger* sanctioned these suggestions by the Beaver press and pointed out that the state wanted no repetition of the conduct that marked the close of Hiester's administration when appointments similar in character to those that disgraced the "midnight hours of John Adams' reign" were extended to many.[27]

As a result of such agitation, the legislature passed a bill in 1825 requesting that the voters decide whether or not they favored a constitutional convention to study such changes. Although the convention was voted down, all but three [28] of Western Pennsylvania's counties dissented from the decision, and ultimately in 1838 the convention was summoned and the governor's personal powers curbed. Since the state-wide vote was only four to three against the convention in 1825, the western counties were encouraged to pursue their reform objectives and to work for increased support elsewhere in the Commonwealth.

---

[26] Klein, *Pennsylvania Politics,* p. 195.

[27] *Western Argus* quoted in the *Crawford Messenger,* December 2, 1823; *Crawford Messenger,* December 30, 1823.

[28] The three counties were Armstrong, Butler, and Warren. In Butler there were only 84 votes separating the number favoring a convention and the number opposed; the vote was much closer in Warren, 400 to 398.

This anticipation of limiting the personal powers of the governor was equally meaningful to the adherents of party discipline. In the expectation of divorcing the governor from his dominant position in local and national politics, these advocates recognized that added power and responsibility would accrue to party organizations. Not since the collapse of Federalist and Democratic-Republican cohesion were the prospects for healthy party conflict so bright. The transition from party warfare under these banners to warfare under Jacksonian and Adams-Clay Republican banners was nearing completion at the end of this decade. In the short span of ten years Western Pennsylvania had passed through a cycle from hope to disappointment and despair and back to hope again.

BIBLIOGRAPHY

The following abbreviations have been used to indicate the location of manuscript collections, newspaper files, magazine articles, etc.:

Car. Pub. Lib.: Carnegie Public Library, Pittsburgh.

Craw. Co. Hist. Soc.: Crawford County Historical Society, Meadville.

Hist. Soc. Pa.: Historical Society of Pennsylvania, Philadelphia.

Hist Soc. West. Pa.: Historical Society of Western Pennsylvania, Pittsburgh.

Lib. Cong.: Library of Congress, Washington.

Pa. Mag. of Hist. & Biog.: The Pennsylvania Magazine of History and Biography.

State Lib. Pa.: State Library of Pennsylvania, Harrisburg.

West. Pa. Hist. Mag.: The Western Pennsylvania Historical Magazine.

Manuscript Materials

Henry Baldwin Correspondence. In the possession of James R. Shryock, Meadville.

Denny-O'Hara Papers. Hist. Soc. West. Pa.

Patrick Farrelly Letters. Craw. Co. Hist Soc.

Harm Jan Huidekoper Papers, 1796-1854. Hist. Soc. Pa.

William Reynolds Scrapbook. Vol. II. Craw. Co. Hist. Soc.

William Reynolds Manuscripts. In the possession of James R. Shryock, Meadville.

Jonathan Roberts Memoirs. Two photostated volumes in Hist. Soc. Pa.

Jonathan Roberts Papers. His. Soc. Pa.

Newspapers

Baltimore:
Niles' Weekly Register, 1814, 1816-1820. Darlington Library, Univ. of Pittsburgh.

Brownsville:
American Telegraph, 1814-1818. New York Historical Society.

Butler:
The Butler Palladium and Republican Star, scattered issues, 1819-1820. Lib. Cong.

Erie:
Erie Gazette, 1820-1825. Lehigh Univ. Library and Erie Public Library.

Greensburg:
Greensburg Gazette, 1815-1825. Princeton Univ. Library and State Lib. Pa.
The Westmoreland Republican, 1818-1824. Tribune Review Publishing Co., Greensburg, Pa.

Harrisburg:
The Commonwealth, 1824. Lehigh Univ. Library.
Harrisburg Chronicle, scattered issues, 1818-1824. State Lib. Pa.
Meadville:
The Crawford Weekly Mesenger, 1814-1825. Craw. Co. Hist. Soc.
Western Standard, scattered issues, 1820-1822. Craw. Co. Hist. Soc.
Morgantown:
The Monongalia Spectator, scattered issues, 1816. Lib. Cong.
Philadelphia:
Aurora: General Advertiser, 1814-1825. Hist. Soc. Pa. and Lib. Cong.
The Democratic Press, 1815-1825. Hist. Soc. Pa.
Poulson's American Daily Advertiser, 1815-1825. Hist. Soc. Pa.
Pittsburgh:
Allegheny Democrat, 1824-1825. State Lib. Pa.
The Commonwealth, scattered issues, 1815-1818. Car. Pub. Lib.
The Mercury, 1814-1824. Car. Pub. Lib.
Pittsburgh Gazette, 1815-1825. Car. Pub. Lib.
Statesman, scattered issues, 1818-1825. Carnegie Library of Allegheny, Lib. Cong., and Darlington Library, Univ. of Pittsburgh.
Steubenville:
The Western Herald, scattered issues, 1815-1817. New York Historical Society.
Uniontown:
The Genius of Liberty, scattered issues, 1815-1822. Uniontown Public Library and New York Historical Society.
Washington:
The Reporter, 1815-1825. Observer Publishing Co., Washington, Pa.
Washington Examiner, 1817-1825. Washington County Historical Society.
Wheeling:
Virginia North-Western Gazette, scattered issues, 1821-1825. Lib. Cong.

Other Published Sources

Adams, Charles F. (ed.). *Memoirs of John Quincy Adams, comprising Portions of His Diary from 1795 to 1848.* Vols. IV, V, and VI. Philadelphia: J. B. Lippincott & Co., 1875.
Adams, Henry (ed.). *The Writings of Albert Gallatin.* 3 vols. Philadelphia: J. B. Lippincott & Co., 1879.
Address to the Democratic Republican Citizens of Crawford County. A political pamphlet bound with the *Crawford Weekly Messenger* for the period 1818-1821 in Craw. Co. Hist. Soc. and published at an undetermined date in 1823.
Annals of Congress: The Debates and Proceedings in the Congress of the United States; . . . 42 vols. Washington: Gales and Seaton, 1834-1856.
Atkinson, Thomas. *To the Democratic Republican Citizens of Crawford County.* A political pamphlet bound with the *Crawford Weekly Messenger* for the period 1818-1821 in Craw. Co., Hist. Soc. and published October 9, 1823.

Baldwin, Henry. *Hypocrisy Unmasked.* Philadelphia: S. Probasco, 1832.

Bassett, John Spencer (ed.). *Correspondence of Andrew Jackson.* 6 vols. Washington: Carnegie Institution of Washington, 1926-1931.

"Benjamin Franklin." *To the Electors of Fayette County.* A political pamphlet bound with the *Genius of Liberty* in the Uniontown Public Library and dated October 7, 1823.

Birkbeck, Morris. *Notes on a Journey in America, from the Coast of Virginia to the Territory of Illinois.* 2d ed. Philadelphia: M. Carey & Son, 1819.

Brackenridge, Henry M. *Recollections of Persons and Places in the West.* 2d ed. Philadelphia: J. B. Lippincott & Co., 1868.

Carey, Mathew. *The New Olive Branch: or, An Attempt to Establish an Identity of Interest between Agriculture, Manufactures, and Commerce;* . . . 2d ed. Philadelphia: M. Carey & Sons, 1821.

Cramer, Zadok. *The Navigator: or The Traders' Useful Guide in Navigating the Monongahela, Allegheny, Ohio and Mississippi Rivers;* . . . Pittsburgh: Zadok Cramer, 1806-1824.

Cuming, Fortescue. *Sketches of a Tour to the Western Country through the States of Ohio and Kentucky.* Vol. IV of *Early Western Travels 1748-1846.* Edited by Reuben G. Thwaites. 32 vols. Cleveland; The Arthur H. Clark Co., 1904-1907.

Evans, Estwick. *A Pedestrian's Tour of Four Thousand Miles through the Western States and Territories during the Winter and Spring of 1818.* Vol. VIII of *Early Western Travels 1748-1846.* Edited by Reuben G. Thwaites. 32 vols. Cleveland: The Arthur H. Clark Co., 1904-1907.

Fearon, Henry Bradshaw. *Sketches of America: A Narrative of a Journey of Five Thousand Miles through the Eastern and Western States of America;* . . . 2d ed. London: Longman, Hurst, Rees, Orme and Brown, 1818.

Flint, James. *Letters from America, containing Observations on the Climate and Agriculture of the Western States, the Manners of the People, the Prospects of Emigrants, &c, &c.* Vol. IX of *Early Western Travels 1748-1846.* Edited by Reuben G. Thwaites, 32 vols. Cleveland: The Arthur H. Clark Co., 1904-1907.

Flint, Timothy. *Recollections of the Last Ten Years, Passed in Occasional Residences and Journeyings in the Valley of the Mississippi, from Pittsburg and the Missouri to the Gulf of Mexico, and from Florida to the Spanish Frontier;* . . . Boston: Cummings, Hilliard, and Company, 1826.

Ford, Paul L. (ed.). *The Works of Thomas Jefferson.* 12 vols. New York: G. P. Putnam's Sons, 1904-1905.

Hansard, Thomas C. *The Parliamentary Debates from the Year 1803 to the Present Time.* Vol XXXIII. London: T. C. Hansard, 1816.

McGrane, Reginald (ed.). *The Correspondence of Nicholas Biddle dealing with National affairs 1807-1844.* Boston: Houghton, Mifflin Co., 1919.

Mills, Samuel J., and Smith, Daniel. *Report of a Missionary Tour through That Part of the United States Which Lies West of the Allegheny Mountains;* . . . Andover: Flagg and Gould, 1815.

Palmer, John. *Journal of Travels in the United States of North America, and in Lower Canada, Performed in the Year 1817; . . .* London: Sherwood, Neely and Jones, 1818.

Parke, John E. *Recollections of Seventy Years and Historical Gleanings of Allegheny, Pennsylvania.* Boston: Rand, Avery & Co., 1886.

Pennsylvania. *Journal of the House of Representatives of the Commonwealth of Pennsylvania,* 1808-1831.

——————. *Journal of the Senate of the Commonwealth of Pennsylvania,* 1810-1827.

Pittsburgh Directory, 1815, 1819.

Speeches of Henry Baldwin, Esq. in the House of Representatives on the Bills Reported by Him as Chairman of the Committee of Manufactures. Pittsburgh: R. Patterson & Lambdin Printers, 1820.

U. S. Bureau of the Census. *Census for 1810.* Washington, 1811.

——————. *Census for 1820.* Washington, 1821.

Waldo, S. Putnam. *The Tour of James Monroe, President of the United States, in the Year 1817; . . . together with a Sketch of His Life, His Inaugural Speech and First Message; and Historical and Geographical Notices of the Principal Places through which He Passed.* Hartford: F. D. Bolles & Co., 1818.

General Works, Monographs, Articles

Andrews, J. Cutler. *Pittsburgh's Post-Gazette.* Boston: Chapman & Grimes, 1936.

Babcock, Kendric Charles. *The Rise of American Nationality, 1811-1819.* Vol. XIII of *The American Nation: A History.* Edited by A. B. Hart. 28 vols. New York: Harper & Brothers, 1904-1918.

Bining, Arthur C. "The Rise of Manufacture in Western Pennsylvania," *West. Pa. Hist. Mag.,* XVI (1933), 235-256.

Bining, William J. "The Glass Industry of Western Pennsylvania, 1787-1860." Unpublished Master's Thesis, History Department, University of Pittsburgh, 1936.

Bishop, Leander. *A History of American Manufactures from 1608 to 1860.* 2 vols. Philadelphia: Edward Young & Co., 1864.

Brigham, Clarence S. *History and Bibliography of American Newspapers 1690-1820.* 2 vols. Worcester, Massachusetts: American Antiquarian Society, 1947.

Brown, Everett S. "The Presidential Election of 1824-1825," *Political Science Quarterly,* XL (1925), 384-403.

Crall, F. Frank. "A Half Century of Rivalry between Pittsburgh and Wheeling," *West. Pa. Hist. Mag.,* XIII (1930), 237-255.

Dangerfield, George. *The Era of Good Feelings.* New York: Harcourt, Brace & Co., 1952.

De Grand, P. P. F. "Side-Lights upon the Presidential Campaign of 1824-25," *The Magazine of American History,* VIII (1882), 629-632.

Diller, Theodore. *Pioneer Medicine in Western Pennsylvania.* New York: Paul B. Hoeber, Inc., 1927.

Egle, William H. *Pennsylvania: Civil, Political, and Military;* . . . Harrisburg: DeWitt C. Goodrich, 1877.

Eiselen, Malcolm Rogers. *The Rise of Pennsylvania Protectionism.* Philadelphia: Malcolm R. Eiselen, 1932.

Elder, Margaret. "Pittsburgh Industries That Used To Be," *West. Pa. Hist. Mag.,* XII (1929), 211-225.

Ferguson, Russell J. *Early Western Pennsylvania Politics.* Pittsburgh: University of Pittsburgh Press, 1938.

Gray, Juliet G. "Early Industries and Transportation in Western Pennsylvania 1800-1846." Unpublished Master's thesis, History Department, University of Pittsburgh, 1919.

Hailperin, Herman. "Pro-Jackson Sentiment in Pennsylvania, 1820-1828." Unpublished Master's thesis, History Department, University of Pittsburgh, 1925.

Hartz, Louis. *Economic Policy & Democratic Thought: Pennsylvania, 1776-1860.* Cambridge: Harvard University Press, 1948.

Higginbotham, Sanford W. *The Keystone in the Democratic Arch: Pennsylvania Politics 1800-1816.* Harrisburg; Pennsylvania Historical and Museum Commission, 1952.

Hockett, Homer C. *Western Influences on Political Parties to 1825: An Essay in Historical Interpretation.* Columbus: Ohio State University, 1917.

Holdsworth, John Thorn. *Financing an Empire: History of Banking in Pennsylvania.* 4 vols. Chicago: S. J. Clarke Publishing Co., 1928.

Hulbert, Archer B. *The Cumberland Road.* Cleveland: The Arthur H. Clark Co., 1904.

Hunter, Louis C. "Financial Problems of the Early Pittsburgh Iron Manufacturers," *Journal of Economic and Business History,* II (1930), 520-544.

——————. "Influence of the Market upon Technique in the Iron Industry in Western Pennsylvania up to 1860," *Journal of Economic and Business History,* I (1929), 241-281.

Jordan, Philip D. *The National Road.* New York: Bobbs-Merrill Co., 1948.

Kehl, James A. "The *Allegheny Democrat* 1824-1836." Unpublished Master's thesis, History Department, University of Pittsburgh, 1947.

Klein, Philip Shriver. *Pennsylvania Politics 1817-1832: A Game without Rules.* Philadelphia: The Historical Society of Pennsylvania, 1940.

Lynch, William O. *Fifty Years of Party Warfare 1789-1837.* Indianapolis: Bobbs-Merrill Co., 1931.

MacDonald, William. *From Jefferson to Lincoln.* New York: Henry Holt & Co., 1913.

McKinney, William W. *Early Pittsburgh Presbyterianism: Tracing the Development of the Presbyterian Church, United States of America, in Pittsburgh, Pennsylvania, from 1758-1839.* Pittsburgh: Gibson Press, 1938.

Myers, James Madison. "Committees of Correspondence in Western Pennsylvania as Forerunners of Party Organization." Unpublished Master's thesis, History Department, University of Pittsburgh, 1949.

Niebaum, John H. "The Pittsburgh Blues," *West. Pa. Hist. Mag.,* IV (1921), 110-122, 175-185, 259-270.

Reader, Francis S. *History of the Newspapers of Beaver County, Pennsylvania.* New Brighton, Pennsylvania: F. S. Reader & Son, 1905.

Reiser, Catherine E. *Pittsburgh's Commercial Development 1800-1850.* Harrisburg: Pennsylvania Historical and Museum Commission, 1951.

Reynolds, John Earle. *In French Creek Valley.* Meadville, Pennsylvania: The Crawford County Historical Society, 1938.

Searight, Thomas B. *The Old Pike: A History of the National Road.* Uniontown, Pennsylvania: Thomas B. Searight, 1894.

Sharpless, Isaac. *Two Centuries of Pennsylvania History.* Philadelphia: J. B. Lippincott Co., 1900.

Shelling, Richard I. "Philadelphia and the Agitation in 1825 for the Pennsylvania Canal," *Pa. Mag. of Hist. & Biog.,* LXII (1938), 175-204.

Smith, Catherine B. "The Terminus of the Cumberland Road on the Ohio River." Unpublished Master's thesis, History Department, University of Pittsburgh, 1951.

Stanwood, Edward. *A History of the Presidency.* 2 vols. New ed. revised by Charles K. Bolton. Boston: Houghton, Mifflin Co., 1928.

Stonecipher, Frank W. "Pittsburgh and the Nineteenth Century Tariffs," *West. Pa. Hist. Mag.,* XXXI (1948), 83-98.

Swetnam, George. *Pittsylvania Country.* New York: Duell, Sloan & Pearce, 1951.

Tinkcom, Harry Marlin. *The Republicans and Federalists in Pennsylvania 1790-1801: A Study in National Stimulus and Local Response.* Harrisburg: Pennsylvania Historical and Museum Commission, 1950.

Turner, Frederick Jackson. *The Frontier in American History.* New York: Henry Holt and Co., 1921.

Young, Jeremiah Simeon. *A Political and Constitutional Study of the Cumberland Road.* Chicago: University of Chicago Press, 1902.

Biographical Materials

Adams, Henry. *The Life of Albert Gallatin.* New York: J. B. Lippincott & Co., 1879.

Bassett, John Spencer. *The Life of Andrew Jackson.* New ed. New York: Macmillan Co., 1928.

Commemorative Biographical Record of Washington County, Pennsylvania. Chicago: J. H. Beers & Co., 1893.

Ewing, Robert M. "Hon. Walter Forward," *West. Pa. Hist. Mag.,* VIII (1925), 76-89.

Houtz, Harry. "Abner Lacock." Unpublished Master's thesis, History Department, University of Pittsburgh, 1937.

Roadman, George. "Daniel Sturgeon, A Political View." Unpublished Master's thesis, History Department, University of Pittsburgh, 1950.

Schoyer, George P. "James Ross, Western Pennsylvania Federalist." Unpublished Master's thesis, History Department, University of Pittsburgh, 1947.

Schramm, Eulalia Catherine. "General James O'Hara Pittsburgh's First Captain of Industry." Unpublished Master's thesis, History Department, University of Pittsburgh, 1934.

Slick, Sewell. "The Life of William Wilkins." Unpublished Master's thesis, History Department, University of Pittsburgh, 1931.

Stevens, John Austin. *Albert Gallatin.* Vol. XIII of *American Statesmen.* Edited by John T. Morse. 40 vols. Boston: Houghton, Mifflin Co., 1889-1917.

Taylor, M. Flavia. "The Political and Civic Career of Henry Baldwin 1799-1830." Unpublished Master's thesis, History Department, University of Pittsburgh, 1940.

————. "The Political and Civic Career of Henry Baldwin 1799-1830," *West. Pa. Hist. Mag.,* XXIV (1941), 37-50.

Walters, Raymond. *Alexander James Dallas: Lawyer-Politician-Financier 1759-1817.* Philadelphia: University of Pennsylvania Press, 1943.

Local History

Albert, George D. (ed.). *History of the County of Westmoreland, Pennsylvania, with Biographical Sketches* . . . Philadelphia: L. H. Everts & Co., 1882.

Baldwin, Leland D. *Pittsburgh: The Story of a City.* Pittsburgh: University of Pittsburgh Press, 1937.

Bates, Samuel P. *History of Erie County, Pennsylvania,* . . . Chicago: Warner, Beers & Co., 1884.

Boucher, John Newton. *A Century and a Half of Pittsburg and Her People.* 2 vols. Chicago: Lewis Publishing Co., 1908.

————. *History of Westmoreland County, Pennsylvania.* 3 vols. New York: Lewis Publishing Co., 1906.

Brown, Robert C. (ed.). *History of Butler County, Pennsylvania* . . . [Chicago]: R. C. Brown & Co., 1895.

————. *History of Crawford County, Pennsylvania* . . . Chicago: Warner, Beers & Co., 1885.

Crumrine, Boyd (ed.). *History of Washington County, Pennsylvania, with Biographical Sketches of Many of Its Pioneers and Prominent Men.* Philadelphia: L. H. Everts & Co., 1882.

Dahlinger, Charles. *Pittsburgh: A Sketch of Its Early Social Life.* New York: G. P. Putnam's Sons, 1916.

Fleming, George T. *History of Pittsburgh and Environs.* 4 vols. New York: American Historical Society, Inc., 1922.

Forrest, Earle R. *History of Washington County, Pennsylvania.* 3 vols. Chicago: J. S. Clarke Publishing Co., 1926.

Hadden, James. *A History of Uniontown, the County Seat of Fayette County, Pennsylvania.* Uniontown: James Hadden, 1913.

Jones, Samuel. *Pittsburgh in the Year Eighteen Hundred and Twenty-six,* . . . Pittsburgh: Johnston & Stockton, 1826.

Killikelly, Sarah. *The History of Pittsburgh: Its Rise and Progress.* Pittsburgh: B. C. & Gordon Montgomery Co., 1906.

Riesenman, Joseph. *History of Northwestern Pennsylvania.* 3 vols. New York: Lewis Historical Publishing Co., 1943.

Schenck, J. S. (ed.). *History of Warren County, Pennsylvania.* Syracuse: D. Mason & Co., 1887.

Smith, Robert Walter. *History of Armstrong County, Pennsylvania.* Chicago: Waterman, Watkins & Co., 1883.

Thurston, George H. *Allegheny County's Hundred Years.* Pittsburgh: A. A. Anderson & Son, 1888.

White, J. C. *A Twentieth Century History of Mercer County, Pennsylvania.* 2 vols. Chicago: Lewis Publishing Co., 1909.

Wilson, Erasmus (ed.). *Standard History of Pittsburg, Pennsylvania.* Chicago: H. R. Cornell & Co., 1898.

APPENDIX A
Western Pennsylvania Population Picture

County	Area in sq. mi.	Population[a] 1810	1820	Pop. per sq. mi.[b]	Taxables in 1815[d]
Allegheny	754	25,317	34,921	46	5,518
Armstrong	941	6,143	10,324	11	1,454
Beaver	646	12,168	15,340	24	2,398
Butler	785	7,346	10,193	13	1,493
Crawford	974	6,178	9,397	10	1,184
Erie	720	3,758	8,553	12	858
Fayette	824	24,714	27,285	33	4,579
Greene	497	12,544	15,554	26	2,412
Indiana	770	6,214	8,882	11	1,398[e]
Jefferson	1,203	161	561	0.5	
Mercer	830	8,277	11,681	14	1,734
Venango	1,114	3,060	4,915	4	889[f]
Warren	832	827	1,976	2	
Washington	888	36,289	40,038	45	6,780
Westmoreland	1,064	26,392	30,540	28	5,370
W. Pa. Totals	12,942	179,375	230,160	18.5[c]	35,067
Aggregate for Pennsylvania	43,950	810,091	1,049,458	24[c]	164,807
W. Pa. Per Cent of Aggregate	29%	22%	22%		21%

[a] U. S. Bureau of the Census, *Census for 1810* and *Census for 1820,*
[b] Averages computed on the basis of 1820 census.
[c] Represent population averages.
[d] *Crawford Messenger,* February 22, 1815.
[e] Includes taxables of Jefferson County.
[f] Includes taxables of Warren County.

APPENDIX B

County Development in Western Pennsylvania

County	Rank in Size	Rank in Population[a]	Erection Dates[b]	County Towns	Population of County Towns[a]
Allegheny	12	2	1788	Pittsburgh	7,248
Armstrong	5	8	1800	Kittanning	318
Beaver	14	6	1800	Beaver	361
Butler	10	9	1800	Butler	225
Crawford	4	10	1800	Meadville	649
Erie	13	12	1800	Erie	635
Fayette	9	4	1783	Union (town)	1,058
Greene	15	5	1796	Waynesburg	298
Indiana	11	11	1803	Indiana	317
Jefferson	1	15	1804		
Mercer	8	7	1800	Mercer	506
Venango	2	13	1800	Franklin	252
Warren	7	14	1800	Warren	182
Washington	6	1	1781	Washington	1,687
Westmoreland	3	3	1773	Greensburg	771

[a] Based on *Census for 1820.*

[b] Pennsylvania, *Genealogical Map of the Counties.* 2d. ed. York, Pennsylvania: n. p., 1936.

APPENDIX C

Gubernatorial Balloting in 1817 and 1820

	1817[a]			1820[b]		
	Findlay	Hiester	Differential	Findlay	Hiester	Differential
Allegheny	1,593	1,630	37	1,702	1,749	47
Armstrong	759	347	412	1,016	495	521
Beaver	951	679	272	858	1,100	242
Butler	735	273	462	779	438	341
Crawford	387	393	6	581	580	1
Erie	358	261	97	519	415	104
Fayette	1,982	898	1,084	2,120	1,463	657
Greene	1,095	412	683	1,229	507	722
Indiana	718	274	444	977	432	545
Jefferson........	with Indiana			with Indiana		
Mercer	832	343	489	868	582	286
Venango	547	146	401	514	190	324
Warren.........	with Venango			175	96	79
Washington	3,111	1,306	1,805	3,037	1,814	1,223
Westmoreland ..	2,242	1,421	821	2,366	2,104	262
W. Pa. Totals ..	15,310	8,383	6,927	16,741	11,965	4,776

State Totals ... 66,520

[a] *Mercury,* November 21, 1817
[b] Pennsylvania, *House Journal* (1820-1821), I, 131f.

APPENDIX D

The Vote For Presidential Electors in 1824

County	Jackson	Crawford	Adams	Clay	Totals	Jackson Percentage
Allegheny	1,386	402	19	26	1,833	76
Armstrong	286	6	16	1	309	93
Beaver	485	165	0	0	650	75
Butler	506	234	2	3	745	68
Crawford	312	8	40	0	360	87
Erie	302	10	55	3	370	82
Fayette	849	52	16	278	1,195	71
Greene	374	9	6	30	419	89
Indiana	258	2	27	0	287	90
Jefferson	with Indiana				with Indiana	
Mercer	438	142	0	0	580	76
Venango	265	15	1	1	282	94
Warren	153	3	7	0	163	94
Washington	970	184	120	208	1,482	65
Westmoreland ...	963	6	34	3	1,006	96
W. Pa. Totals....	7,547	1,238	343	553	9,681	78
State Totals	36,100	4,206	5,441	1,690	47,437	76

INDEX

Composed in Caslon Intertype, printed on Mead's 60 pound white eggshell by Waverly Press, Inc., Baltimore. Moore & Company, Baltimore, bound the book in Holliston's Roxite Vellum.